Looking Back at

Leisure

EDITORIAL PLANNING
AVR

M
MACMILLAN

First published 1988

Published by
MACMILLAN EDUCATION LTD
Houndmills, Basingstoke, Hampshire RG21 2XS
and London
Companies and representatives
throughout the world

Author: Anne Mountfield

Designed and typeset by The Pen and Ink Book Company Ltd, London

Illustrations by Jane Cheswright, Kay Dixey, Stuart Hughes and Trevor Ricketts

Picture research by Faith Perkins

Printed in Hong Kong

British Library Cataloguing in Publication Data

Looking Back at leisure –
(Looking back at)
1. Recreation - History – Juvenile literature
I. Title
306'.48'09 GV174

ISBN 0-333-43944-9
ISBN 0-333-43946-5 Series

Photographic Credits

t=top b=bottom l=left r=right

The author and publishers wish to acknowledge, with thanks, the following photographic sources: 4, 5*l*, 24, 28 J Allan Cash Photograph Library, London; 11*l*, 37*l* BBC Hulton Picture Library, London; title (Knusthisorisches Museum), contents (Christopher Denniston), 6*l*, 6*r* (Bethnal Green Museum), 7 (London Museum), 9 (Louvre), 12 (Guildhall Library), 13*l* (Edward James Foundation), 14*l* (Christopher Denniston), 15 (Rijksmuseum), 19*t* (National Gallery of Art, Washington), 25*b* (American Museum in Britain), 26*b* (Attingham Park, Shrewsbury), 29*r* (Jeu de Paume), 34 (Sotheby's Belgravia), 39*t* (Paddington Green Hospital), 39*b* (Royal Holloway College), 40*l* (Victoria Art Gallery, Bath) Bridgeman Art Library, London; 21*t*, 21*b* (photograph Terence Le Goubin), 33*b* (photograph Paul Conklin) Colorific, London; 8, 13*r*, 36 E.T. Archive, London; 17*t*, 19*b*, 23*l*, 30*r*, 33*t* Mary Evans Picture Library, London; 35*t*, 35*b* Ronald Grant Archive, London; 18, 22, 23*r*, 25*t*, 26*t*, 30*l*, 38, 41 Michael Holford; 29*l* Hutchison Picture Library, London; 32 Mansell Collection, London; 16, 17*b* Peter Newark's Historical Pictures; 14*r*, 40*r* Picturepoint (UK); 27 David Redfern; 5*r* S and G Press Agency, London; 10 Ronald Sheridan Picture Library; 42, 43 Alan Thomas; 31 (Vienna Museum) Weidenfeld Archive, London

Cover illustration courtesy of the Bridgeman Art Library, London and the Kunsthistorisches Museum, Vienna.

The publishers have made every effort to trace the copyright holders, but if they have inadvertently overlooked any, they will be pleased to make the necessary arrangement at the first opportunity.

Note to the reader
In this book there are some words in the text which are printed in **bold** type. This shows that the word is listed in the glossary on page 46. The glossary gives a brief explanation of words which may be new to you.

Contents

Introduction

How do you spend your spare time? Do you like to play a sport? Do you like to go out with friends? Perhaps you stay at home and read a book, or watch television. All these are ways to use the time you have to yourself, when school or work is over. It is a time when you can choose how to enjoy yourself. It is your **leisure** time.

▼ These dancers are in Bali, in Indonesia. They are dancing as part of their religion.

Leisure in the past

In early times, people had very little time for leisure. It took them most of the day to hunt for food and to find shelter. Even then, people made time to do things for fun. They painted on cave walls. They carved knife handles or cut patterns on cooking pots. Many of these **decorated** objects have been found.

Some of our leisure activities began as part of a religion. People danced and sang to please their gods and goddesses. They also danced and sang to show their feelings, or to amuse each other.

▼ Many people enjoy running. It is a way of keeping fit. In some cities, there are marathon races. Thousands of people run together for several kilometres. Other people prefer to run alone.

Alone and in a group

Some people like to be alone. They like time to think, or to invent new objects or ways of doing things. They may enjoy going for a walk, a swim or a jog, on their own. They may enjoy watching birds or other animals. Poets, artists and scientists are some of the people who like to spend their leisure imagining or making things.

Some people like to spend their leisure time with other people. They enjoy playing games in a team with others. They like to see which team wins. This is called **competing**. Competitions used to be very important. The best hunter, runner or fighter would be the leader of a group of people who lived together. The loser might be killed. Today, many

▼ The Harlem Globe Trotters are a world famous basketball team. They began playing in New York City, in the United States. All the players are very tall. They play all around the world.

sports are dangerous, but there are rules to make them as safe as possible. Competitions are now held for fun. The pleasure is not just in winning the game, but in being part of a team.

There are ways to feel part of a group, even when you are alone. Television and radio bring plays, football matches and music into people's homes. Sick people in hospital or people who cannot move around easily can feel they are sharing their leisure with millions of others.

Toys

Young children have more leisure time than most other people. In the past, however, children had to work when they were quite young. Children who were four, five or six years old spent long hours in fields, factories and mines. In some countries, children still have to work like this.

Toys in the past

Many kinds of toys and games have changed very little over the years. Thousands of years ago, children in Egypt had wooden toys that were moved by strings, like puppets. Greek and Roman children had rattles, hoops, and dolls made from clay or rags. In South America, children had pull-along dogs that ran on wheels. These toys existed long before the children's parents had carts with wheels.

Most toys that are played with wear out, or break. We know about some toys of the past from pictures. Other toys have been buried. They have been found hundreds of years later. Some old toys are on show in **museums** today. No one is allowed to play with them in case they break.

◀ This doll is more than 2000 years old. It was made for a child in Egypt. It is made of carved wood. The doll still has its hair.

◀ Dolls' houses have always been popular. This one was made in the 1700s. We can learn many things from dolls' houses. They show us how people lived. This is the children's room. We can see what sort of toys children liked to play with.

Hand-made toys

The first simple toys were made at home from wood, clay, grass or rags. In Egypt, balls were made from a plant called **papyrus**. Children in North and South America played with dolls made from cobs of corn.

From about the 1600s, children in rich families had toys such as rocking horses, Noah's Arks, farm sets and armies of toy soldiers. These were often carved from wood or modelled in wax. They were bought from people who made toys to sell. These toys took a long time to make. They cost a lot of money. Some of the old dolls and dolls' houses that are on show in toy museums were not made as toys. They were used to show the latest fashions in clothes and furniture. Today, old toys are often collected by adults as well as children.

Factory-made toys

In the 1800s, toys became cheaper. This was because they began to be made in factories. There were machines in the factories. They made toys very quickly. Many toys were made from tin, lead and china.

Children have always liked cuddly soft toys. In the early 1900s, teddy bears became very popular. The President of the United States at that time was Theodore Roosevelt. He was known as 'Teddy' Roosevelt. In 1903, the President was out hunting. He stopped the hunters from shooting a baby bear. A newspaper drew a picture of him with the bear. This gave a German toy-making company an idea. They named a new soft toy after the President. They called it the 'Teddy bear'.

Toys that can move and make a noise were made. Some of these toys work by **clockwork**. They are wound up by a key. Other toys have an electric **battery** inside them. The battery makes them work.

▶ This Noah's Ark was made more than 100 years ago. It has nearly 100 animals and a Mr and Mrs Noah. They can all be packed inside the ark. The ark, the animals and the people are carved out of wood.

Board and card games

Both children and adults enjoy playing board games. The first board games were played by throwing pebbles or fruit stones at shapes marked out on the ground. Later, bones, glass and ivory were used to make marbles, counters and dice. Coins were sometimes used as counters for games.

Most games need two or more players. The game of draughts is at least 2000 years old. The Greek poet Homer wrote a story called *The Odyssey*, more than 2500 years ago. In the story, many men wanted to marry a queen. So these men played draughts while they waited for the queen to decide what to do.

▲ Awari is a board game played in Africa and the Caribbean. The Awari board is cut from a log and is made smooth by the fingers of the players. Seeds are put in the cups on each side. The aim is to get the other player's seeds by skilful play.

Chess is another very old board game. It was played thousands of years ago in India, China and the Middle East. Chess spread to Europe from Asia years ago. 'Check mate', the move that ends the game, was first called 'shah mat'. These are Persian words that mean 'The King is dead'. In the 1700s, the kings and queens of France played chess with huge pieces. You can see chess played like this in parks and other open spaces. Sometimes, people pretend to be the chess pieces.

A few board games can be played alone. Solitaire uses 33 marbles. It is said to have been invented in the 1700s by a prisoner in France.

◀ Chess is one of the oldest games in the world. This picture was painted in ancient Egypt thousands of years ago. It is on the inside of a tomb. It shows people playing a game like chess. The chess pieces look very like those we still use today.

New board games are being invented all the time. In 1935, one of the most popular games, *Monopoly,* was invented by an American who was out of work. More than 50 years later, the game is played by millions of people.

Card games

In ancient Egypt, about 3000 years ago, Tarot cards were used. People guessed what would happen to them by turning over the cards. These cards showed pictures such as Death, the Chariot, the Wheel of Fortune and the Fool. The Fool card became the Joker, which is still found in some packs of playing cards today.

Playing cards did not reach Europe until the 1300s. They were first used in France and Italy. Early packs of playing cards were painted by hand. There were 78 or more cards in each pack. There were also some picture cards, like the Tarot cards. As well as Kings, Queens and Jacks, there were Knight cards. This suggests that playing cards may have links with the game of chess, which also has Kings, Queens and Knights.

Puzzles and learning games

In the 1800s, parents began to look for learning games for their children. Some of these were jigsaws, which had pieces that could be fitted together to show famous scenes, or maps of the world. Others were board games which taught counting, or the ABC. Today, although there are many new card and board games, the old games are still played all over the world.

▶ These people were playing a card game over 300 years ago. The way of playing many of the games and the design of the cards has not changed much. The cards were marked with hearts, diamonds, clubs and spades even before this time.

Sports and races

People have always tried to keep fit. They have taken part in sports to win a game or a prize. In ancient Greece, sports grounds were often near temples. People went to the temples to pray and to the sports grounds to exercise their bodies. Other sports trained young fighters for battle. These practice fights were also exciting to watch.

The Olympic Games

The Olympic Games are a famous sports event that still take place today. The Games began in Greece over 2500 years ago. They were held every four years at Olympia, near a holy river called the Alpheus. Thousands of people came to cheer the young people who took part in the races. They were called **athletes**. Men, boys and girls competed in separate groups. Women could not compete in the Games, or watch them, after they were married.

On the first day of the Games, the athletes had to make a promise. They promised not to cheat and not to quarrel with the judges. The second day was for gymnastics. On the third day, there were horse races. Five different skills were tested that day, as part of one race. This was called the **pentathlon**. The fourth day was a holy day, when the athletes prayed to the gods. On the fifth day, there were running races and boxing and wrestling matches.

The winners were crowned on the last day of the Games. They were given circles of olive leaves to wear in their hair. The winners did not receive any prizes.

When the Romans conquered the Greeks, they took over the Olympic Games. Then, the Roman emperor,

▲ This vase is about 2000 years old. It was made in Greece. It shows men on horseback throwing javelins.

Theodosius, stopped the Games. He was a Christian, and he did not like the idea that the Games had begun in honour of Greek gods. For 1500 years, there were no Games. Then, in 1896, the Olympics were started again. Today, they are held in a different country every four years. The Games begin with a runner who carries a flaming torch. This torch comes all the way from Olympia. It is a way of remembering how the Games began in Greece.

▲ This picture shows Jesse Owens of the United States in the 1936 Olympic Games. Jesse Owens won this 200 m race in the record time of 20.7 seconds.

▶ In the main picture, knights are jousting with each other on horseback. The knights are practising for war. Underneath, we can see a game in which people ride on hobby horses.

Fighting sports

The Greeks and Romans enjoyed war-like sports, such as fights between armed men. These fighters were called **gladiators**. They often fought until one of them was killed by the other.

In Europe, about 500 years ago, knights practised for the wars by holding competitions. These were called **tournaments**. The knights' weapons did not have sharp ends. They could hurt, but did not usually kill. Sometimes, two knights rode against each other with spears. This was called **jousting**.

Ball games

The first ball games probably began when people threw fruit or balls of grass to each other. Games which use sticks or bats, like hockey and cricket, may first have been played with animal bones or sticks. Ball games have been played for a very long time. We know that the Chinese army played a kind of football 1500 years ago.

British football

In England, in the 1500s, football was played at fairs and on holidays. The ball was the stomach, or **bladder,** of an animal. It was blown up like a balloon. There was no special number of players, and no marked field. The game was an excuse for hundreds of people to play around roughly!

In the mid-1800s, British schools began to play football. Rules were invented by the schools, to make the game safer. Each team had to have the same number of players. There was a person in each game who made sure that both teams played fairly. This person was called a **referee**.

There are different kinds of football. **Rugby** got its name from Rugby School, in Britain, where it was first played. This game has 15 players on each side. The aim is to get the ball over a line, or above the crossbar of tall goal posts.

Soccer football is a game that follows rules drawn up by the Football Association in 1863. The game has 11 players on each side. The first soccer football goal posts were just two wooden posts. Later on, nets were fixed between the posts to stop arguments about whether the ball had passed between them or not.

American and Australian football

American football has 11 players in each team. The players can run with the ball. The teams wear padded clothes, with helmets and knee pads. The first American football match was played in 1869, between the universities of Princeton and Rutgers.

◀ Not many games are invented in prison! In London, in the 1800s, prisoners invented a game where the prison walls were used. That game was called rackets. Today, people play a similar game called squash.

In Australia, football has 18 players on each side. Australian football was first played by men who were looking for gold. They had nothing else to do in their spare time.

▼ Golf is a very old game. No one really knows how it began. This picture was painted in the 1600s. We can see from this picture that children as well as adults played golf.

Baseball and tennis

Baseball is the North American national sport. It was first played in 1839 at Cooperstown, New York. The diamond-shaped playing ground, or **pitch**, was invented by a man called Abner Doubleday.

Baseball and tennis began as games mostly played in summer. In the 1500s, tennis was played indoors. It was played by people at the courts of kings and queens in France and England. This game is still known as Royal tennis. It uses different rules from the lawn tennis that is mostly played today. Lawn tennis, in spite of its name, may be played on hard courts as well as on grass. Each year, many people enjoy watching the best players in the world compete. They play in major tournaments, such as Wimbledon in Britain.

▲ This is the first cricket match between England and Australia. It was played in Melbourne, Australia, in 1862. Cricket is played in many parts of the world.

Water and winter sports

People in the past had to live near water. Rivers and lakes often gave them the water they needed. It was also often easier to travel on water than on land. Children had to know how to swim and how to paddle canoes and rafts. So water sports began as a way to teach children to survive on or near water.

About 2000 years ago, the Greeks and the Romans had public baths in many cities. These were not just swimming pools, but were health clubs, too. Other people thought that public bathing was unhealthy. For hundreds of years, no one used public baths for sport.

In the early 1800s, sea-bathing became a popular sport. The new railways made it easy for people who lived in towns to travel to the seaside. People found that paddling and swimming in the sea was a healthy exercise. They began to build indoor and outdoor pools in towns, so that they could swim more often.

▲ Modern racing yachts sail very fast. They are specially designed to move through the water very easily. This picture shows the Sydney to Hobart Yacht Race in Australia.

Sailing and water sports

Today, many boats have engines to help them travel and race at speed. Even so, people still enjoy sailing, using only the wind as power. Sometimes, fast boats with sails, called racing **yachts**, compete with each other. A famous yacht race is held every four years, called the America's Cup.

Surfing is also a popular sport. It began on the coasts of Australia and America, where there are strong, high waves. Surfers balance on boards and let the waves carry them to the shore.

◀ This picture shows swimmers in the sea. It was painted about 80 years ago. You can see how much fashions in clothes for swimming have changed since then!

Many people also enjoy water-skiing. This sport was started in the 1930s by French soldiers. They had been trained to travel on skis over snowy ground. For a change, they tried skiing on water. They were pulled along behind a boat.

Winter sports

In parts of Asia, Europe and North America, the rivers freeze in winter. Skates were first invented as winter footwear, for journeys over ice. In the Netherlands, people used skates to travel on the frozen rivers and canals. They also skated and raced for fun.

▼ Ice skating has always been a popular sport. This picture shows a frozen canal in the Netherlands in the 1600s. The people are taking part in many activities on the ice. How many activities can you see?

Some people like to skate gracefully, making difficult movements. When they skate in this way, their skates make patterns in the ice. This is called figure skating. It was brought to Europe by an American dance teacher called Jackson Haines.

Skis were used thousands of years ago in North America and North Europe as a way to travel quickly on snow. Long distance ski races began in Norway nearly 200 years ago. Downhill skiing as a sport came later, in the early 1900s. It was begun by British people on holiday in Switzerland. In 1938, a race on skis between marked flags, the **slalom**, became part of the Winter Olympic Games. Today, many people enjoy skiing and skating as part of a winter holiday.

Hunting and fishing

For thousands of years, people have hunted animals for food and skins. Today, some people enjoy spending their leisure hunting and fishing.

Hunting big game

Wild animals, birds or fish that are hunted are called **game**. In the past, it was a test of courage to hunt wild animals, such as lions and tigers. In ancient Egypt, hunters were armed with arrows, poles and nets. They chased and trapped the animals, ready for their masters to kill them. North American Indians hunted with bows and arrows, sometimes on horseback. Killing a bear or a bison was a test for a young man.

In the 1800s and 1900s, people from Europe went hunting lions, tigers, rhinos and elephants in India and Africa. This was called 'big game hunting'. Now, many of these animals are kept in special parks called wild game **reserves**. It is against the law to harm these animals. Sometimes, people steal animals from the reserves, or kill them and take away their skins.

Birds and forest animals

More than 4000 years ago, people in China hunted small animals, using birds called falcons. This sport was called **falconry**. It was also popular in India and the Middle East. Falconry still takes place there today. Hunters in other countries now kill birds with guns.

Falconry was a sport for kings and queens in Europe over 1000 years ago. Then, it became a sport for all, and a way to hunt for meat. Hoods were put over the birds' eyes. When the hoods were removed, the birds flew off. They swooped down on their **prey**. In old paintings, you can often see men and women on horseback, with a hooded bird sitting on their wrists. The hunters wore long leather gloves to protect them from the birds' sharp claws.

Kings and queens enjoyed hunting in royal forests. They chased on horseback after deer or wild pigs. Other people were forbidden to hunt there.

◀ These are hunters in Persia in the 1400s. They hunted wolves and foxes.

◀ The falconer in this hunting party is calling back his hawk. He wears a thick glove to protect his arm when the bird lands on it. Another bird is waiting to be flown. It is kept quiet by the red hood covering its eyes.

From the 1700s, many other kinds of hunting became popular. Foxes were chased by riders with dogs called **hounds**. Otters and hares were hunted, too. In Australia, the kangaroo was hunted. Many of these animals are still hunted to death today.

Some people think hunting for sport should be banned. Even people who enjoy hunting agree that they should no longer hunt rare animals. If these animals cannot breed, they will one day die out.

Fishing

People have always fished for food. Some people like to catch fish more than they like eating them. We know from writings and wall paintings that the Egyptians fished as a sport. They used rods, nets and spears. The Greeks and Romans also fished. They made **flies** from feathers to attract the fish. Fishing methods have changed very little in hundreds of years.

Fishing is one of the most popular sports. People enjoy fishing beside rivers and from the sea shore. They also use boats if they are hunting larger fish. Fishing clubs hold competitions to see who can catch the heaviest fish. People do not fish in the breeding season. This is to make sure that there will be enough fish to catch each year.

◀ This picture shows duck-shooting in 1854. By this time, people were using guns for hunting. Wild animals and birds are still hunted in this way. The dogs have the job of fetching the ducks after they have been shot.

Circuses and fairs

The word 'circus' means a ring. The Romans built stone circuses. They were open air places where people went to watch fights. Today, circuses are often held in round tents.

The sports which were held in Roman circuses were watched by thousands of people. Races in light carts pulled by horses were popular. These carts were called **chariots**. There were fights between armed gladiators. Sometimes, the gladiators fought wild animals, such as lions and bears.

At one circus, a Roman monk called Telemachus, ran into the ring to stop a fight. He thought it was cruel and wrong. The crowd threw stones at him and killed him. The Christian emperor thought the monk was right. He made Telemachus a saint. After that, gladiator fights were ended.

Circuses

In 1783, an ex-army rider, Philip Astely, and his wife, began to give horse riding displays in London. They also hired a clown to take part in the shows. Astley's 'circus' became so popular that many others began to copy it. Circuses began to travel by covered wagons in France, Russia and America. They held their shows in tents. A very large, round tent, called 'the Big Top' was used. There were also smaller tents for stables and side shows.

In the early 1800s, collections of wild animals and displays by trained animals became popular. These were often part of the circus. North America was the home of the very big circuses. 'Buffalo Bill's Wild West Show' and 'Barnum's Travelling Circus' were famous in the late 1880s.

When a circus came to town, crowds would gather to watch as the lions, elephants and chimpanzees were led through the streets. Not many people had seen these animals before. There

▲ This ruined building is the Colosseum in Rome. It was built by the Romans for their fights. It could even be flooded for 'sea battles'. It held 50 000 people. The floor has gone and we can see that there were small rooms and passages underneath. When there were wild animal shows, the animals were kept there.

were no wildlife parks to visit, as there are now. There were no cheap books with coloured photographs or pictures of the animals.

Today, it is difficult to travel with performing animals. There are laws about cages and exercise for the animals. Animals cannot be taken abroad because of laws about disease. So many circuses no longer use them.

▼ Circuses were very popular in the 1800s. Here, we see a clown, the ringmaster and two bareback riders. Acts like these can still be seen in today's circuses.

Fairs

In Europe, for hundreds of years, fairs were places where goods were bought and sold, or **traded**. Fairs were held on saints' days and at festivals when people did not go to work. There were stalls at the fair which sold food and drink. Plays were performed in the street. The street shows at a fair became almost as important as the trading.

In London, the River Thames sometimes froze in very cold winters. Then, a frost fair would be held on the ice. There have only been six frost fairs in the last 400 years. The last one took place in 1814.

In the 1700s, roundabouts appeared at fairs. The first ones were turned by hand. Later, steam engines turned the 'merry-go-rounds'. Many holiday centres still have huge fairgrounds which are open all year round.

▼ The River Thames in London no longer freezes right over. It used to do so, in the coldest winters. The winter of 1684 was especially cold and there was thick ice all over the Thames. People put up stalls and tents and held a frost fair. They even lit fires on the ice.

Pets and zoos

People first kept animals to hunt with, and for food. They also kept small animals for company, too. Pet dogs have been found buried with their owners in graves that are 10 000 years old. In the countries of ancient Egypt and **Persia**, monkeys were kept and dressed like humans.

Cats were popular pets in many countries, as the names of breeds such as Persian, Siamese and Burmese show. The Egyptians worshipped cat-headed gods. They believed that cats went to a cat heaven. They were very sad when a pet cat died. They shaved their eyebrows and wore special **mourning** clothes to show how sad they felt.

Sometimes, pets like small birds and insects are kept because people like to listen to the sounds they make. The Aztec people of Central America kept parrots as pets. The parrots were also useful as guards. They squawked loudly when there was any danger.

Other pets are kept for their unusual colour. Chinese emperors put brightly coloured fish, called carp, in their fish ponds. Travellers to China brought some of these fish back. They are now called goldfish and are kept in ponds all over the world. In the 1700s and 1800s, many rich people liked to keep peacocks because of the colour and size of their lovely tail feathers.

▼ In the past, people kept unusual pets. In Egypt, queens had baboons as pets. In Rome, the Emperors had lions. Today, in India, mongooses are still kept as pets. They are very good at killing snakes.

▲ The Kentucky Derby is one of the most famous races in the United States. People from all over the world come each year to watch the horses race around the track at Louisville, Kentucky.

Racing animals

Horses have been raced for thousands of years. Most racehorses today have been bred from Arab horses. In the last 100 years, 'going to the races' has become a favourite leisure pastime. Some people enjoy dressing up to meet their friends at the race course. Others go to watch the races and cheer the winners.

Greyhound dogs were first used to chase and catch small animals, such as hares. The dogs were often raced against each other to see which was best. In the late 1800s, people began to race greyhounds around a track. A model of a hare was tied to a rail and pulled along by a rope. The first greyhound racing track was built in Arizona in the United States in 1909. Now, there are greyhound tracks in many countries.

▶ This is how London's Regent's Park Zoo used to look. All the animals were in bare cages. Today, zoos are different. The animals have larger areas to move around in and objects to climb on. Most are not kept behind bars.

Zoos

Wild animals are sometimes captured and kept in parks called zoos. The earliest zoos we know about were in Iraq and Egypt, over 2000 years ago. Rulers from different countries often sent each other lions and tigers as gifts. Some kings of England kept camels, lions and elephants in the grounds of the Tower of London. People were allowed in to see the zoo.

When it became easier to travel, people went to new countries. More animals were captured and put in zoos. In the early 1800s, large zoos were opened in cities all over the world. Now, there are over 500 zoos around the world. There are also large collections of fish to visit. The places where these fish are kept are called **aquariums**, or sea zoos.

Zoos and wildlife parks now try to be like the animals' natural homes. They are places where animals can live and breed in safety. Some kinds of animals have been hunted so much that there are very few left in the world.

Painting and sculpture

▲ This picture of a bison is on the wall of a cave in Altimira, in Spain. It was painted about 14 000 years ago.

Many people like to paint or to look at pictures. Some pictures which are thousands of years old have been found painted on the walls of caves. These cave paintings can tell us a lot about the way people lived at that time.

Some of the most famous cave paintings are at Lascaux, in France. They were discovered on a walk. One day in 1940, two boys and their dog, Robot, were out in the hills. Robot chased a rabbit and went down a hole. The boys found the hole. It was a hidden cave entrance. In the cave, there were paintings of cows, bulls, red deer and horses. The pictures showed hunting scenes. These paintings were 20 000 years old. People, called Bushmen, who live in Southern Africa still paint pictures like these in caves.

Painting and portraits

Painting has always been a popular pastime. People all over the world have enjoyed spending their leisure time in this way. In China, paintings were made on long **scrolls** of paper or silk. These could be unrolled, a little at a time, to show pictures of the countryside and of flowers. The Aborigine people of Australia are also famous for their paintings. They painted on the bark of trees.

In the 1700s and 1800s, most girls did not get the same kind of education as boys. The girls were taught at home. They were given lessons in drawing, and painting in **water-colours**. This was thought to be a useful skill for young ladies. Some of these paintings were very good, but they were never put on show.

Some people like to have a picture painted of themselves. This is called a **portrait**. These portraits often show a great deal about leisure in the past. People were painted with their favourite books, or dogs, or horses. Children were often shown holding toys or pets. We can see how people dressed and what their homes were like from these pictures.

▼ People of all ages enjoy painting. They often paint the things they see in the countryside. This girl has used water-colour paints. When she is older, she may be taught to use oil paints. They make the colours look stronger and thicker.

Sculpting as a hobby

Sculpting has also always been a popular hobby. Two thousand years ago, the people of the Indus valley, in Pakistan, sculpted toy figures and animals from clay. In Mexico, about 1000 years ago, statues of gods, goddesses and people were often carved from a hard, dark-coloured stone.

People also liked to make carvings or statues from wood, or metal. These statues were often of famous hunters, athletes or rulers. The Greeks and the Romans liked to decorate public places with statues for the people in the streets to admire.

Today, many people paint with oil paint on canvas, or with water-colours on paper. They make sculptures from wood, clay, stone or metal. People find these activities a good way to relax, or to share their thoughts and feelings with others.

▼ The ancient Greeks made statues of gods and goddesses. These statues are in the ruins of a temple in Athens. They are copies of the ones which were made more than 2000 years ago. The real ones are in museums, so that they will not be damaged.

Crafts

People wanted the objects they used to be beautiful as well as useful. When everyone made pots or tools, they tried out ways of decorating them. Some people were very skilled in this way. Their skills at making things is called a **craft**. People still enjoy making things for themselves 'by hand', even though factory-made objects may now be cheaper.

Early crafts

Some of the first crafts were making baskets, pottery and clothes. Many thousands of years ago, workers plaited reeds into long thin strips. Then, they twisted the strips around to make a basket shape. Cooking pots were shaped out of wet clay. Sometimes, the clay was just pushed into shape. Sometimes, the work was done on a flat wheel. The potter's wheel was spun around so that the clay could be shaped smoothly and easily into jugs or bowls. Wheels like these have been used for about 6000 years.

The Pueblo Indian women of Arizona and New Mexico painted beautiful patterns in red, brown and black on cooking pots. Some of these designs are symbols of rain and clouds.

Sewing and embroidery

Needlework has been a popular craft for thousands of years. Clothes were often decorated with stitched patterns. This is called **embroidery**. The patterns were passed on from one family to another. Sometimes, people embroidered pictures to hang on walls. There is a famous embroidered wall hanging which is kept at Bayeux, in France. It is called the Bayeux Tapestry. It shows the French army fighting the English, over 800 years ago.

▶ This Mexican woman is shaping wet clay to make a dish. Pottery is still made by hand in many parts of the world. People make pots for their own use, or because they like making them.

▲ This is an embroidered map from Kashmir. It is a map of Srinagar, the capital city of Kashmir. Thousands of stitches and many coloured threads have been used to make the picture.

In North America, in the 1700s, people made bed covers called **quilts**. They used scraps of leftover dress material to make the **patchwork** quilts. Often, there were quilt-making parties, where women sewed and talked. They all helped to make quilts for a special event, such as a wedding.

Knitting and printing

Knitting is a very old skill. It began in Asia. Sailors and shepherds in Europe used to knit to keep themselves busy. Shepherds in France used to knit with five needles at once. Today, people use two or four. Sometimes, they use a needle which bends around into a circle. Different knitting patterns are found in different parts of the world.

Some patterns are made by dyeing and printing cloth. In Indonesia, patterns are made on cloth, using wax and coloured dye. This is called **batik**. Batik printing has become very popular.

Woodwork

Carpenters often decorated their work with beautiful carvings. In many places, such as Africa, people carved wooden birds and animals. They made masks to wear when they were dancing.

The North American Indians made the largest wood carvings in the world. These were called **totem poles**. They were tall, carved tree trunks, 25 metres high, with pictures all the way up. The pictures were often scenes from well-known stories. Sometimes, they were in memory of members of the family who had died.

◀ In the 1700s and 1800s, young girls were taught how to embroider. They had to sew a picture. It showed that they could do all kinds of stitches. The picture was an example of their work, so it was called a sampler.

Music

Many people like to sing and to play music themselves. Others go to hear music being played at a concert. Music is one of the oldest pleasures in the world.

▲ This picture shows musicians playing in an Egyptian court. They are playing reed pipes and a stringed instrument like a lute.

Music around the world

People often sang and played musical instruments in temples. They thought music was a way to get their gods to listen to their prayers. Many different types of music developed around the world. Eastern, African and South American music has a strong tune, or **melody**. The beat, or **rhythm**, is added by drums and brass instruments. In Indian music, the **sitar** often provides the melody. It is a stringed instrument with a long wooden neck, and seven main strings.

Folk music

In the past, people often made up songs to sing as they worked. They taught the song to their families and friends. These **folk songs** were never written down. They were passed on to other singers. Folk songs were sung by travelling singers, called **minstrels**. Many songs tell of battles or brave deeds. Some are love songs, or songs to put babies to sleep.

▶ In this group of musicians of about 500 years ago, we can see an early type of violin. It is not quite the same shape as a modern one. The other stringed instrument is a lute.

Concert music

In ancient Greek theatres, the place where the musicians sat was called the **orchestra**. It was right in front of the stage. Today, the word means a group of people who play music together. People who make up music are **composers**.

Over the years, orchestras and bands grew to about 80 players. In the 1800s, many big cities set up orchestras. Public concerts became a leisure activity for music lovers.

Sometimes, people like to go to see a story acted and sung to music. This is called an **opera**. One of the newest and finest opera houses in the world was opened in Sydney, Australia, in 1973. The building looks like a ship's sail.

Popular music

In the early 1900s, a new kind of music was popular. It started in New Orleans, in the United States. The working songs of black Americans were mixed with other folk tunes. African drum beats and the sounds of brass instruments were mixed in, too. This music was called **jazz**. It is now popular in many other countries.

Many young people today learn an instrument and form their own 'pop' group. Some of these 'pop' groups have become very famous. This music has given pleasure to millions of people around the world.

▼ Jazz is now popular all over the world. There are many jazz bands. This is the Count Basie Orchestra.

Dancing

In the past, people believed they could make things happen by dancing for their gods and goddesses. They sometimes danced in a circle because this was the shape of the Sun and the Moon. They also danced for fun and to amuse each other. Sometimes, they danced to tell a story.

Many dances began as a part of a spring festival, or to celebrate bringing in the crops at **harvest** time. Other **folk dances** were danced at weddings and festivals. Different styles of dancing grew up around the world.

▲ Morris dancing is one of the best-known British folk dances. The dance was often performed on May Day. In this dance, the girls have bells on their aprons and shoes.

In Britain, people danced around a tall pole on the first day of May. This was to welcome the spring. They held long ribbons that were tied to the top of the pole. As they danced, they twisted the ribbons into a pattern. **Morris dancing** was danced in spring, too, but only by men. They wore flowers in their hats and bells on their legs. The bells and the handkerchiefs they waved were first meant to frighten away evil spirits. Later, the morris dances became country dances, like the square dances of the United States. Both men and women now take part in the dances.

Trained dancers

Dancers in countries like Japan, India and China, were trained from childhood. Chinese dancers had to be able to jump and tumble. They were called **acrobats**. In Japanese dances, it was important to use a fan gracefully. Hindu dancers in India needed to learn nine movements of the head, eight movements of the eyes, six of the eyebrows and four of the neck. There were 4000 movements of the hands, called **mudras**.

In the 1400s, trained dancers began to perform in royal courts in Europe. The French king, Louis 14th, liked dances which told stories. These dances were called **ballets**. They were danced to music in a theatre. The king and his friends even took part in ballets at the royal court.

Ballet became most popular in Russia. The Russian dancer, Anna Pavlova, was one of the world's most famous

▲ Hawaii is the name of a group of islands in the Pacific Ocean. Many people go there on holiday. These dancers are performing one of their traditional dances for tourists.

ballerinas. Many people of all ages enjoy watching ballet dancers. The dancers must train every day for hours to learn all the difficult steps. Ballet dancing is very hard work, although it looks so easy and graceful.

Popular dancing

In Europe, country dances were often danced by ordinary people at weddings and feasts. In the 1600s and 1700s, new dances were invented. They were based on old country dances. Ladies and gentlemen at royal courts took lessons in dancing. Palaces and grand houses were built with special ballrooms for dancing.

Popular dancing has changed over the years. For a long time, people danced apart from each other. Only their hands touched. In the 1800s, the new popular dances were the waltz and the polka.

▲ This is a picture by the painter Edgar Degas. It shows a ballet school in Paris in the 1800s.

These dances were based on folk dances from Germany and Poland. Many people were very shocked because these were danced with the couples putting their arms around each other!

Then, in the 1950s people once again danced away from each other. This dance was rock-n-roll. It was very fast and the boys threw the girls into the air. It was usually only danced by young people.

Theatre

Plays are stories told by actors. The actors dress up and pretend to be the people in the story. Sad stories are called **tragedies**. Funny stories are called **comedies**. Acting out stories, or **drama**, has always been a way of entertaining people.

In Asia, over 2000 years ago, there were many kinds of drama. Some of these different types of drama can still be seen today. In Japan, for hundreds of years, people have gone to see **Noh** plays. The actors are all men. They paint their faces and wear masks. The actors sing the words of the story. Sometimes, these plays go on all day.

▲ This Greek vase shows a comedy. The actors are wearing padded clothes which were worn to make them look funny. The 'woman' at the window is played by a boy.

▲ In Japan, the oldest kinds of plays are Noh plays. The actors wear masks.

Greek drama

Greek drama was some of the earliest drama in Europe. It began as a religious dance. There were only a few main actors in the play. Other people danced and sang in the background. These people were called the **chorus**. All the actors wore masks. The plays took place in open air theatres. These theatres were often built on a hillside. The seats were steps built into a curved half-circle around the stage. Some of these Greek plays are still acted today.

Drama and religion

Often, religious stories are made into plays. In India, actors still act the stories of gods and goddesses of the Hindu religion. One famous play is the tale of Rhada and Krishna.

Many early plays in Europe were acted in Christian churches. Others were acted on wooden carts. These were wheeled through the streets. The plays were each performed by a different group of

◀ Some theatres were very big and very grand. This is a picture of a theatre in Germany in the late 1800s. People often dressed in their best clothes to go to the theatre. It was a special occasion.

workers. The carpenters all acted one story. The stonecutters acted another story, and so on. They always acted the same play. The plays were stories from the Bible. They were called **mystery plays**.

Travelling theatre

Sometimes, actors travel to their audience. In the 1800s, many actors in the United States travelled westwards. They went to the new towns which were growing up. At the time of the Great Gold Rush, a little girl called Lotta Crabtree toured mining camps to perform. She started when she was only ten years old. William Chapman put on exciting and funny plays for the passengers on Mississippi river boats. In Australia, the first theatre performance was given in 1789 by prisoners who had been sent there from Britain.

In Britain, many small groups of players went to towns and villages. They performed in barns or farmyards. Sometimes, they acted in the courtyard of an inn or in a town square.

Theatres

In the late 1500s, theatres were built in Europe. These theatres had no roof. If it rained, the play had to stop. Women did not act. Their parts were played by young boys. Instead of ice-cream, oranges were sold to the audience. If the people did not like the play, they laughed and booed and threw the oranges at the actors. In the 1800s, indoor theatres were built. This meant that painted scenery could be used. The theatre was now a more comfortable place. A theatre visit became a favourite way for people to spend their leisure time.

Storytelling and reading

Before people knew how to read or write or make books, stories were told or sung around the fire. These stories were remembered and passed on. Storytellers travelled from place to place, telling their stories.

Early writings were copied out by hand. This took a long time. In many parts of the world, laws and holy writing were kept on long **scrolls**. In Europe, some writings were bound together to make books. Books and scrolls were very precious. They were often locked away. Very few people could read, and there were no books for amusement.

▲ Children in the past had no reading books like ours today. Instead they had horn books. These were not really books at all. They were boards covered with horn. They usually had the alphabet or prayers written on them.

Printed books

Chinese people were the first printers. They carved wood into the shapes of symbols or letters. Then, they dipped these blocks into paint or ink. When they pressed them on to a sheet of paper or cloth, the ink left a mark. The first book to be printed by a machine appeared in Germany in 1455. The machine was called a **printing press**. Printing presses could print many copies of the same book. When books were cheaper to make and there were more of them, more people could learn to read.

To begin with, the presses printed mostly holy books and information books. By the 1700s, story books were being printed, and were very popular. People could now enjoy reading stories, plays and poems. Later, as the presses were improved, newspapers, magazines and comics were also printed. The first magazine for children was published in 1777, in London. It was called *The Young Gentleman's Magazine*. In 1832, the *Boys' and Girls' Penny Magazine* was sold weekly in Britain. Coloured comics came later.

Children's books

The first books for children were teaching books, not books for leisure. At the end of the 1800s, books were written for children to enjoy. Nursery rhymes, fairy tales and story books with pictures were printed. Today, thousands of new children's books are printed every year.

▲ Children's books today have attractive pictures in them. The picture here is from a book of nursery rhymes, printed in the 1800s. It shows a scene from the rhyme 'Jack and Jill'.

Public libraries

In the 1800s, many countries set up free public libraries. People could borrow the books from the libraries. They did not have to buy them. So poor people could enjoy the books, too. Today, big cities, like Washington, Sydney and London, have huge libraries that hold millions of books.

Many towns also have small libraries. There are even travelling libraries. Vans take books to people who are sick, or to people who live in lonely places. In some towns, there are special children's libraries where only children can borrow the books.

Many people enjoy writing stories for fun. They may keep a **diary**, in which they write down the things that happen each day. These writings may be kept just for families and friends. Some diaries have been printed so that other people can read them.

▶ Many countries have a national library, where millions of books are stored. People may look at these books, but they may not take them away. This is a public library in New York City.

Photography and cinema

In the 1800s, people found out how to use light to make pictures of real people and things. This was called **photography**, from Greek words meaning 'to draw with light'. Taking and printing photographs started to become a pastime.

The first photographs

In 1827, a Frenchman, Joseph Niépce, took the world's first photograph. This was of the view from his window. He used a metal plate that changed slowly as light fell on it. This change could take as long as eight hours to happen. Only places and objects could be photographed. People could not sit still for that long!

In the earliest photographs of people, they often look frozen and stiff. This is because they had to sit still for half an hour. By the 1840s, photographs could be taken in ten to twenty seconds.

The first cameras were very large and heavy. When **film** on a roll was invented in the 1890s, cameras could be made smaller. They became easier to carry about. People could then take their own photographs. Now, people take pictures of friends and families. They take them of their homes and their holidays, too. Some people also develop their own pictures. They must have a place where no daylight can get in. This is called a darkroom. Light would spoil the film.

▲ This is an early photograph. It was taken in 1853. The person being photographed had to sit quite still in front of the camera, for about a minute.

Slide shows

In the 1840s, people went to see 'magic lantern' shows. Light was passed through a small piece of glass called a **slide**. The slide had a picture drawn on it. The picture then showed clearly on a screen. It was much larger than the slide. The light machine, or 'magic lantern' was the first type of **projector**.

Magic lantern pictures did not move. In the early 1800s, the Wheel of Life, or **zoetrope**, was a popular toy. A strip of paper was spun very fast. Viewers peeped through a hole. The figures in the moving pictures seemed to be of one picture, moving by itself.

Photographs could also be moved quickly and projected on to a screen. Auguste and Louis Lumière were the first to charge money for showing moving photograph pictures. They did this in a café in Paris, on 20 February 1896. It was the beginning of 'the movies'.

▲ There are cinemas in almost every town. The first ones were just like shops, with rows of chairs. Later, large, grand cinemas were built. There was an organ or piano in front of the stage. It was played during the silent films.

Going to the pictures

In 1901, the first film story was shown in France. It was called 'The Story of a Crime'. From then on, going to 'the pictures' or 'the movies' became popular. At first, films did not have any sound. A piano player played music to make the film feel more exciting or sad. In 1927, the film *The Jazz Singer* was made. This was the first film with sound. People called these new films 'talkies'. By 1932, films were being made in colour. Many families went to the cinema at least once a week. Millions of people still like to watch old films on TV and to visit the cinema.

◀ These are early film makers. The year is 1923. In those days, films were still silent. Millions of people enjoyed going to see these films.

Radio and television

In 1892, Guglielmo Marconi discovered that he could send sound through the air by **radio waves**. In 1925, John Logie Baird showed scientists that he could send a picture of a person through the air. This was called television. At that time, no one guessed how important these two inventions would be. Now, listening to the radio and watching television are among the most popular ways to spend our leisure time. They help people to get the latest news. They bring music, plays and shows into homes around the world. They even let people hear or see a sporting event at the same time as it is happening in another part of the world.

Radio

The first radio station opened in Pennsylvania in the United States in 1920. Four years later, there were 1000 new stations in the United States. In Britain, the British Broadcasting Company, the BBC, made its first broadcast in 1922.

At first, radio was called the wireless. This was because sound travelled to it through the air and not along a wire. Listening to the wireless was very exciting. Families would sit around a large machine. People might only hear faint sounds. Even so, it seemed amazing to hear voices coming from the radio set. The first programmes were sent out as they happened, or **live**. If something went wrong in the studio, everyone at home could hear!

Television

TV broadcasts began in Britain in 1936, in the United States in 1939, and in Australia in 1956. The first televisions were large wooden boxes with very small screens. TV programmes also went out live. All the plays and shows took place in a TV studio. There was no way of making a TV programme outside in those days. The first television programmes were shown only in black and white. By

◀ Radios in the 1920s were quite different from radios today. They were larger and heavier than modern ones. This one has a separate speaker. It was made to look like a flower. Radios like this are very valuable today.

◀ This is a combined radio and television set. It was made in 1938. Few people at that time had a television set. The sets were very large and heavy, and there were not many programmes to watch.

1953, a way of sending out colour pictures was in use in the United States. Today, colour TV sets are in use all over the world.

Programmes

Today, there is a wide selection of TV programmes. You can choose what you watch. It may be a play, a comedy programme or a quiz. It might also be news, music or a programme about real life. These programmes are called **documentaries**.

Satellites are machines in outer space. Using satellites, TV pictures can be sent all over the world. They can even be sent from outer space. When Neil Armstrong stepped on to the Moon in 1969, 723 million people were watching on TV. Soon, many homes will have satellite receivers of their own. People will be able to choose from the TV programmes which are being shown in other countries.

People's leisure time has been changed a great deal by television. They can now see many sights from other parts of the world. This makes them keen to travel. They can see many sports and activities which they would not know about without television. Many people try these new activities. Television has also helped many people to learn about many difficult subjects. In future, TV may also be used as a kind of telephone. We will be able to see the person we are speaking to, as well as hear them.

▲ In the future, we may be able to talk to our friends on the phone and see them on a television screen at the same time.

Vacations

The word holiday first meant a "holy day." The first Christian holidays were the saints' days, and festival times like Christmas and Easter. On these days, no one had to work. They were times to rest and have fun. People would go to fairs, watch street shows, or eat and drink with friends.

The word "vacation" also means a time of relaxation away from work. Until about thirty years ago, very few people took vacations away from home. These cost too much money. People were not paid for days when they did not work. Today, many people go away on vacation. Some people travel to other countries. It is now possible for people to fly to the other side of the world for their vacation.

Travelers

People have always traveled. Two thousand years ago, a journey was easy in the parts of Europe that were ruled by the Romans. The roads were good. There were places that sold wine, cheese, and bread to travelers. There were inns where people could eat and sleep, and where their horses were looked after.

When people visited new towns, they liked to look at the places of interest. There were many guides who were eager to show them the sights. Throughout the Roman Empire, almost everyone could speak the Roman language, called Latin.

▲ The poet Geoffrey Chaucer wrote his most famous poem, the *Canterbury Tales*, about pilgrims in the 1300's. Their pilgrimage was like a vacation tour. The pilgrims had a tour guide to show them the way. This picture of the pilgrims was drawn in the 1500's.

A thousand years after the Roman Empire ended, travel in Europe was not so easy. Many roads were just muddy tracks. The idea of traveling "to see the sights" was almost unknown.

Between the 1100's and the 1400's, some people did go on long journeys. They went to visit the places where holy people had lived or died. Christians went to Jerusalem or Rome. Muslims went to Mecca. These special journeys were called **pilgrimages**. Many people also went along to see the sights.

Tours

In the 1800's, young men were sent to Europe as part of their education. The journey was called the **Grand Tour**. They visited important cities to see famous buildings and works of art. These journeys took many months. People could travel only at the speed of a horse.

Railways, steamers and hotels

Railways and steamships made it possible to travel faster and in more comfort. Large hotels opened near railway stations and in big cities. Railways took people to the seaside or into the countryside. Often, they only went for the day. People who lived at the seaside began to allow people to stay, or board, overnight very cheaply. Families began to take cheap holidays, staying at these boarding houses. Very few people could afford a holiday abroad.

▲ Now that travel was easier and cheaper, people could go on holiday. From the 1800s on, people began taking seaside holidays. This is a picture made in tiles. It shows that children used to enjoy making sandcastles in the past, just as they do today.

Package holidays

In 1861, an English man named Thomas Cook, tried a new idea. He offered holidays in Paris. The price of the holiday was a package including travel, five nights in a hotel and all meals. Today, many people fly away on package holidays. There are summer holidays now specially for children. Many children spend holidays at a camp each year, where they go swimming, sailing and pony riding.

▼ Travel became much easier in the 1800s. All over the world, people were building railways. More people could afford to travel. Here, we see how crowded a station could get.

Open to visitors

▲ These tourists are in the Metropolitan Museum of Art in New York City in the United States. They are looking at a collection of armour from other countries.

People made beautiful things for temples, churches and palaces. Then, rich people began to collect these objects for their homes too. Today, many of these beautiful objects from the past are on show to everyone.

Early collections

The Greek goddesses of the arts were the **Muses**. They gave people ideas for making things. A museum first meant a temple of the Muses. They were buildings where interesting and beautiful objects were kept.

In the 1400s, people in Europe began to collect objects from the past and keep them in museums. These museums were not open to the public.

▼ These people are at Bath, in Britain, in the 1700s. Bath had many visitors because of its hot-water springs. People believed that bathing in the springs made them healthier.

Public museums and art galleries

In the 1700s, some good collections were put on display to the public. By the 1800s, many towns and cities had public museums. Some had scientific displays. Some looked after paintings and sculptures. Others were places for animals and plant life.

Some of the famous picture galleries began as the private picture collections of kings and queens. The Louvre, in Paris, was a royal palace. When the king of France was killed in 1792, the Louvre was taken over by the government.

In other countries, wealthy people gave money to buy paintings and sculptures for the public to enjoy. The Metropolitan Museum in New York began in this way. So did the Australian National Gallery in Canberra, and the British National Gallery in London.

One of the newest and richest art galleries in the world was built in Malibu, California, in 1953. It was a gift from the oil millionaire, John Paul Getty. The art gallery holds a collection of French furniture of the 1700s. There are also many famous paintings that date from the 1400s to the 1600s.

Great houses

Many of the palaces and great homes of the past are now owned by the government and are open to the public. Sometimes, an entry fee is charged. A few small homes are open, too. In this way, visitors can see how rich and poor people lived many years ago. Some are places where famous people have lived. Some were built or decorated by famous craftsmen. Often, the buildings are filled with beautiful furniture. Many people like to spend their leisure time visiting these famous homes and palaces.

Monticello, near Charlottesville, in the United States, is a famous house. The United States President, Thomas Jefferson, designed it for himself in the late 1700s. Jefferson was an inventor. At Monticello, visitors can see some of his inventions. They include one of the first 24-hour clocks and a chair that could swing around, so that the President could read in the light.

▼ Many people enjoy looking around grand houses. This is Burghley House built in 1589. Visitors can see how rich people used to live in the past. They can look at the fine paintings and pictures. They can walk in the beautiful gardens.

Collecting as a hobby

Many people enjoy collecting objects. People have been collecting things for hundreds of years. Collectors like to study things, and to find out about when and where they were made. Perhaps you have a collection of your own.

▲ You can collect almost anything. This boy collects match-box tops. There are many different kinds, from all over the world. If you tell everyone about your collection, they may help you add to it.

Coin collecting

People started to collect coins in the 1500s and 1700s. It is easy to tell how old a coin is, and where it comes from. Most coins are stamped with the date when they were made and the head of the country's ruler. Thousands of small Roman coins still exist. This is because Roman coins were used in all parts of the Roman Empire.

Old coins were often made of silver and gold. Sometimes, people clipped the edges off. They melted the clippings down to make new coins. About 600 years ago, coins in Britain were made with rough, or **milled**, edges. They could not be clipped without losing the milling.

Stamp collecting

In Britain, on 6 May 1840, the One Penny Black stamp went on sale. It was the world's first postage stamp that could be stuck down, using the glue on the back of the stamp. Sixty-eight million were printed, but they are rare today. Most of them were thrown away when they had been used.

The first stamps did not have the rows of holes, or **perforations**, that make sheets easy to tear. They had to be cut out with scissors. Today, if the printing goes wrong, stamps come out the wrong colour, or without perforations. This makes them worth more to collectors. Some people would pay hundreds of thousands of pounds for a rare Swedish stamp of 1855. This is because it was printed in yellow by mistake.

Today, stamps all over the world are printed with pictures of birds, flowers, views and famous people. Some people collect stamps from one country only. Others like to collect flower stamps or bird stamps, or stamps showing sports and games.

Names and letters

People's signatures, or **autographs**, are often collected. Some people have made autograph collections of well-known people from the past. In the United States, the set of autographs of all the men who signed the Declaration of Independence is very rare. Sometimes, people collect autographs of friends, and they become famous later. People also collect old letters from famous people.

Your own museum

Almost anything can be collected. Some people collect old rocks called **fossils**. Some people collect old clothes, jewellery or furniture. Others collect paintings or books. Some people even collect old bus tickets or grocer's bills. You need not spend a great deal of money on a hobby like this. Try to find something fairly cheap, like old marbles or coloured glass bottles. Find something that no one else has thought of collecting. Remember, if you keep something for long enough in your family, it will turn into history.

▲ Some collections are worth a lot of money. This man collects clocks. If he is lucky, he may find a rare clock for sale. He may be able to buy it cheaply, and repair it.

▼ Children all over the world enjoy making their own collections.

Quiz

How much can you remember? Try this quiz and use the glossary and index to help you check your answers.

1. Here are the names of some toys with the letters mixed up. Try to find the correct names.
   a) TARETL, b) SLODL OSHEU,
   c) GINCKOR OSHER, d) DETYD RABE,
   e) UPPETP, f) POHO

2. Match the description given in (a) to (f) with the words numbered (1) to (6) below them.
   a) a downhill ski race
   b) places where fish are kept
   c) patterns made on cloth, using wax and coloured dye
   d) armed men who fought in Greece and Rome to entertain crowds
   e) movements of the hands in Hindu dancing
   f) large wood carvings made by North American Indians

   1) aquariums
   2) gladiators
   3) totem poles
   4) poachers
   5) batik
   6) mudras

3. Complete the following sentences with
   (a), (b), (c) or (d):

   1) The Olympic Games were first held in
      a) Rome.
      b) Egypt.
      c) Asia.
      d) Greece.

   2) Carp were
      a) drinks.
      b) coats.
      c) goldfish.
      d) statues.

   3) A melody is
      a) a ballet.
      b) a strong tune.
      c) a story book.
      d) an animal.

   4) Thomas Cook was
      a) the inventor of television.
      b) a President of the United States.
      c) a famous ballet dancer.
      d) a man who sold package holidays.

   5) The Bayeux Tapestry is
      a) a famous embroidered wall hanging.
      b) a folk dance.
      c) a greyhound racing track.
      d) a famous zoo for bears.

   6) A play sung to music is called
      a) an orchestra.
      b) an opera.
      c) a ballet.
      d) a chorus.

4. Which is the odd one out?
   a) cinema, theatre, slide shows, harvest
   b) knitting, patchwork, sitar, embroidery
   c) wood, falconry, stone, clay
   d) waltz, polka, charleston, baseball
   e) woodwork, coins, stamps, autographs

5. Are the following statements true or false?
   a) Many early plays in Europe were acted in churches.
   b) A satellite is a kind of armchair.
   c) Documentary programmes on television are about real life.
   d) A museum is a place where races are held.
   e) Parrots were kept as guards by the Aztecs.
   f) A portrait is a kind of sailing ship.

6. Name the game that
   a) ends in a move called check mate.
   b) was invented by a French prisoner.
   c) was played by men in *The Odyssey*.
   d) was invented in America in 1935.
   e) has pieces that fit together.

7. How many
   a) races are there in a pentathlon?
   b) players are there in a rugby team?
   c) players are there in an Australian football team?
   d) players are there in an American football team?

8. Here are ten words written backwards. Which five are dances?
   a) AKLOP, b) LLABESAB, c) OOZ, d) TORTXOF, e) ZTLAW, f) TELLAB, g) GNITSUOJ, h) SIRROM, i) SIKS, j) ERUSIEL

9. Where
   a) was Royal tennis played in the 1500s?
   b) were skates first used as winter footwear on ice?
   c) did musicians first sit in front of a stage, in a place called an orchestra?
   d) are Noh plays popular?
   e) are the cave paintings discovered by a dog in 1940?

10. Who
   a) paid for an art gallery at Malibu, California, in the United States?
   b) toured mining camps to act at the time of the Gold Rush in the United States?
   c) was a famous Russian ballerina?
   d) took the world's first photograph?
   e) opened a circus in London in 1783?

ANSWERS

1. a) RATTLE, b) DOLL'S HOUSE, c) ROCKING HORSE, d) TEDDY BEAR, e) PUPPET, f) HOOP
2. (a) 4, (b) 1, (c) 5, (d) 2, (e) 6, (f) 3
3. (1) d, (2) c, (3) b, (4) d, (5) a, (6) b
4. a) harvest, b) sitar, c) falconry, d) baseball e) woodwork
5. a) true, b) false, c) true, d) false, e) true, f) false
6. a) chess, b) solitaire, c) draughts, d) Monopoly e) jigsaw
7. (a) 5, (b) 15, (c) 18, (d) 11,
8. a) POLKA, b) FOXTROT, c) WALTZ, d) BALLET, and e) MORRIS
9. a) France and England, b) the Netherlands, c) Greece, d) Japan, e) France
10. a) John Paul Getty, b) Lotta Crabtree, c) Anna Pavlova, d) Joseph Niépce, e) Philip Astely

Glossary

acrobat: a person who entertains people with jumping and balancing acts
aquarium: a tank or a building with tanks for keeping water plants and animals
athlete: a person who takes part in exercises and sport. Athletes like to enter running and jumping contests
autograph: a person's name, written in her or his own handwriting

ballet: a dance that tells a story in steps and actions. There is music, but there are no words spoken
batik: a way of making designs on cloth using wax and dye
battery: makes electricity which makes things move or light up or make a noise
bladder: the skin or bag in which urine collects in human's and animals' bodies. Animal bladders were filled with air to make a ball for throwing and kicking

chariot: a light, two-wheeled cart drawn by one or more horses. Chariots were used by the Romans for war and for racing
chorus: the people in Greek plays who chanted and danced in between the acts of the play
circus: 1) a round stone building. 2) a show held in a circular tent
clockwork: to have a working part that is like a clock
comedy: a play or film that is funny and has a happy ending
compete: to try and do better than someone else
composer: a writer of music
craft: a job or skill that needs special cleverness with the hands

decorate: to paint or carve an object to make it look more beautiful
diary: a written daily record
documentary: a film showing an activity from real life without using actors
drama: a story acted out on a stage by actors

embroidery: the art of making designs by needlework on cloth

falconry: to train or hunt with falcons or hawks
film: material with a special coating on it. When light falls on the film a picture is formed on it
fly: a small hook made to look like a small insect. It is used to catch fish
folk dances: dances handed down from one generation to the next. Folk dances often tell stories of a country area
folk songs: songs handed down from one generation to the next
fossil: the remains of an animal or plant, usually found in rock. A fossil may be the bones of an animal, or the shape left by the animal's body in the rock

game: wild animals, birds or fish which are hunted by people
gladiator: a man whose job was to fight with other men or animals in an arena in ancient Rome
Grand Tour: a long journey from place to place around Europe, for pleasure and education

harvest: the time when crops are gathered in
hound: a dog used to hunt animals

jazz: music first played in the New Orleans area of the United States. Jazz comes from the music of Africa and from other folk music
jousting: a fight between two knights on horses. The knights used long spears called lances

leisure: time when people do not have to work
live: a performance which is broadcast while it is happening

melody: a tune of music
mill: to put grooves on the edge of coins
minstrel: a singer or player who used to travel around
morris dance: a very old English dance. It was usually danced on May Day. The dancers have bells attached to their clothes
mourning: wearing special clothes to show sadness for someone's death
mudras: Hindu dance movements of the body
Muse: one of a group of nine goddesses. These goddesses stood for the arts such as poetry, song, drama and dance

museum: a building used to store and show collections of antiques, natural history and art
mystery play: a drama which told a story from the Bible or the life of a saint

Noh: drama from Japan which came from a religious dance

opera: a form of drama where the story is told in song
orchestra: the front of the stage where the chorus danced in Greek theatre. Now, the orchestra means the musicians who play together with a conductor

papyrus: a reed plant. The Egyptians made writing paper from the stem of papyrus. The word 'paper' comes from 'papyrus'
patchwork: cloth made by sewing together small pieces of fabric
pentathlon: an athletic contest which has five parts. Each athlete must enter all five events
perforations: holes made in a line in paper to make it easier to tear apart
Persia: the old name for the country now called Iran
photography: using light to make a lasting picture on a special surface
pilgrimage: a journey to a holy or special place
pitch: a place set aside for playing or practising a game. In baseball, the pitch is called the 'diamond'. In cricket it is called the 'wicket'
portrait: a drawing, painting or photograph of a person or animal
prey: an animal or bird that is killed by another animal or bird
printing press: a machine for putting words on paper. The letters are covered with ink and pressed down on the paper
projector: a machine for showing light or pictures on a screen

quilt: a bed-cover made of pieces of cloth with padding sewn in between

radio wave: an invisable ray that travels through air and space. Radio waves can carry messages
referee: a person who makes sure games are played fairly. Both sides in a game listen to the decision of the referee
reserves: a special area of land in which wild animals can live in safety
rhythm: a beat or pattern of beat in music
rugby: a game of football between two teams using an oval-shaped ball. The ball can be kicked or picked up and carried by the players

satellite: a small body in orbit around a larger body in space. The Moon is a satellite of the Earth. We also call spacecraft that orbit the Earth satellites
scroll: a length of linen or parchment with writing on it. It could be rolled around a piece of wood or metal
sitar: a stringed instrument with a long neck
slalom: a downhill or zigzag race. Skiers go between posts or trees down a slope. Canoeists paddle between poles or 'gates' on a river
slide: a picture which can be shown on a screen by a projector
soccer: a kind of football. The players kick the ball. They cannot carry it or touch it with their hands

totem pole: a pole carved and painted by Indian peoples in North America
tourist: a person who goes on a tour or is on holiday in a country
tournament: 1) a practice fight between two groups of men on horses. Their weapons were not sharp so they did not seriously hurt each other. 2) a competition between a number of players or teams
trade: to buy and sell goods
tragedy: a film or play that has an unhappy ending

water-colour: a type of paint which is mixed with water

yacht: a light, fast sailing boat. Yachts are often built for racing

zoetrope: a machine in which pictures inside a moving case are seen through slots. These pictures look as though they are moving

Index

Flower Arranging

Basics to Advanced Design

Walter E. Larmie

Professor and Chairman
Department of Plant and Soil Science
University of Rhode Island

PRENTICE-HALL, INC., Englewood Cliffs, New Jersey 07632

Library of Congress Cataloging in Publication Data

Larmie, Walter E
Flower arranging: basics to advanced design.

Includes index.
1. Flower arrangement. I. Title.
SB449.L35 1980 745.92 79-14936
ISBN 0-13-322438-4

Editorial/production supervision and interior design
by Barbara A. Cassel
Cover design by Jerry Pfeiffer
Manufacturing buyer: Gordon Osbourne

Printed in the United States of America

10 9 8 7 6 5 4 3 2 1

Prentice-Hall International, Inc., *London*
Prentice-Hall of Australia Pty. Limited, *Sydney*
Prentice-Hall of Canada, Ltd., *Toronto*
Prentice-Hall of India Private Limited, *New Delhi*
Prentice-Hall of Japan, Inc., *Tokyo*
Prentice-Hall of Southeast Asia Pte. Ltd., *Singapore*
Whitehall Books Limited, *Wellington, New Zealand*

Contents

Contents

Preface

Flowers are a part of almost everyone's life. A single rose or even a daisy placed in a bottle of water can bring enjoyment to many, no matter how humble the surroundings might be. As flowers become available from the garden, fields, roadside markets, or the florist, the homemaker endeavors to arrange them to achieve maximum effectiveness. Having seen arrangements at flower shows, those from florists, and pictures of them in many magazines, one is confronted with a desire to know how to proceed to accomplish these results.

For prospective florists, a thorough understanding of the basics of floral design is necessary if they are to succeed in this endeavor. Through the proper interpretation and modification of this groundwork, the florist will produce noteworthy designs.

The experienced designer can learn new ideas from the work of others. Design schools are held in many localities to help these designers—not only with the use of new products but to present new concepts as well as a general review of older ideas. If the designer can pick up only a few hints that can be used in future arrangements, the sessions have been worthwhile.

The same situation exists with new books such as this text, pamphlets, magazines, and flower shows.

The objective of this book is to help all those interested in floral design. Beginning with an abbreviated history of flower arrangement and its relationship to the present-day, description of principles of arrangement, basic lines, and construction details, this book will launch the reader in the right direction and will help to avoid confusion in the basic understanding of proper flower arrangement. Photographs of prize-winning arrangements as well as those showing common errors are included to provide a better insight into the art for the beginning designer and to present new ideas and common pitfalls to the more experienced or professional designer. A thorough study of each of the photographs is of prime importance throughout the book.

After studying the first six chapters, it is suggested that the student practice several designs employing the various principles of flower arrangement, basic lines and shapes, and color combinations. Upon completion of these, the designer is ready to proceed to more complicated situations involving the manipulation of the basic procedures.

Flower shows are always a challenge to the floral designer and involve all types of arrangements. Various types of shows are discussed, along with hints to aid the designer who might be entering for the first time and suggestions for those who are seasoned veterans.

Modern arrangements, those for the home and those for special occasions and holidays, are discussed in some detail. The use of flowers for personal adornment, the preparation and construction of corsages, and methods of drying flowers and making artistic arrangements with these materials are discussed in some detail.

Purchasing and handling cut flowers to get maximum longevity from them are concerns of all designers. The author has offered some suggestions to help the designer enjoy flowers for as long as possible.

The floral designer should make arrangements at every opportunity—whether for a special occasion or only for practice. This is a continuing process and the more arrangements that are made, the greater will be one's improvements in the art. Observe arrangements made by others. Attend flower shows. Study pictures of arrangements—and, above all, look for new ideas and ways to improve your floral designs.

Acknowledgments

I would like to express my sincere appreciation to the individuals listed below who gave me permission to use pictures of their arrangements throughout this book, to Mr. David Brown for his help in reproducing pictures and to Mrs. Evelyn Curran, Mrs. Marlene Niederman, Mrs. Rogean Nicolai, and Miss Regina Reckling for the seemingly never-ending task of typing manuscripts. Without the cooperation of the members of many garden clubs who helped and guided me at their flower shows, it would have been impossible for me to complete this book. I am especially grateful to my wife and to our children for the encouragement and understanding that was necessary to bring this book to a successful completion. I also wish to thank Barbara Cassel of Prentice-Hall for her help in the preparation and production of this text.

Many of the arrangements made by the author and some by others are used to show some of the errors or pitfalls one might encounter in the art of flower arrangement. Because of these factors, names of individuals have been listed alphabetically rather than in order of pictures. They are: Mrs. M. Akelewicz; Mrs. J. I. Andre; Mr. F. Andreozzi; Mrs. F. A. Archibald, Jr.; Mrs. E. Armstrong; Mrs. P. Batrow; Boston Museum of Fine Arts; Mrs. D. L. Browning; Mrs. D. Burt; Mrs. R. Chojin; Colonial Williamsburg; Mrs. J. P. Colton; Mrs. W. Croce; Mrs. W. DiPrete; Mrs. K. W. Douglas; Mrs. H. B. Duckwell; Mrs. A. Francis; Mrs. F. L. Giard; Mrs. D. Glover; Mrs. A. Gufler; Mrs. R. Gustafson; Home Garden Club of Wethersfield, Ct.; Mrs. J. L. Hylander; Mrs. A. Jamiel; Mrs. L. Jarvis; Mrs. C. Larmie; Mrs. H. Lebeck; Mrs. D. W. Ledbetter; Mrs. G. B. Long; Mrs. B. Lowe; Mrs. A. Mahoney; Mrs. S. G. Marsocci; Mrs. D. G. McCoy; Mrs. E. Melnick; Mrs. W. W. Minton; Mrs. P. Nichols; Mrs. E. Norton; Mrs. E. O'Neil; Mrs. E. S. Parks; Mrs. L. Pease, 2nd; Mrs. A. Pike, Jr; Mrs. M. Pitterman; Mr. and Mrs. J. Potter; Mrs. T. T. Prior, Jr; Mrs. G. Ray; Mrs. R. K. Richardson; Mrs. A. E. Rose; Mrs. H. Salisbury; Mrs. J. D. Shumway; Mrs. D. L. Smith; Mrs. J. Smith; Mrs. W. J. Smith; Mrs. J. W. Spinner; Mrs. W. D. Taylor; Mrs. E. Theberge; Mrs. R. S. Thompson; Mr. C. A. Todesco; Mrs. N. Wallack; Mrs. D. A. Weaver; Mrs. R. Whitford; Mrs. G. Whitelaw; Mrs. H. Wilbur; and Mrs. A. F. Yates.

Walter E. Larmie

History of Flower Arranging

1

The American type of flower arrangement has been influenced by many of the styles of arrangements throughout the world. As different ethnic groups migrated to this country, they carried with them the cultural achievements, including floral art, of their homelands. With the homogeneous mixing of these various groups, the art of flower arrangement was subject to many changes. Characteristics of many of these were incorporated into an entirely new form of floral art called the American type of floral arrangement. Until just a few years ago, this so-called hybrid type of arrangement was distinctly American and was seldom seen beyond our shores. However, with the vast increases in travel since the development of high speed aircraft, the American type of arrangement is known throughout the world and is not uncommon on the European continent, Japan, and as far away as New Zealand.

The styles that have most influenced the American type are those that predominated on the European continent in the

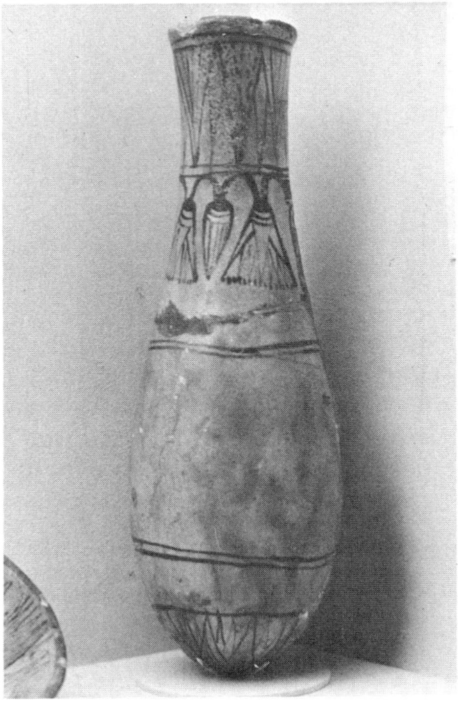

FIGURE 1-1. Blue glazed vessel from the tomb of King Tuthmosis IV, 1423-1410 B.C. Note the decorative lotus blossoms. (Courtesy Museum of Fine Arts, Boston)

late 18th and 19th centuries and the Japanese styles of floral art of that same era. The typical American arrangement today is a line-mass type. The mass shows the occidental and the line, the oriental influence.

As long as history has been recorded, there has been reference to the use of flowers for beautification of the home, for personal adornment, for ceremonial occasions, and for offerings. Discoveries of ancient remains tell us that flowers played an important part in these cultures. Pottery adorned with floral decorations dating back more than 3000 years has been found. Egyptian tombs reveal the use of flowers for their decorative effect, and other works of art from this era indicate a general use of flowers for many occasions. The lotus is often referred to and is shown used singly and massed in vases for general decorative effects. See Figures 1-1 and 1-2.

FIGURE 1-2. Faience Lotus Cup with foot from the Abydas Dynasty. (Courtesy Museum of Fine Arts, Boston)

Materials from Ancient Rome and Greece show little evidence of placing cut flowers in vases; cut flowers were used primarily in wreaths and garlands. Garlands were extensively used by the populace for weddings and other festive occasions, while wreaths were awarded to athletes, victorious sailors and soldiers, as well as to other prominent individuals.

The use of flowers declined along with the other arts during the fall of the Roman Empire, and it was not until medieval times that recordings indicate a revival of their popularity. Gardening and the use of flowers progressed rapidly behind monastery walls during this period. The arts, including use of flowers, were limited primarily to the church. Paintings and writings indicate a strong religious influence and significance. In the 15th century, vases were made especially for holding flowers, but flowers were not limited to these containers only. These special vases held many types of floral groupings which were used for both decoration and symbolism, with the latter being the primary purpose of using flowers.

During the Renaissance (14th–16th centuries) gardening and floral design spread from the monastery, and the general population became involved. The Italian gardens were quite extensive and were grown for beauty as well as for herbs and other purposes. As might be expected, the early gardens of this period were quite similar to those of the medieval walled gardens. As time progressed, a closer relationship arose between the house and the garden. Fountains, sculptures, terraces, and flower vases were incorporated into the area, all integrating into an overall formal setting. Flower beds near the house but in a rather inconspicuous location were used in the latter part of the 16th century, probably as a source of cut flowers for use in the home.

A book *Flora-ouero Cultura di Flori,* written by P. Giovanni Battista Ferrari of Vienna and published in Rome in 1633, contains chapters on gardening and methods of decorating with flowers. Several of the methods of caring for cut flowers described in this publication are basically the same as those practiced today. The book describes the construction of arrangements, the tying together of bouquets, the placement of flowers, and methods for preserving and drying them. It also indicates that flowers were inserted in vases containing holes placed equidistant in a removable top. Only the flower heads were exposed, resulting in rigid unnatural groupings.

In the latter part of this era, as shown in Figure 1–3, the style changed to more graceful types, pyramidal or triangular in shape, colorful, and many made of combinations of fresh and dried materials.

Much of our information regarding this period comes from paintings by Dutch and Flemish artists. They created hundreds of works depicting floral arrangements, and it is from these that much of our present-day knowledge of floral design begins. Their works were not always reproductions of actual arrangements, but in reality were artists' conceptions of them. Flowers of different seasons were combined; placement and curvatures were not practical or probable with living material but were easily accomplished with an artist's brush.

The arrangements of this period were strictly mass. It appears that materials, including quantities of various flowers

FIGURE 1-3. Italian 17th century painting "Poppies in a Wine Flask" by a follower of Caravaggio. Flowers were treated in a natural manner with graceful flowing stems and foliage. (Courtesy Museum of Fine Arts, Boston)

and fruits, as well as accessories of various kinds were literally jammed into the container. Butterflies, shells, stuffed birds and animals, and bird nests containing eggs were used extensively in them. Examples can be seen in Figures 1-4 and 1-5.

Most of the arrangements were colorful and oval in shape. This is the first indication of a true design form being used in floral design. Early designers of this period concentrated more on individual flowers rather than color, which in turn resulted in a spotty effect. Later artists concentrated more on the use of color, creating a more even flow or movement of the eye throughout the arrangement. This resulted in the rhythmic motion we see in today's arrangements.

Containers used for arrangements during this period varied considerably. Early arrangements were made in various jugs, bottles, and other common objects. However, with time came

FIGURE 1-4. "Vase of Flowers" painted by Jim Van Huysum (1682-1749). Many kinds of flowers are literally stuffed into the container which is typical of the Dutch school. (Courtesy Museum of Fine Arts, Boston)

FIGURE 1-5. Elaborate containers were often used in Flemish arrangements. The use of many accessories such as shells, butterflies, birdnests, and stuffed birds are common.

FIGURE 1-6. French 18th century Rococo type arrangement. A note of massiveness but not heaviness or bulkiness exists. Containers gilded with gold leaf were popular.

elaborate containers with beautiful shapes and markings. Massive containers, including the classic urn, were used extensively to support the size of the arrangements made in them.

Unlike life in the low countries, the center of attention in France in the 17th and 18th centuries was focused on the court and the reigning monarch. The arts were focused upon luxury and extravagance and flourished during this period.

Flower arrangements were in keeping with the furnishings of the time. They were large, colorful, and in ornate containers but never as massive as those of the Flemish. Distinctive forms and graceful lines were employed. Flowers loosely arranged with many open spaces, with the resulting overall airy effect, created the typical arrangement of this era. See Figures 1-6 through 1-8. Most were oval in shape and somewhat taller than the container. Pastels were commonly used, although each of the reigning monarchs had favorite colors or flowers. Blues, pinks, soft red, mauve, green, and white were used extensively. The rose appears to be the favorite flower along with peony, delphinium,

FIGURE 1-7. "Mixed Flowers in a Vase" by Pierre Auguste Renoir (1841-1919). From the French school during the latter part of the 19th century. (Courtesy Museum of Fine Arts, Boston)

FIGURE 1-8. "Flowers and Fruit" by Henri Fantin-Latour (1836-1904) shows the openness of the flowers when combined with the heavier fruit. (Courtesy Museum of Fine Arts, Boston)

tulip, iris, and lilac. Napolean favored violets, and these were used extensively during his reign.

Many types of containers were used for flower arrangements. Bronze urns, potteries, Chinese vases, marble and alabaster vases, epergnes, cornucopia, and glassware were common. Most were highly decorated with paintings, scenes, or figures and fit in well with the areas where they were used.

The English have expressed a love for gardens and flowers for centuries, and, unlike the areas on the continent, where gardening was done in enclosed walls by the monks, homeowners or tenants had their own gardens where they grew plants for food, fragrance, flavoring, cosmetics, medicine, and cut flowers. Early records indicate that cut flowers were used in garlands similar to those of ancient Rome and Greece and that these were used in church rituals and processions. Those with fragrance were used for nosegays and were placed throughout the home for their agreeable aromas.

In the 1636 edition of John Gerarde's *Herball,* the frontispiece shows two flower arrangements composed of many varieties of garden flowers arranged in decorated urns. Arrangements are large and compact, but do show a certain amount of gracefulness. In this publication, he gives us much information on cut flowers and their uses.

The Georgian period (1714–1820) is characterized by large, massive, symmetrical, triangular arrangements as shown in Figure 1–9. These were tastefully designed to fit in with the furnishings designed by Hepplewhite, Chippendale, and others. Flowers were plentiful, and many new varieties were imported from foreign countries during this time. The rose was the most popular, but carnations, primroses, campanulas, hyacinths, tulips, irises, and other varieties were used in great numbers. Although fresh flowers predominated, dried bouquets were common and were used extensively during the winter months.

Containers of glass, silver, pewter, porcelain, and pottery were used. It was during this period that many flower vases were made by such well-known manufacturers as Wedgewood, Bristol, and Chelsea. They were made in urns, epergnes, bottles, and special flower holders, with most of them decorated with figures and paintings of va- ous kinds.

FIGURE 1–9. An arrangement of the Georgian period (1714–1820) made with dried flowers in a marble urn. Arrangements were symmetrical and triangular in shape

FIGURE 1-10. The Victorian period (1830–1900) saw many types of arrangements. This typical arrangement in a Chelsea porcelain container shows the massive character of this period.

The Victorian era encompassed almost the entire 19th century (1830–1900). During this period there were considerable changes in flower arranging as well as the other arts. Early Victorian arrangements were distinctly of French influence with many voids and open spaces throughout. As seen in Figure 1-10, flowers were plentiful and much of the flower materials we have today were in cultivation by the time Queen Victoria ascended the throne.

This was the time when the middle class came into wealth and power, and the arts were no longer limited to the nobility. With this rise in power, the status symbol of the arts, including flower arrangement, declined. Flower arrangements were heavily overdone. Dried, fresh, and artificial materials were literally jammed into the same arrangement in heavy ornate containers. Short-stemmed flowers were used, resulting in circular- or oval-type arrangements, many wider than their height. Often the height of the flowers and foliage was less than that of the container. Strong color contrasts were used throughout the designs; colors were bold and rich, and materials of a velvety texture were preferred.

Many types of containers were used; most of them were

heavy and well decorated. Baskets and epergnes, elaborate porcelain vases, glass etched with designs, and many highly decorated pottery containers were in vogue. Footed trumpet vases decorated with gold are a good example of the more popular vases of the day.

As time progressed, Victorian tastes grew progressively worse. Containers, flowers, and arrangements became heavier and more elaborate, and more and more materials were stuffed into the vases. To help keep the arrangement "fresh," many were placed under glass domes.

In 1883, W. Robinson, author of *The English Flower Garden,* wrote that in arranging flowers one should "seek unity, harmony and simplicity of effect, rather than complexities, many of which involve much wearisome labour." This served as an indication of the thoughts of many of the true English designers, yet the massive designs continued in many areas.

Toward the end of the Victorian period, a drastic change took place in floral arrangements. Instead of the heavy, ornate type in earlier years, the use of only a few flowers in cut-glass containers was common. Arrangements were oversimplified, oftentimes to the detriment of the art. See Figure 1–11.

FIGURE 1–11. "Flowers and a Bowl of Fruit" by Paul Gauguin (1848–1900). From the French school but typical of suggestions during the latter part of the Victorian period. (Courtesy Museum of Fine Arts, Boston)

Twentieth century occidental arrangements vary considerably. Many retain the mass effect of their earlier counterparts, although, except for specific occasions, the heaviness of the Victorian era has disappeared. Light- and heavy-appearing flowers are used together, with the heavier and deeper hues concentrated toward the center of the arrangement. The arrangements may be round, oval, or pyramidal, their final placement determining the overall shape. The container should blend well with the flowers and foliage as well as with the room and its furnishings. Lilies, irises, delphiniums, roses, and peonies are among the favorite flowers used in these arrangements.

Arrangements from other parts of the world show their influence on present-day occidental floral designs. The oriental and the American line-mass styles have been accepted to some degree, and it is not uncommon to see compositions with only a few flowers. These are usually found in homes or offices of modern or contemporary design.

While the Europeans were concentrating on massive, colorful arrangements used primarily for their decorative purposes, styles or types of arrangements almost directly opposite of their European counterpart were developed in the Orient. There is some confusion among historians regarding the beginning of oriental flower arrangement. However, it appears that it began in China and was later carried to Japan by Buddhist monks. Chinese arrangements are known for *simplicity, preservation of life,* and *symbolism.* Simplicity comes from Confucius' teachings that too much beauty leads to distraction. In these arrangements, each flower is considered as a detail in itself and is viewed as such. Buddhism teaches the preservation of life, and original arrangements are made with flowers broken from the plants as a means of continuing their lifespan. Specific trees, plants, and flowers are highly symbolic in Chinese culture because of their longevity and durability. Symbolism is the result of Chinese folklore. A certain meaning is expressed in each flower and the way it is used.

All of these three facets, incorporated into arrangements, have led to a restrained type of arrangement, the elimination of unnecessary materials, and simplifications. Figures 1-12 and 1-13 illustrate this.

Japanese floral design is an old art brought to Japan by Buddhist monks about 500 A.D. At that time arrangements were crude and were primarily a way of prolonging the lifespan of flowers that had been broken from the plant by wind, rain,

FIGURE 1–12. Carved wood screen. Ching Dynasty (1700). Overall scene of a Dutch hunting party. The top of each panel and end panels have flower arrangements carved in them. (Courtesy Museum of Fine Arts, Boston)

FIGURE 1–13. Ko-Shaped Beaker, Porcelain decorated in enamels. China, Ming Dynasty, Wan-Li Period (1573–1620). (Courtesy Museum of Fine Arts, Boston)

or other means. The flowers were used in temples, and the arrangements were made by monks.

From this humble beginning developed a system of arranging flowers by the priests called *shin-no-hana,* meaning central flower arrangement. All material evolved about a central stem, and these arrangements expressing a certain amount of symbolism were used on the altars.

In 552 A.D., Ono-no-imoka, a Japanese scholar and an envoy to China, brought back to Japan from China an appreciation of the arts, including the Buddhist practice of floral altar worship. Later, upon the death of his cousin the prince regent, he retired to a residence beside one of his garden lakes and devoted much of his time to praying for his benefactor's soul and to arranging flowers. He was responsible for formalizing styles of arranging and rules to follow, and he later established the first school of flower arrangement in Japan known as Ikenobo, "hermitage by the lake." The school is still in existence today (see Figure 1–14), and the principles of its founder are still carried out by his decendants. The arrangements are based upon a tri-lineal design consisting of three main lines or groups of lines joined at the base and having the appearance of a living plant. The lines known as *heaven, man,* and *earth* are incorporated in most present-day Japanese arrangements. Ikenobo arrangements expressed the idea of universal life by the use of long-lasting sturdy pine which formed a background for short-lived flowers representing man. This principle is practiced by the current Japanese artists.

The size of these arrangements varied considerably. The overall visual weight of the container and plant material, its habit of growth, and the purpose of the arrangement were all instrumental in determining its size. Height varied from one and one half to six or seven times that of the container.

Containers were usually of bronze, although other materials were sometimes used. Decorations often adorned them, but they were always considered subordinate to the plant material in the arrangement.

From its humble beginning, floral art progressed rapidly in Japan after the formation of its first school. Many other schools were founded throughout the years, and in the 17th century Japanese flower arrangement reached its highest degree of perfection. At this time it was considered one of the Japanese ancient cultural achievements, which also included the tea ceremony, incense burning, and sand painting.

FIGURE 1-14. An interesting modern-day version of the Ikenobo School.

Since the 17th century, floral design has been considered one of the fine arts in Japan, just as music and painting have been considered in other parts of the world. Many young people have become involved, and it is said to have been a requirement for many high-ranking military officers during the late 19th century and early into the middle 20th century.

Originating from the Ikenobo school have been many schools and styles of flower arrangement. Each has followed the asymmetrical, tri-lineal designs with some variations, each has its own rules, and all have a certain amount of significance attached to them. Formal and informal as well as classical and naturalistic types have developed. Some have been extremely complicated, while others have stressed simplicity.

One of the first styles that developed was known as the Rikka (Rikkwa). The arrangements were elaborate, highly stylized, formal, and sometimes more than six feet tall. It is said that some were as tall as 40 feet. They were extremely complicated arrangements suggesting complete landscapes, and often taking several days to complete. Rules were rigid and complex, and no deviations from them were allowed. These "standing up" arrangements were usually completed in heavy bronze vases. Although they originated in the temples, they soon became popular with the nobility and upper classes. Because of their size, there was a very limited use for them outside of the temples. This style with some modification is still practiced today by many designers, as shown in Figures 1-15 and 1-16.

The Seika (Seikwa) style shown in Figures 1-17 and 1-18 was a development of the Rikka because of the desirability of having simpler and less complicated arrangements. During this period floral arrangements for the home were placed in built-in alcoves called "tokonoma," a household religious shrine especially built to hold floral arrangements or other forms of art.

The arrangements of the Seika style were formal, of trilineal design, and they followed rigid rules. As time progressed, several schools using this style were developed, each having its own rules. It might be expected that because of rigid rules, there would be a tendency toward "oneness," and all arrangements would look alike. This is not true, and many interesting

FIGURE 1-15. Rikka. A highly stylized, elaborate arrangement.

FIGURE 1-16. Rikka. A highly stylized, elaborate arrangement.

FIGURE 1-17. Lines in a Seika arrangement. The center line is heaven; lower right is man; and lower left, earth. The other lines are called attributes.

FIGURE 1-18. Typical of the early classical arrangements. The use of aspidistra leaves creates the basic lines for this Seika-style of arrangement.

arrangements can be made. Height of arrangements in the Seika style varies among the schools. Some stress that plant material should be one and one half while others might be three or four times the height of the container. The degree of formality of the arrangement is determined by the spread of the three basic lines. The closer the lines, the more formal the design.

The arrangement may consist of only three stems or may be three groupings all originating from the same point. All stems remain together for four to six inches above the rim of the container before branching out, to give the appearance of a living plant. The idea is to create a rhythmic motion and a clear, unconfused line.

Many kinds of flowers are used in Seika arrangements, but they must conform to the time of year when they are growing naturally. As might be expected, chrysanthemum is the favorite flower of the Japanese and is the most popular flower for these arrangements.

Along with the Rikka and Seika arrangements, which are considered classic or formal, another distinct or naturalistic style was developed. This was called the Nagiere and is known as the "thrown in" style. It has been popular for centuries as part of the tea ceremony.

In this type of arrangement, nature is claimed to be expressed more realistically than in the more formal styles. The natural beauty of the stem and flower is used rather than the manipulation of stems to form desired curves. All types of plants are used, including those that naturally climb or hang.

Plant material is placed in a container in such a way that it leans against its side and comes out in a natural manner. Flowers are used as well as other plant materials, and color is an important part of the design.

The principles of Heaven, Man, and Earth are expressed in these arrangements; but unlike those of a formal nature, they are often difficult to interpret. In many of these arrangements, the lines may form more of a diagonal line than the typical triangular pattern. Close examination, however, will reveal the triangular form, modified in various ways.

Nagiere arrangements may consist of one well-shaped branch with a few flowers at the base or several branches and flowers incorporated into them. However, arrangements of most schools have one dominant branch, with a secondary one used at the base where a few flowers are added. All should originate from the same point to give the feeling of a single plant and of stability. Tall narrow vases are commonly used for this style.

The Moribana type of arrangement is the modern style of naturalistic flower arrangement. The idea is to create a landscape or garden scene using miniature ponds and various types of plant material. Although the name refers to "piled up flowers," the amount of material used is small when compared to occidental or American types of arrangements.

The design is tridimensional, and each segment of the arrangement follows the tri-lineal pattern. Arrangements are made in shallow containers and closely follow the season of the year by selection of plants, amount of water exposed, and general placement of material. Many times only flowers are used with their own foliage. They can be grouped according to varieties or if only one kind of flower is used, different groupings can be used throughout.

From among these styles, along with others, have developed many of the present-day schools of Japanese flower arrangement. Examples of these as shown in Figures 1-19 and 1-20 are the *Sogetsu* and *Ohara,* two of the more popular

FIGURE 1-19. The Sogetsu School has many forms. Some express the natural feeling while others are completely in the opposite direction.

FIGURE 1-20. Another example of the Sogetsu school.

schools of Japanese flower arrangement today. Each has its own rules and styles of arranging flowers and has many followers, not only in Japan but throughout the world.

There are few pictures and a meager amount of literature telling us about flower arrangement in colonial America (1620–1800). However, we do know that three cultural centers developed including New England, New Amsterdam, and Virginia, and in each, different types of flower arrangement developed.

In New England where homes were small, living conditions rough, and contact with the outside world limited, there was little time for flower arrangement or other forms of art. Gardens were small and were limited primarily to the necessities of life including food, medicine, cosmetics, and dyes. Cut flowers were incidental and were obtained from those plants grown for other purposes. Roses, peonies, hollyhocks, and marigolds were grown for medicinal use, but some of the flowers were brought indoors for their decorative value. The countryside provided many native flowers such as goldenrod, black-eyed Susans, laurel, and dogwood, which also served as cut flowers.

Arrangements were simple—mixed bouquets arranged in any type container available including wooden and earthenware bowls, pewter and tin mugs and pans, and an occasional treasured vase brought from the homeland. Sharp color contrasts were employed instead of color harmonies.

New Amsterdam was the center of Dutch culture in the New World, and many of the cultural practices of Holland were followed in this settlement. Many horticultural efforts were started, including the planting of orchards and gardens. Garden flowers included roses, carnations, tulips, lilies, anemones, violets, and marigolds.

Homes and gardens in this area were larger than their counterparts in New England. Servants were plentiful, and outside dangers were not as great as were those in other areas, leaving more leisure time for the enjoyment of gardens and flowers. Little is known about the arrangements made by these colonists; but since ties with the homeland were strong, it is expected that they followed rather closely those of Holland. Most floral containers were probably brought from Holland, but along with them, pewter and pottery containers and stoneware jugs were used.

Unlike the colonists in New England, those in Virginia remained affiliated with the Church of England and were never separated from the Mother Country. Cotton, tobacco, and other crops were grown on a large scale with the help of slave labor

FIGURE 1-21. Colonial Williamsburg. A fan-shaped arrangement of dried flowers.

and were exported to other countries. In return, fine furniture, tapestries, wall paper, chinaware, and other materials were imported, and a favorable balance of trade was developed. Wealth obtained from trade resulted in more gracious living and more leisure time than that of the New England colonists; consequently, fine homes were built and extensive gardens developed.

Flower arrangement of this period has been researched considerably more than that of the other colonies, and through books, diaries, portraits, floral prints, and correspondence, much has been learned about the arrangements of this period. Williamsburg was considered the cultural and horticultural center of the South during most of the 18th century, and much of the information available centers around this area.

Arrangements were made to fit specific locations. In the homes of the wealthy, there were many areas in which to place floral displays. Large hallways, dining rooms, and other areas were suitable for large arrangements, as shown in Figure 1-21, while smaller, more delicate arrangements were found in bedrooms. Sideboards served as attractive areas for small vases and bowls of flowers and fruits as well as for potted plants.

Many kinds of flowers and many colors were used for arrangements: Peonies, carnations, roses, tulips, daffodils, and many other flowers were available. Arrangements were triangular or fan-shaped, and height of the flowers was about the same as the height of the containers, although there were some deviations from this. Many arrangements consisted of only one kind of flower with a filler such as baby's breath added, while others contained many kinds and colors: Blues and pastel colors were popular, although many deeper hues were used to some extent.

Dried and fresh flowers were seldom used together, but dried material was used extensively for winter bouquets. By drying properly, color was retained and attractive arrangements made.

Many types of containers were used. These included China imports, fingered posy holders, blue and white "bricks," and various bowls made of silver, pewter, pottery, Delftware, and Wedgewood. Most were decorated in various ways.

During the 19th centry the French influence was seen in the American arrangements. See Figure 1-22. The arrangements became lighter, more airy, and more formal than in the preceeding years. Urns and bowls in silver, glass, pewter, and porcelain were used.

In the early part of the 20th century the Japanese influence began to show in the American floral arrangement. However, the general style was that of the European nature. With the integration of the East and West, rapid changes took place in the American style; at flower shows new types of arrangements were displayed, and whole sections were later devoted to them.

The early 1930s saw the birth of a new style of American flower arrangement as shown in Figure 1-23. The line of the Japanese arrangement was incorporated with the mass of the European style to form the line-mass type which has continued as the basic American style since that time. This caught on rapidly, probably because of the result of the National Council of State Garden Clubs. It is to this organization that we owe the high status and the popularity of the art of flower arrangement today.

The art of flower arrangement is constantly in a state of change. We see many variations in the American type today; we not only have the line-mass style, but we find many strictly line types and others only mass. Freedom of expression along with a basic understanding of the art are the underlying elements of the American type of arrangement. See Figures 1-24, 1-25, and 1-26.

FIGURE 1-22. "Still Life—Flowers in a Basket" by Severin Roesen (1847-1871). The French influence is depicted in the airyness of the arrangement from the American school, (Courtesy Museum of Fine Arts, Boston)

FIGURE 1-23. A line-mass arrangement typical of the American type of the early 1930s.

FIGURE 1-24. Line-mass. A later version of the American form of flower arrangement.

FIGURE 1-25. A line arrangement using chrysanthemums and sumac, typical of many of the present type of American arrangements. [See also Color Plate.]

FIGURE 1-26. A mass-type arrangement used in many present day colonial homes. Note the massive but airy effect throughout.

Principles of Flower Arranging

2

In all the arts, composition is based upon a series of principles or elements. To the beginner, a thorough understanding of these is necessary. As one progresses in the art, distinction is recognized by the various ways these principles are manipulated to fit one's own personality.

As the painter uses his paints, and the musician his notes, the floral designer uses his flowers, and each has certain principles or basics he must follow. In the area of floral arrangement these basics are referred to as *principles of flower arranging.* It is the employment of these principles that distinguishes an arrangement from a bunch or a bouquet of flowers.

When one takes a handful of flowers and drops them into a container, the result is not an arrangement but a haphazard grouping of flowers. This is usually referred to as a "bunch" of flowers. If these flowers are then manipulated according to size, shape, color, or other factors, the "bunch" becomes a "bouquet." This is a term that has several connotations and is

FIGURE 2–1. A bouquet of roses. The flowers have been arranged strictly by spacing; no principles of flower arrangements have been applied.

often used for any type of cut flower display. It is the type often found in many of our homes today. Long-stemmed roses mixed with baby's breath and/or foliage in a deep vase as shown in Figure 2–1 demonstrate this category.

The bouquet becomes an arrangement when various principles of floral design are applied. The number of principles varies among authors. Some list as many as a dozen, others as few as four.

The terms *arrangement* and *composition* are often used interchangeably. *Arrangements* are usually considered as a combination of flowers and foliage in a container, whereas if accessories, dried materials, or nonfloral items such as sculptures and figurines and backgrounds are applied, *composition* is the correct connotation. When one is entering an arrangement in flower show competition, the show schedule should be clearly understood, to distinguish between these two and to eliminate the possibility of disqualification.

The remainder of this chapter will be devoted to a discussion of the principles of flower arranging.

As with the architect, *design* is the overall plan of the arrangement to be created. It may be good or bad but is neverthe-

FIGURE 2–2. Design. The use of bright red geraniums in an old-fashioned lamp indicates a well-thought-out plan to carry out the theme of the class, "One Bright Corner—old-fashioned and lovely."

less present in every flower arrangement. Figures 2–2 and 2–3 illustrate both good and poor designs.

The tailor does not take a piece of cloth and start to cut with no preconceived idea of what the finished product will be. He follows a pattern and anticipates the overall outcome of his

FIGURE 2–3. Weak design. The vertical line placed at an angle, the heaviness of the foliage on the lower right, and the placement of the four chrysanthemums above the rim of the container that is too small—all contribute to the overall weak design of the arrangement.

efforts before he makes the first cut. The same should be true of the floral designer. Before beginning construction, the designer should have a clear idea of the complete arrangement. The idea might be obtained in a number of ways; perhaps the best source is in determining the purpose of the arrangement—what it is expected to accomplish. The specific setting or physical space where it is to be used is also a good source of ideas; since the arrangement should harmonize with its surroundings, the decor should have a strong influence upon the design.

The container can be a source of ideas. By studying its shape, texture, color, and other prominent features, an inspiration for the design might come forth. The flowers and foliage are other areas that can influence the design; and the shape or color of the flowers available will prove valuable. Accessories are also worthy of consideration and can be an inspiration for design. At flower shows, the general theme of the show will influence the design of the arrangements. Figure 2–4 illustrates a flower show theme.

FIGURE 2-4. The theme of the show, an event, containers, etc, are sources of ideas. The Gasparella Regatta in Tampa, Florida, is the inspiration for this arrangement depicting a boat under full sail.

FIGURE 2-5. The beginner should make a rough sketch to follow. As experience is gained, this will not be necessary.

FIGURE 2-6. This arrangement closely follows the sketch seen in Figure 2-5.

The beginner will find it helpful to make a rough sketch of the expected arrangement, as shown in Figures 2-5 and 2-6, and then try to manipulate the flowers to achieve this end. As one gains experience, crude drawings will no longer be necessary, although an overall mental picture of the completed arrangement will prove beneficial. A good design is not something that just happens—it is the result of much thought and planning!

Scale (see Figures 2-7 to 2-9) may be defined as the size relationship of all the parts of the composition. This includes (1) the flowers themselves—gladiolus combined with lily of the valley would be out of scale because the tiny, delicate lily of the valley would be completely overpowered by the large size of the gladiolus florets and the total size and mass of the entire gladiolus stalks. However, a combination of medium-sized gladioli and carnations or chrysanthemums would prove satisfactory; (2) the flowers and foliage—French marigolds and canna leaves would be out of scale. The large, heavy canna

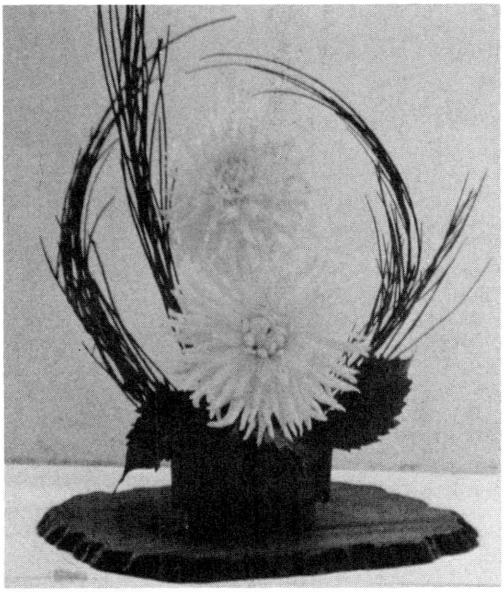

FIGURE 2-7. Scale. The size of each part of the arrangement is influenced by the overall size of the arrangement and their relationships to each other. Each dahlia in the above arrangement is too large for the overall size and is out of scale with the container.

FIGURE 2-8. Roses tend to open quickly when placed in a warm room. Because of this situation, the dark roses now predominate in an arrangement where all flowers were in scale only a few hours earlier.

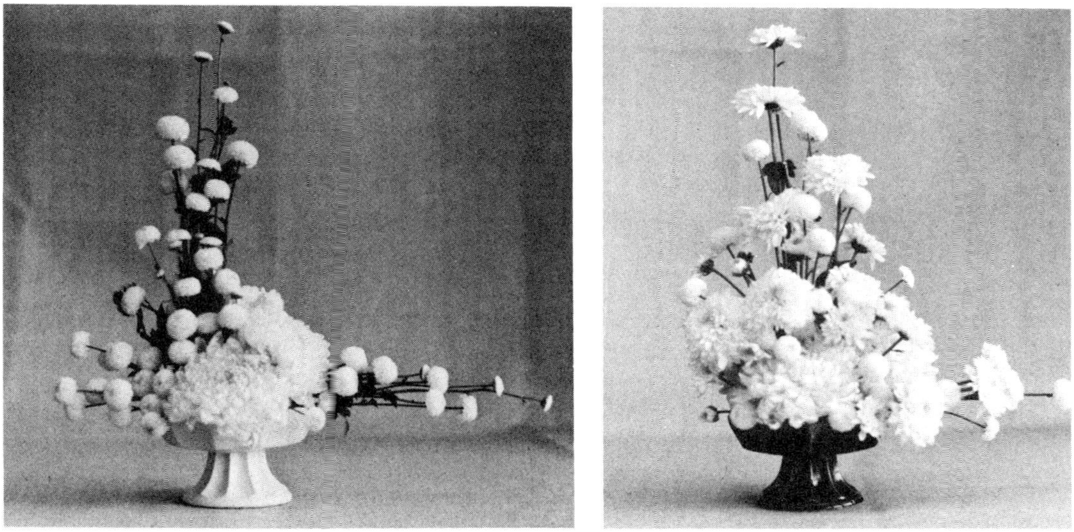

FIGURE 2-9. Scale. Large chrysanthemums combined with pompon type. By placing the large flowers deep into the arrangement and covering them with a few smaller ones, they remain in scale. If the large flowers were placed in the forward position, they would dominate the arrangement and be out of scale.

leaves would predominate, and the small marigolds would be rather inconspicuous unless used in large masses. If the marigolds were used with boxwood or huckleberry foliage, the combination would have a satisfactory scale relationship; (3) the arrangement and/or flowers and container—large chrysanthemums in an average-sized tea pot or large flowers in a small arrangement would be out of scale because the large flowers would completely overshadow the container or dominate the arrangement. A general guide is to have no flower larger than one third the size of the container or the arrangement of flowers. Calendulas or carnations would be in scale with the tea pot mentioned above.

When selecting flowers for an arrangement, one must be careful to select a size and visual weight of flowers that work together. Visual weight is that element due to color, texture, size, and other characteristics that can make one object appear heavier than another. This element should be considered for all parts of the arrangement including flowers, foliage, container, and accessories, and all should be in the proper relationship to each other. With two flowers of equal size and color—cosmos and single pompon chrysanthemum—the chrysanthemum would appear heavier because of its coarser texture and therefore

FIGURE 2-10. Two carnations of equal size. The darker one appears to be heavier.

should be used accordingly in the arrangement. With carnations of equal size but different colors, the darker colored flowers will appear heavier than the lighter colored ones as indicated in Figure 2-10. There is a tendency among designers, probably originating with the 19th century era, to use many so-called "fillers" such as baby's breath in their designs. If not used properly, these materials can be out of scale with the other parts of the arrangement and may destroy the whole effect.

Foliage is often overlooked, especially by the beginner, and anything readily available is stuck into the arrangement, almost as an after-thought. Many of the foliages used are either too fine or too large for the design and, therefore, are out of scale. See Figure 2-11. Asparagus fern with its fine rather delicate texture is often a poor choice for use with many of the

FIGURE 2-11. Zinnias with rhododendron foliage. The weight of the rhododendron leaves dominates and overpowers the zinnia flowers.

flowers in today's arrangements; however, it might prove satisfactory with some of the more delicate flowers such as sweet peas. The use of magnolia leaves has been popular in some areas; they can be preserved easily and used in dried arrangements. One of the major problems in using them is that they are often out of scale with the other dried material and predominate in the arrangement.

The designer should choose foliage carefully. Many good materials are available, and with a little care and patience it is possible to select one that will be in scale with the other parts of the arrangement.

Proportion (see Figures 2-12 and 2-13) is the size relationship of one part of the arrangement or composition to another. It deals with the arrangement or composition as a whole rather than the individual items within. The arrangement of plant material should be in proportion to the size of the container, and the whole design should be in proportion to its setting.

As a general rule, the arrangement should be one and one half to two times the height or length of the container, whichever is greater. Horizontal arrangements can be up to four times the length of the containers. However, because of the type of material being used (pottery, glass, etc.), color and texture of the container, and the type of plant material used,

FIGURE 2-12. An interesting combination of chrysanthemums, wild asters, and ivy seen from all sides. The arrangement would be in better proportion if displayed on a larger table.

FIGURE 2-13. Proportion. Geraniums and daisies combined with several kinds of foliage make an interesting centerpiece in good proportion to its setting.

these measurements may be exceeded to keep the arrangement in proportion. A tall arrangement in a short container may appear top heavy, whereas a small arrangement in a large container would create the same relationship as does a cork in a bottle. Both arrangements are out of proportion with the containers.

Arrangements should "fit" into a selected setting and should be the correct size for the location, as shown in Figure 2-14. Household furnishing will influence the size of the arrangement. If the room is decorated in the Victorian style with its ornate, fussy, and generally heavy appearing furnishings, the

FIGURE 2-14. An arrangement of dried strawflowers and statice in good proportion to its surroundings.

arrangement should have a corresponding appearance in order to be in proportion with the surroundings. If a contemporary decor is being used, the arrangement, although perhaps as large as that of the Victorian style, would not present the heavy, fussy appearance and would remain in proportion with the lighter modern furnishings.

Careful placement of the completed arrangement in the room is necessary if it is to be in scale or proportion with its surroundings. The arrangement should not be crammed into a space nor should it be 'lost'' in the available area. A massive arrangement in an average-sized hallway would be out of proportion with the surrounding area. This would also be true for a miniature arrangement on an averaged-sized coffee table.

Balance is the visual stability of the arrangement and may be considered in a number of ways. The arrangement should appear to be stable in the container. The flowers should not give the impression of falling forward out of the container, nor should they be leaning too far back in it. To achieve this type of balance in a one-sided arrangement, the stem of the first flower (the tallest in most arrangements) should be inserted into the holder toward the back of the container and should either be straight up or leaning slightly toward the back. The flowers at the sides should be placed slightly in back of the center line position and those in front, forward in the container. A cross section of the arrangement as viewed from one side should have the appearance of a triangle, as shown in Figure 2-15.

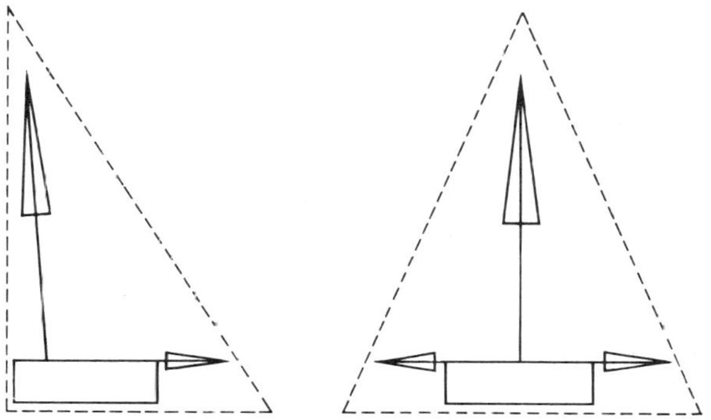

FIGURE 2-15. To obtain stability, the top flower in a one-sided arrangement should be either vertical or slightly leaning toward the back. (left) In an arrangement seen from all sides, the top flower should be in a vertical position. (right) Both form a triangle when seen in cross section.

If the arrangement is to be viewed from all sides, the first flower should be secured firmly in the center of the container extending vertically. The flowers forming the horizontal line or length of the arrangement should radiate from the center forming a 180 degree arc. The width of the arrangement is obtained by placing flowers an equal distance forward and backward. A cross section of this arrangement, when viewed from one side, will be seen as an isosceles or equilateral triangle. This is illustrated in Figure 2-15. With this beginning, the arrangement should appear to be stable in the container and will not give the appearance of falling out at the first slight movement or breath of air. The arrangement is completed as described in Chapter 4.

Other types of balance are symmetrical and asymmetrical. These are achieved when all the material on one side of the imaginary center line of the arrangement has a visual weight equal to that of the material on the other side. An equilateral or isosceles triangle, a circle, or an oval are examples of symmetrical balance. A line drawn through the center from the high point perpendicular to the base of the triangle and a diameter in the circle or oval divides them into two equal and similar parts. In the arrangement, to achieve symmetrical balance as shown in Figure 2-16, it is not necessary that both sides be exactly alike but merely similar. The high point in the arrangement should be directly in the center of the container, and the basal lines should be of equal length from the center.

FIGURE 2-16. Balance. An interesting use of Bells of Ireland, snapdragons, and roses in a holiday arrangement possessing symmetrical balance.

FIGURE 2-17. Balance. The vertical lines on the left are counterbalanced by the lower lines on the right giving this arrangement asymmetrical balance.

Asymmetrical balance can be created with any triangle other than those mentioned above, with a Hogarth curve, a crescent, or a diagonal. With this type of arrangement, a line dropped from the high point divides the arrangement into two *un*equal parts. Height on one side of the centerline is counterbalanced by width or weight on the other side of the line; thus, the high point in most of the designs is placed to one side of the imaginary centerline. This would be the vertical line of the design while the counterbalancing line would be the low horizontal line on the opposite side of the center. Counterbalance is illustrated in Figure 2-17.

The inverted T as described in Chapter 3 is an example of symmetrical balance and the L described in the same chapter is an example of asymmetrical balance.

Focus is the point or area of emphasis in the arrangement. It is commonly referred to as the focal point. Although found in all arrangements, it may be more outstanding in some types than in others. Those seen from one side usually have a more pronounced focal point than those seen from all sides. A centerpiece viewed from all directions will have an all around focal area.

The focal point or focal area is placed low in the design, many times overlapping the rim of the container. This is the area that has the bulk of the weight and supports the rest of the arrangement. All lines in the arrangement should give the appearance of leading to this area.

There are many ways to create a focal point. One large flower, a group of flowers, contrasting color, or a figurine can be used effectively for this purpose. The use of one large flower at the base of the arrangement and slightly overlapping the rim of the container is the easiest way to establish a focal point. This method is employed when flowers of varying sizes are used in the arrangement. Zinnias or marigolds cut at various stages of maturity from buds to fully opened flowers work well. This can be seen in Figure 2-18, where the lighter-appearing buds are used at the extremities and the heavier, fully opened flower is used as the focal point.

FIGURE 2-18. Focus. One single marigold forms the focal point for this vertical arrangement. By gradually increasing the size of flowers from the top to the base and decreasing the spaces between them, the eye is led to the large marigold at the base.

FIGURE 2–19. Focus. By concentrating the weight of the dark colored sweet william near the base, a focal area is formed. The lines of the scotch broom and carnations lead the eye to this area which has been increased in intensity by the dark ti leaves.

When flowers of the same size, i.e., all carnations, are used throughout an arrangement, the focal point can be achieved by using a grouping of flowers at or near the rim of the container. Spacing of flowers as described in Chapter 4 should also be used to establish this focal area.

The use of a contrasting color is the most *difficult* way to successfully establish a satisfactory focal point. In most instances, the use of a different color will tend to overemphasize the focal point and actually take away from the overall arrangement. Careful attention should be given to selection of colors in order to avoid this situation. To make a focal point using contrasting colors, it is best to use several flowers all of the focal point color as you see in Figure 2–19. Work them deep into the arrangement, gradually bringing them forward to emphasize them at the focal point. To use a single flower as a contrasting color for a focal point almost always brings disaster.

FIGURE 2-20. Focus. An arrangement of mountain laurel and a single dahlia. The lines are in good scale, but the use of one large dahlia for the focal point is overpowering. Overemphasis of the focal point is a common error among designers.

Care must be taken when using figurines; if not used properly they can seriously detract from the rest of the arrangement. They should be incorporated in such a way that they do not command all of the attention and take all the significance away from the other parts. When used correctly, they can be a definite asset.

One of the big problems, especially with beginners in the art of floral design, is overemphasis of the focal point; this is shown in Figure 2-20. They tend to become overly conscious of the focal point and concentrate on this area at the expense of other parts of the design. As one gains experience, this fault is gradually overcome.

Unity is a sense of togetherness. All parts of the composition, including flowers, foliage, container, background, and setting, should fit together in such a way that there is no discord or conflict among them. Figure 2-21 is a good example of unity of design. Daffodils combined with Dutch iris is another often used combination . The color combination of soft lavender-blue iris and bright yellow daffodils is good. In addition to unity of color, unity of season of bloom is expressed, and the textures of the flowers go well together. The combination of daffodils and fall asters (New England Aster), although being nearly the same color combination as above, would be out of unity because of the combination of spring and fall flowers and the different textures of materials. It is possible to have rather striking effects in arrangements by combining different textures, but one should consider this approach as carefully as when selecting color combinations. Crotin leaves and chrysan-

FIGURE 2–21. Unity. The use of carnations, daisies, foliage, and riding apparel (hat, gloves, and crop) all combined to express a unifying effect of materials in the arrangement. [see also Color Plate.]

the mums make a fine combination, but the colorful crotin leaves can be out of unity when used with many other flowers such as roses, delphinium, and sweet peas.

Contemporary arrangements would be out of unity in a Victorian type container as would a Victorian arrangement in a modern living room.

Rhythm involves the feeling or sense of motion flowing through the arrangement. See Figures 2-22 and 2-23. It is created when the eye flows through the design because of the harmonious placement of the lines and color. The lines may be straight or curved but there is always that feeling of movement, usually toward the focal point. By proper manipulation of flower sizes and placement—small or partially opened flowers

FIGURE 2-22. Rhythm. Placement and size of flowers help to create a rhythmic motion leading toward the focal area in this beautifully designed arrangement for a church at Palm Sunday or Easter.

at the extremities and fully opened flowers at or near the focal point—and the blending of colors from the lighter colors to darker colors within and toward the base, the feeling of motion can be obtained.

Curved lines in themselves do not necessarily create the principle of rhythm but do provide a quality of gracefulness to the arrangement. However, it is easier to create the feeling of motion with flowing lines rather than straight lines which indicate a quality of strength and direction. Crossing lines should be avoided whenever possible. They usually interrupt the flowing movement and may result in static areas.

Although the principle of rhythm is not always employed, without it, the arrangement might be rather static or uninteresting. See, for example, Figure 2-24.

FIGURE 2-23. Rhythm. The curvature of the lines suggest movement or a whipping of the whale's tail.

FIGURE 2–24. Rhythm. An interesting arrangement without using the principle of rhythm.

Repetition, as the term implies, is the repeated use of an element throughout the arrangement as illustrated in Figure 2–25. It can be accomplished by the multiple use of lines, colors, forms, and sizes. Although important in creating interest, it can be easily overdone and may create a disaster in some compositions. Equal spacing of colors, forms, and sizes throughout the arrangement can become monotonous and detract from the whole. Repeated use of lines of the same length and curvature has the same effect. In applying this principle to any arrangement, it is important that variations be made to avoid the above situations.

One blue cornflower might look lost in an arrangement of yellow marigolds, but if several are used throughout the arrangement, the combination ties together into an attractive unit. The use of this principle would help when using a contrasting color for a focal point: Using a few flowers of the color of the focal point down deep in the arrangement would help tie things together and would reduce the possibility of overemphasis of the focal point.

A common error often found in Christmas arrangements is the use of a single glass ball or other ornament attached near the extremities of an evergreen branch. This usually looks lost or out of place in this position. However, if a few more are worked into and toward the center of the arrangement (the principle of repetition), the whole arrangement is tied together, and a more attractive creation results.

Dominance is the use of one element in the arrangement

that stands out above all others. All other elements become subservient to it but remain a necessary part of the whole. Line, color, size, or shape of flowers may be dominant, or some other factors may be used to create this commanding effect. Mass alone does not necessarily create dominance.

Lines of equal height will compete for dominance. To avoid this situation one stem should be used to establish the vertical line or uppermost portion of the line in the arrangement. If gladioli are used to establish the line, one spike should predominate above all others as shown in Figure 2-26. Curved lines are interesting, but care should be taken in their use to avoid confusion and loss of the dominating factor.

FIGURE 2-25. Repetition. The use of pine cones throughout the arrangement employs the principle of repetition. If only the one cone on the uppermost branch were present, it would not fit in with the rest of the arrangement. [see also Color Plate.]

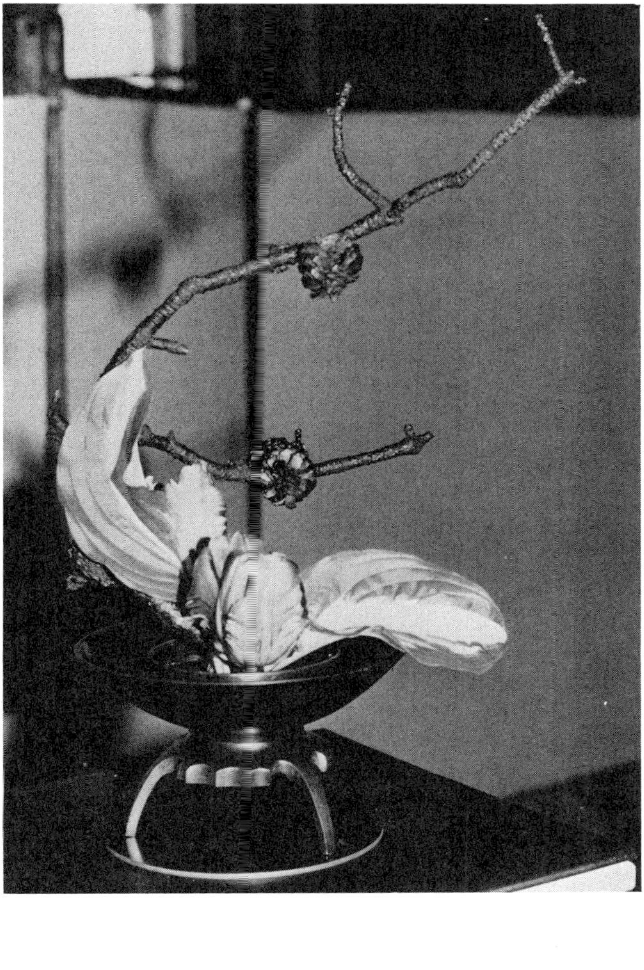

Color used effectively throughout the arrangement can be the dominating element in it. Equal amounts of color should be avoided because of competition for prominence.

An arrangement consisting of all the same type of spikey or round flowers may be quite ineffective because of the lack of dominance. If only one type of plant material is available, dominance may be achieved by manipulating the flowers at different angles and making use of line or color. If a combination of round and spikey material is used, one type should predominate. Perhaps the easiest way of creating dominance is the use of flowers of unequal size. In such a situation, the larger flowers will dominate and the smaller ones will be subordinate to them.

FIGURE 2-26. Dominance. The vertical line of the gladioli and horizontal position of the fern create a dominating effect of line in this arrangement. The uppermost gladiolus is primarily responsible for this effect. If both gladioli were the same height, they would be competing for dominance.

3 Lines and Shapes

Artists and architects alike base their plans or designs upon a series of simple geometric forms which are modified in various ways to meet desired ends. These forms serve as useful guides to the floral designer in determining the overall outline or shape of the arrangement to be created. The pyramid, the cube, and the sphere are the basis for these designs. These are manipulated in many ways by the floral designer to form various abstract shapes which are created with the use of flowers, foliage, and supplementary materials. Seen in the two-dimensional aspects, they form the triangle, square, and circle shown in Figures 3-1 and 3-2. Most flower arrangements will fit into one of these categories or into some modification of them. For example, the various triangles—isosceles, equilateral, symmetrical, or asymmetrical—may be derived from a pyramid; a rectangle or a vertical from a cube; and the oval, crescent, spiral, or Hogarth curve from a sphere. Arrangements on the following pages show the several basic shapes in flower designs.

FIGURE 3-1. Basic shapes. The three basic shapes—triangle, square, and circle—can be modified to form many variations of each, including an asymmetrical triangle, a rectangle, or an oval.

FIGURE 3-2. The use of dried material in this Colonial Williamsburg type of arrangement suggests the overall basic shape of a circle. [see also Color Plate.]

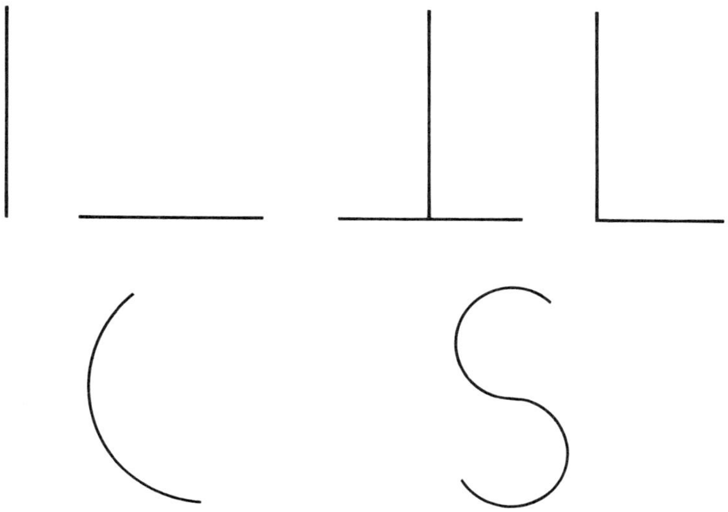

FIGURE 3-3. Basic lines in flower arrangement. Top, left to right: Vertical, horizontal, inverted T, and L. Bottom, left to right: Crescent, Hogarth curve.

The basic line is the main line or backbone of the arrangement. It is the foundation upon which the whole arrangement is built. Its construction is the first step in the actual making of the arrangement, and from this the desired shape of the arrangement is accomplished.

There are six basic lines in flower arrangement, as shown in Figure 3-3. They are the vertical, horizontal, inverted T, L, crescent, and the Hogarth curve. Although many other lines such as the diagonal, zig-zag, spiral, and swirl are often used, most can be traced back to a modification of one or more of these six basic lines. It is possible to combine more than one basic line in an arrangement, as shown in Figure 3-4. However, they tend to compete for dominance, and such combinations should be avoided whenever possible.

The *vertical* line illustrated in Figure 3-5 is perhaps the easiest of all to make. It is a line that possesses the qualities of strength and balance and can best be accomplished by the use of rather bold, spikey-type flowers such as gladioli, snapdragons, or stocks. It is possible to use other types of flowers, but much more effort is required in placing them according to size and shape. The gladiolus, with its fully opened flowers at the base of the stem, flowers in the various stages of maturity in the middle, and buds at the top, makes an ideal flower to use to establish this line. Selection of a tall, narrow container will

FIGURE 3-4. A combination of the vertical and crescent lines. Often times the two lines will compete with each other for dominance.

FIGURE 3-5. Vertical line. The use of a vertical-type container accentuates the vertical line of this arrangement of two daffodils and scotch broom. The overall shape is rectangular.

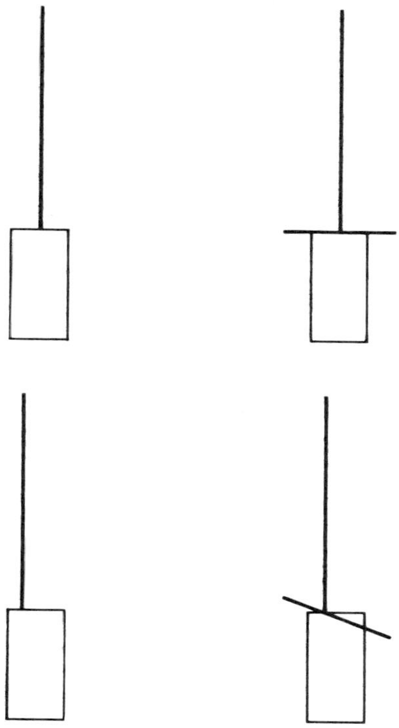

FIGURE 3-6. Top: Symmetrical balance. Left: Placement of the main line in center of container. Right: Horizontal lines of equal length. Bottom: Asymmetrical balance. Left: Placement of vertical line off center of the container. Right: Lines of unequal length for balance.

help to accentuate the line. However, it is possible, although somewhat more difficult, to use other types of containers for this vertical arrangement.

Construction begins with the placement of the tallest flower or foliage. It can be placed directly above or slightly to one side of the centerline of the container depending upon the desired shape of the arrangement. For symmetrical balance, it should be placed directly along and for asymmetrical balance, slightly to one side of the centerline. Figure 3-6 illustrates this. The height of this line is dependent upon the visual weight of the vase. The general rule that the arrangement should be one and one half to two times the height of the container can be varied somewhat with the vertical arrangement. If two vases are the same size and shape but are made of different materials—heavy pottery or delicate glass—the heavier-appearing pottery container will support a larger arrangement than the one made of glass. In fact, it will probably be necessary to *exceed* the above mentioned rule to keep the arrangement in scale with the container. Whether this line forms the basis for a triangle, oval, or rectangular shape, it should possess perfect balance in relation to other parts of the arrangement. The next step will help to determine the shape by placing supporting materials at or near the rim of the container. If the arrangement is to have the overall shape of a symmetrical triangle, short-stemmed material of equal length should be placed on either side of the centerline, thus giving the outline of an isosceles triangle and an overall up and down appearance. The same procedure should be followed in creating an oval shape. If the shape is to be an asymmetrical triangle, the materials placed at the base would be of unequal lengths to create this outline. Again, refer to Figure 3-6. Care should be taken to keep these materials short and close to the container in order not to destroy the vertical appearance. The placement of this material establishes the main line, and the arrangement can then be completed as described in Chapter 4.

There are many places in the home where vertical arrangements can be used. They may be placed at either end of a mantel, in a narrow wall space between two doors or windows, or in a small wall area in a hallway.

The *horizontal* line shown in Figure 3-7 is used for low arrangements when length is needed in preference to height. An

FIGURE 3-7. Horizontal line. The horizontal line is constructed by extending the annual flowers lengthwise from the center of the container and keeping the vertical material relatively low in the above arrangement. The overall shape is that of a symmetrical triangle.

FIGURE 3-8. Horizontal line. A horizontal arrangement using a pedestal-type container elevates the arrangement allowing more space on the table.

arrangement for a mantel, a coffee table, or a dinner table might fit into this category. The line usually creates the feeling of repose and calmness. Most of these types of arrangements have an easy, smooth flow of materials to create the desired shape, and abrupt angles and sharp curves are seldom used. The overall shape using this line may be a symmetrical or asymmetrical triangle, an oval, or a rectangle. The arrangements may be viewed from one side or both depending upon the situation. Those for a mantel are usually seen from one side only; however, if there is a mirror in the background, they should be finished attractively in the rear as well as the front. Table arrangements are usually seen from all sides and should be attractive from every angle.

For the beginner, it is best to start horizontal line arrangements by using a low, flat container. As experience is gained, other types will present more of a challenge. A pedestal-type container with the flowers arranged in a smooth-flowing arc (a modification of the horizontal line) can be used effectively for many occasions. A horizontal arrangement in a pedestal container is shown in Figure 3-8.

Most arrangements based upon the horizontal line will have symmetrical balance. A few locations will require asymmetrical balance, and the procedure followed under the discussion of the L line can be used with some modification. The first step in making an arrangement is to determine its overall length and height. The container and the final placement of the arrangement will have an influence on the overall size. For an arrangement to be seen from one side only and possessing symmetrical balance, place flowers or foliage of equal length on either side of the centerline. The overall length of the stems and container combined can be from one and one half to four times the length of the container. The next step is to place the vertical line in the container. This should be kept relatively low to maintain the overall horizontal appearance. With the installation of these lines, the overall shape has been established, and the arrangement can be completed following the procedures in Chapter 4.

FIGURE 3-9. Horizontal line. An arrangement to be seen from all sides. Note the concentration of darker flowers over the container to give a focal area and to lend stability to the arrangement.

If the arrangement is to be seen from all sides as is the one shown in Figure 3-9, first determine the length, the width, and the height and then add flowers as described in the preceding paragraph; this will establish the basic line of the arrangement. One can now proceed working toward the center by adding supplementary lines and materials. The bulk of the weight should be centered over the vase and also kept low in it for stability. In this type of arrangement, it is the concentration of weight over the container that establishes the focal point or area rather than one or two large flowers.

FIGURE 3-10. Inverted T: The gladioli are used to establish the basic line of an inverted T. Pompon chrysanthemums are incorporated into the arrangement to create interest and to establish a focal area. The overall shape is a symmetrical triangle.

An *inverted T,* as shown in Figures 3-10 and 3-11, is a combination of a vertical and a horizontal line and is the basis for the overall shape of a symmetrical triangle. The line is characterized by strength and balance, which give unquestion-

FIGURE 3-11. Inverted T: Chrysanthemums in a modified inverted T line giving the shape of an isosceles triangle. Note how the container tends to dominate the arrangement and the flowers become secondary to it.

able stability to the arrangement. Although the line can be rather rigid, static, and uninteresting, one can manipulate stems in various ways to form interesting curves. The symmetrical triangle which is built up from this basic line is one of the more popular arrangement styles both in traditional mass and modern line types of design.

The first step in the construction of the line is to determine the height and width. Here, many variations can be employed depending upon the use or final placement of the arrangement. For most arrangements, the vertical line should be somewhat longer than each of the horizontal lines. This will tend to make the arrangement appear more stable. There are situations, however, where it is necessary for the height of the vertical line to be restricted and for the horizontal ones to be extended. Good balance can be achieved in such arrangements.

The next step should be the establishment of the vertical line. It should be placed directly in the center of the container and should be held firmly to avoid movement when other materials are added. If a tall, spikey-type flower is used, one stem might be all that is needed to establish this vertical portion of the inverted T. If other types are used, several flowers will be necessary, starting with buds at the uppermost point and gradually increasing the size to a fully opened flower at the base.

Next is the insertion of the horizontal lines. Two stems of equal length and weight are placed equidistant from the centerline. If the arrangement is to be viewed from one side, these stems should be angled slightly toward the back of the centerline forming an arc of about 200 degrees. If viewed from all sides they should be directly centered. The sketch in Figure 3-12 is illustrative. After establishing these lines, there are several ways to proceed. One method is to fill in the vertical area working toward the center and then the horizontal area working from both ends toward the vertical. Where all lines meet over the center of the container, the focal point is constructed. Other details (Chapter 4) must then be followed to complete the arrangement.

Arrangements using the line of the inverted T can be used in many locations. They are commonly seen as table decorations where a triangular or cone shape is desired. They are often seen at flower shows, and they find many uses throughout the home.

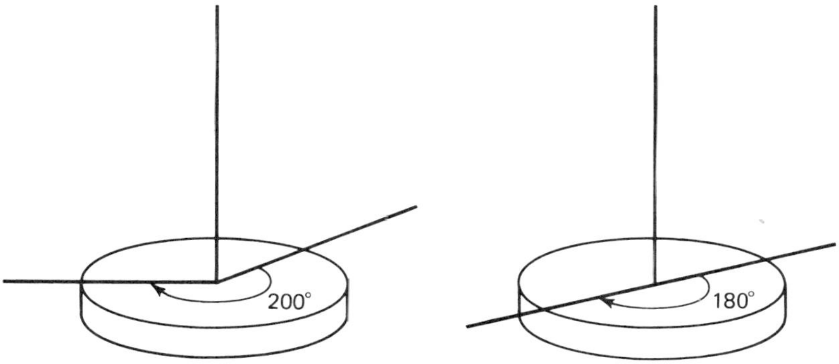

FIGURE 3-12. Placement of stems. For an arrangement to be seen from one side only, the horizontal lines should be angled back from the centerline (200 degrees). If seen from all sides, they should form an arc of 180 degrees.

An *L line* is also a combination of vertical and horizontal lines and is the basic line for the asymmetrical triangle (see Figures 3-13 and 3-14). This line also possesses strength and balance and can be changed in various ways to provide stability and rhythm for the arrangement. Because of the number of

FIGURE 3-13. L line. An L line with an interesting combination of chrysanthemums, cockscomb, goldenrod, and cattails. The heaviness of the cattails is supported by the concentration of flowers at the focal area and the heavy appearance of the container. [See also Color Plate.]

FIGURE 3-14. L line. The L line established with podocarpus and phalaenopsis orchids used as a focal point. Placement of the Madonna helps to create balance.

variations that can be made with this line, the asymmetrical triangle has proved to be one of the more interesting types of flower arrangements.

Construction begins with the placement of the vertical line. It is placed off center in the container and is counterbalanced by the horizontal line. If the design is vertically dominant, the vertical line will be the longer one; if horizontally dominant, the vertical line will be the shorter one as shown in Figure 3-15. In either case a sense of balance between the opposing lines and the container must be achieved by carefully counterbalancing height against width.

The vertical line may be placed either to the right or to the left of the center of the container, depending upon individual choice or ultimate placement of the completed arrangement. It is constructed as described previously under vertical and inverted T lines.

The horizontal line is placed nearly at a right angle to the vertical, passing through the centerline of the container. Length will vary according to the overall shape and size of the arrange-

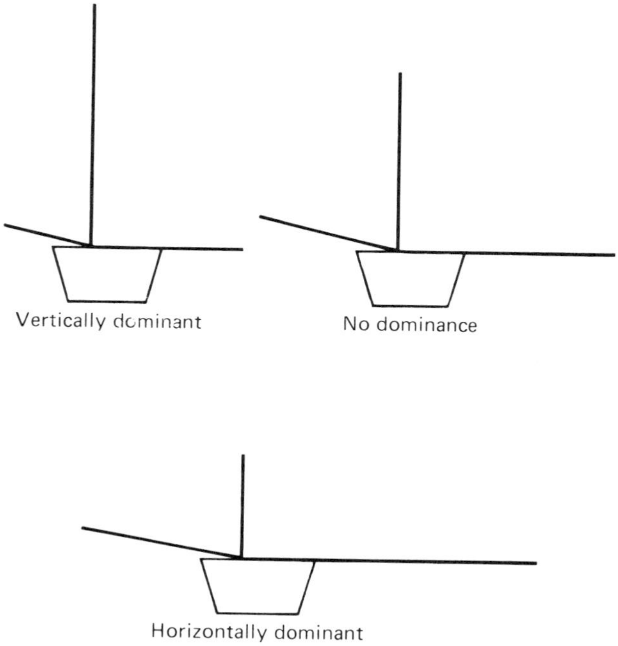

FIGURE 3-15. Establishing vertical and horizontal lines for an L arrangement.

FIGURE 3-16. Crescent line. The crescent line can be formed by using branches that bend easily. Chrysanthemums and scotch broom are used in this crescent arrangement. If the lines were extended, they would form a circle.

ment, but it commonly extends beyond the rim of the container. It is usually necessary to add some weight opposite the longer horizontal line for balance. Fill in from the ends toward the junction of the lines, with eventual placement of the focal point.

This line is suitable for use in many areas throughout the home. Almost any corner or asymmetrical position in a room can support this arrangement. One thing that must be considered is the position of the vertical line; it should be placed nearest the vertical line of the wall with the horizontal line flowing away from it.

The *crescent* line is shown in Figure 3-16. It is one of the more interesting lines in flower arranging. It is characterized by a slow, smooth, rhythmic movement which extends from the high point through the center to the low point of the arc. Both tips curve toward each other; and if these lines were extended, the overall shape of a circle would result. Crescent lines are usually asymmetrical, although it is possible to have symmetrical balance. The opening in the circle can face in any direction; the crescent moon is a good guide to follow when constructing this line.

Construction of the crescent arrangement requires more skill, time, and patience than do those lines previously described. Bending of stems and leaves is usually necessary to secure desired curves, and plant material should be pliable enough to allow this operation. Various ways of bending stems are described in Chapter 4.

As with other types of arrangements, there are several ways to construct the crescent line. One method is to start with lighter materials at the tip, gradually forming a segment of a circle and increasing the width of the line as the center of the crescent is approached. From this point the line diminishes in width toward the other end. The center of this area is directly over or cuts the rim of the container; this becomes the focal area and appears to support the rest of the arrangement. The opening that remains between the two tips can be of any part of the circumference of the circle formed with an imaginary line. The line should be well balanced in the container. Placement of the lines as described for asymmetrical balance should be followed.

Another method that will prove useful in establishing the crescent line is to work from both ends toward the center of the arrangement. Bend stems to the desired curve and insert them at either end; add other flowers and foliage following the curvature of the crescent, gradually thickening the line as the center is approached. The arrangement is then completed as described in the next chapter.

The crescent may be positioned in numerous ways in the vase to create desired effects. The opening can face in any direction as long as the arrangement is well balanced. Almost any type of container can be used for a crescent arrangement. A low flat dish, a tall vase, or a pedestal-type container can prove useful depending upon final placement of the design.

Crescent arrangements are suitable for many places in the home or office. They will fit most places where asymmetrical triangles are used and perhaps will add more interest than other types to the area. Since the overall shape of the crescent arrangement would be a circle if the lines were extended, they are desirable in some locations where symmetrical arrangements are normally used.

The *Hogarth curve,* which derives its name from the English artist William Hogarth, is one of the most interesting and difficult lines in flower arrangement and is shown in Figures 3-17 and 3-18. It is referred to as "the line of beauty," or "lazy S," and is characterized by its graceful rhythmic motion throughout the arrangement. Basically, the line consists of parts

FIGURE 3-17. Hogarth curve. The Hogarth curve or line of beauty. Foliage is often used to form the main line with flowers incorporated at or near the focal point. Scotch broom and rhododendron foliage and black-eyed Susan and rhododendron flowers are used in this arrangement.

of two crescent lines or two half circles or ovals joining at or near the focal point and flowing in opposite directions to form an overall "S" or reverse "S." The curves may be of equal size, or one may be larger than the other depending upon the desired effect. If arranged vertically, the lower half of the "S" is usually smaller than the top and flows across the front of the container as illustrated in Figure 3-17. If a horizontal effect is desired, both sides extending from the centerline will be of equal size. The curvature may vary considerably from just a slight bending of the stems to almost a half circle.

One of the prime requisites of the Hogarth curve is proper balance. This can be achieved by having the ends of the lines equidistant from the centerline and concentrating the weight of the arrangement at or near the rim of the container.

To create the lines for the Hogarth curve, the plant material must have natural curves or be pliable enough to bend to secure the desired curvature. Scotch broom, pussy willow, and heather can be bent or manipulated quite easily for this purpose. Begin the actual construction by placing the longest stems in position at either side of the centerline, being sure they curve in opposite directions and are well balanced. The stem in the topmost position should be leaning backward slightly, and the lower stem should come forward about an equal amount. These lines are gradually filled in following the "S" line toward the focal point, which will be at or near the rim of the container. Final details of construction are described in Chapter 4. Upon completion of the Hogarth curve, an imaginary line drawn from the tips of the upper and lower lines should form the overall shape of an oval or circle.

The Hogarth curve is suitable for use in many areas. In the home, the smooth flowing curve will add interest to most areas and can create a very striking effect. It is one of the most popular arrangements at flower shows and usually is the center of attention at these activities.

FIGURE 3-18. Hogarth curve. The curve can be placed in several positions in the container. Interesting use of goldenrod and black-eyed Susans make up the lazy S in this arrangement.

Construction and Equipment

4

In the previous chapters, the history and theory of floral art have been discussed. Now we approach the most interesting part of the art, the actual construction of the arrangement. This should not be a haphazard operation. It should proceed with a series of steps or stages like any other type of construction.

Good equipment is essential for the floral designer. It need not be expensive, and only a limited amount is necessary for the beginner. As one becomes more involved in the art, the amount of equipment will naturally be increased.

For the beginner, a few containers, flower holders, waterproof clay, wire, knife, and flower shears are basic equipment. Some basic equipment is shown in Figure 4-1. Other materials will prove useful but are not absolute necessities. The shears should be the florist type with relatively short blades and a serrated edge. These heavy duty shears can be used for cutting stems of most plant materials including those of woody shrubs and evergreens; they will also be used for cutting wires. The

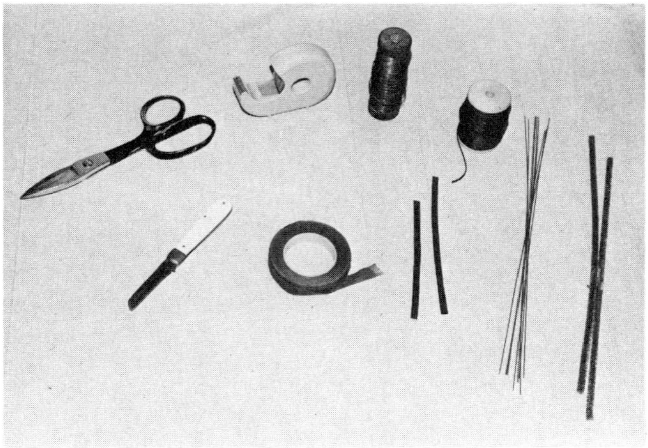

FIGURE 4-1. Tools and equipment. Counter clockwise: Heavy duty florist scissors, sharp knife, floratape, twistems, wire, chenille stems, string, spool wire, and cellophane tape.

serrated blade will prevent or reduce slipping of heavy stems and wires when cutting. The knife should have a short blade made of good steel that will hold a sharp edge. It should fit the hand well and be comfortable to hold. No expense should be spared when purchasing this tool; inexpensive paring knives are too long, the blade will not hold a good edge and will have a tendency to slip, many times resulting in cut fingers. Care should be taken in the proper use of the knife. When cutting stems, draw the blade toward the body, parallel to the side of the thumb, as shown in Figure 4-2. Other tools that will prove beneficial but are not necessary for the beginner are pruning shears, ribbon shears, styrofoam cutters, a small saw, and an atomizer or mister.

Florist wire comes in a number of gauges and lengths. Gauges range from the heavy—number 18—to the very fine—number 32. The wire gauge used should be in proportion to the weight of the flower or foliage being wired. For most designers, gauges 20, 24, and 30 should be sufficient. Number 20 can be used on heavy flowers such as chrysanthemums, 24 on those of medium weight—roses and carnations—and 30 on light and more delicate materials—daisies and sweet peas. Wires are used for repairing broken stems, to get desired curves, to hold flowers upright, for corsages, and many other operations. They can be taped to the back of some foliage with cellophane tape or green

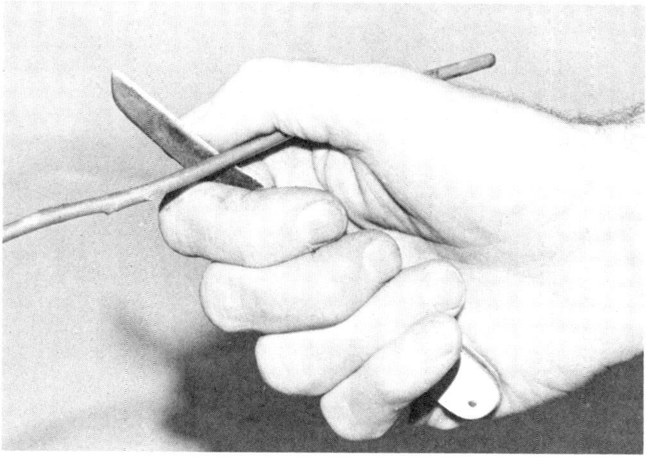

FIGURE 4-2. Correct use of knife. Keep the blade parallel to and against the thumb and pull through the stem, the blade and thumb moving together.

adhesive tape to hold leaves upright or to secure desired curves. They should be used *only when necessary* and should not be visible in completed arrangements.

Florist waterproof clay is used to hold pinpoint holders secure in containers. It is made especially for this use and will not tarnish or have a chemical reaction with most metal containers as might be the case with some other similar materials. For use with the pinpoint holder, a small amount of clay is taken, worked in the hand to make it more pliable, and then rolled between the hand and table to make a length about three eighths of an inch in diameter. This is then placed on the base of the holder along its perimeter, pressing it just enough to hold it in position. The holder is then placed in a dry container and pressed down to hold it firmly in the desired location. See Figure 4-3. It is important that the container be dry when using clay; if it is damp it will not hold.

Twistems, short pieces of wire encased in green paper coverings, will prove useful in repairing bent or broken stems. They are used like a splint, placing one straight piece along the stem and wrapping another around both. They are also useful for tying several stems together, a procedure which may be necessary when thin stems are used with a pinpoint holder.

Pipe cleaners or chenille stems are not only useful for decorations but can also be used as frames for corsages and as

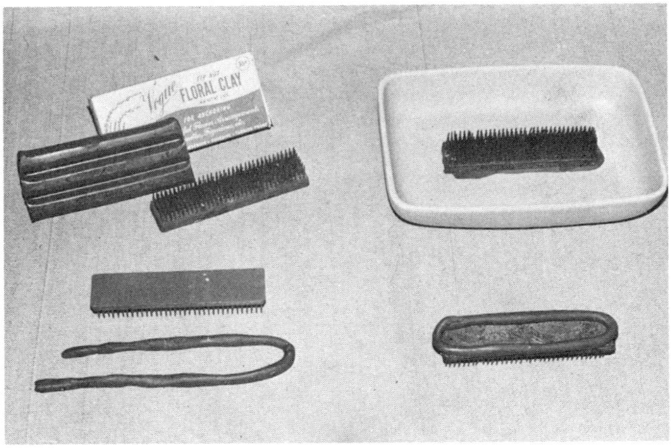

FIGURE 4-3. The pinpoint holder is best anchored with floral clay. Top left: Clay and pinpoint holder. Lower left: Clay rolled out ready to place on the holder as shown at lower right. Upper right: The holder is anchored in the container and is ready for the designer to start construction of the arrangement.

stems for broken-off flower heads. When used as stems, one end is pushed into the base of the flower and the other end placed in water. A certain amount of water will pass through the chenille stem into the flower.

Roll wire, string, floral tape, cellophane tape, etc., can be used by the designer. These are not essential for the beginner but will be useful as one becomes involved in some of the more complicated arrangements. It is permissible for the designer to use these mechanical aids in constructing various designs, providing the aids are well covered and do not show in the completed arrangement. However, one should not become dependent upon them and should use them only when absolutely necessary.

The beginner will need only a few basic containers, but as one progresses many more will be added to the collection. Those shown in Figure 4-4 will serve the novice designer well. They should be of pottery, plastic, wood, or metal, and be of neutral colors. More details on containers will be found in Chapter 5.

There are many kinds of flower holders available to the designer. Some do an excellent job of holding flowers while others leave much to be desired. Glass holders and metal cages as shown in Figure 4-5 are difficult to use. It is almost im-

FIGURE 4-4. Basic containers for the beginner. Beginning top left, counter clockwise: Rectangular or pillow type, horizontal, bowl, vertical, and pedestal.

possible to keep flowers in the desired position when using them.

Pinpoint holders consisting of a basal plate with sharp pointed needles protruding upward are excellent flower holders. They are readily available at department stores, garden centers,

FIGURE 4-5. Evolution of the flower holders. Upper left, then counter clockwise: Strips of lead on a weighted base were wrapped around stems and then held at desired angles. Glass holders, metal cage, metal cage and pin holder, cast lead holder, present day pin-point holder.

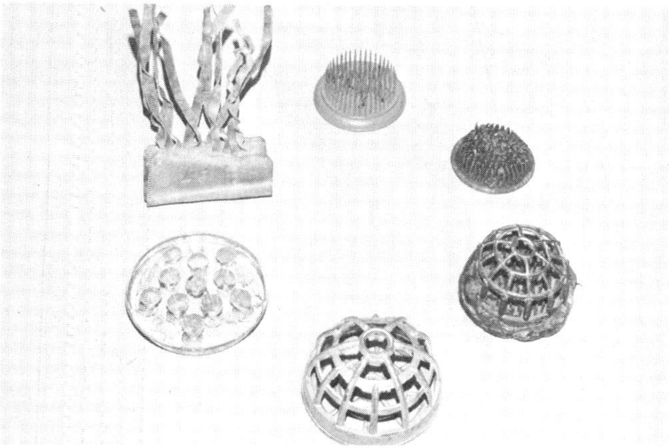

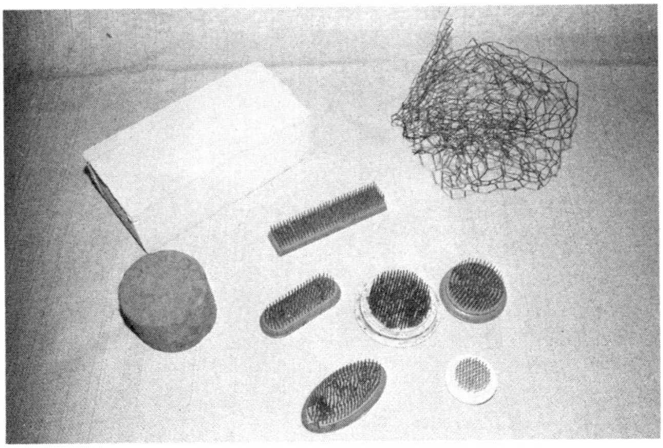

FIGURE 4-6. Flower holders. Counter clockwise from upper left: Standard size block of floral foam, shaped foam, various sizes and shapes of pinpoint holders, and chicken wire. All prove useful for specific types of arrangements.

and florist shops and come in a variety of sizes and shapes. Samples are shown in Figure 4-6. Some have steel or brass needles embedded in plastic; others have a lead, iron, or steel base often with a plastic coating. A holder with brass needles in a lead base with a plastic coating is preferred by most designers. It gives a neat appearance, the needles are more durable than steel, and it will not rust. Needles embedded in a plastic base tend to loosen in a relatively short time making the holder difficult to use and almost worthless.

Needles should be pointed, sharp, fairly long, and close together. Inexpensive holders may be cast as one unit and have no points on the needles; these will not pierce the stems easily and will cause stems to split or break. They may also have needles far apart which will make for difficulty in securing all but thick or heavy stems in them. Remember the expression "you get what you pay for" when buying pinpoint holders. Do not look for bargains. A few extra pennies spent will be rewarded with ease in constructing the arrangement.

Pinpoint holders are best suited for use in low or shallow containers. Here the designer can easily insert stems in the holders to precisely control the angle or direction of the stem. It is difficult or almost impossible to insert stems in them when they are used in deep containers. To prevent pinpoint holders from moving around in the container, they should be secured with florist clay as described earlier.

FIGURE 4–7. To fasten stems to a pinpoint holder, hold the stem firmly near the base and push the end into the needles. For horizontal placement, lay the stem across the holder and push down with the back of the knife or with closed scissors.

To insert stems into a pinpoint holder, cut them directly across or at a slight angle with a clean cut; crushed or damaged stem ends will not hold well. Hold the stem securely near the base with the thumb and finger securing it at the desired angle by pushing the end down as far as it will go into the needles. For stems at extreme angles, the end of the stem may be laid on the holder and pushed into the needles with a knife handle or other implement to avoid injury to the fingers. This procedure is shown in Figure 4–7.

Holding thin-stemmed flowers sometimes presents problems. The stems may be placed between the points and receive little or no support. By tying three or four stems together at their base with twistems, floral tape, or wire, they can be inserted into the holder and be held securely as seen in Figure 4–8. Large stems that tend to move because they are out of balance, or hollow stems that do not hold well, can be held in position by tying a small piece of stem parallel to the base of the stem and inserting them in the holder. This is demonstrated in Figure 4–9 and will help to eliminate twisting and hold the flowers in the desired location.

One-inch mesh chicken wire will make a satisfactory flower holder for tall or medium-height containers. A type made especially for flower arranging is more pliable than the galvanized material made for outdoor use and is available at floral supply houses.

FIGURE 4-8. A group of thin stems may be tied together and inserted into the pinpoint holder securely.

When using chicken wire, it is important that the proper amount be used for the specific container. This will vary according to its size and shape. If too little is used, the wire will tend to move, spaces will be large, and the flowers will not be held securely; if too much is used, there will be no room for the flower stems. A little experience will help you determine the exact amount to use. There are several methods of using this material: One that has proven successful is to cut off the desired amount from the roll and form a ball somewhat larger

FIGURE 4-9. For hollow stems that tend to move or twist on a pinpoint holder, tie a small piece of another stem at the base of the stem.

than the hole in the container. Do not fold into flat sections. The ball is forced into the container in such a way that it extends to or almost to the base and slightly above the rim. It should fit quite tightly to avoid movement when flowers are being inserted. A single piece of waterproof tape placed across the top of the ball of wire and secured to the container is helpful but not always necessary. Sometimes a pinpoint holder is secured in the bottom of the container and the ball of chicken wire forced down into the pins. This will help to prevent the wire from moving when flower stems are inserted.

Flower stems, usually cut on an angle, are pushed through the openings in the ball of wire. By pushing them through two or three spaces, most flowers will be held securely. It is possible to place the flowers at various angles to secure desired lines and shapes. The ends of the stems need not be too deep in the container—only below the surface of the water.

For arrangements that are to last only one or two days or are of an otherwise temporary nature, the container can be loosely filled with branches of evergreens or ferns placed in a vertical position. Here, as with the chicken wire, it is important that just the proper amount of material be used. Flower stems can be pushed into this filler at various angles and be held securely. This material will decay rapidly and shorten the lifespan of the flowers considerably.

Shredded styrofoam can be used successfully in tall containers. Since it does not hold water, the flowers must receive water from the spaces between the pieces of foam. The container should be loosely filled with foam; it should not be packed down tightly or compacted. A piece of chicken wire taped to the top of the container will help hold the foam in the container and the flowers in place. Another method would be to partially fill the container with shredded styrofoam and fill the remainder with one of the water-holding foams described below. Styrofoam has an advantage over the stuffing described above because it does not decay and will not interfere with the lasting quality of the flowers.

There are several water-holding foam materials available for use by the floral designer. These absorb water, which then becomes available to the flowers when they are inserted into it. They can be used in most any type of container, whether deep or shallow, the only requirement being that the container hold water. Wicker baskets and other similar containers which ordinarily do not hold water should be lined with a waterproof substance before using these products in them.

Water-absorbing qualities vary among the different foams. Some absorb their maximum amount of water in a few seconds, while others must be held submerged for a minimum of 30 minutes. A third group requires a special apparatus to force water into the material. Needless to say, this group should be avoided by the flower arranger unless enough arrangements are going to be made to warrant the extra expense and trouble.

Foam materials are usually purchased in a standard block form although special sizes and shapes are manufactured. Again, see Figure 4-6. Most are moist to the touch and should not be allowed to dry out. The desired size piece is cut from the block and immersed in water until the maximum amount has been absorbed. The cessation of air bubbles from most foams will indicate this condition. The remainder of the block should be stored in a plastic bag to prevent dehydration. With several of these materials, once they are wet and allowed to dry out, they will no longer absorb sufficient water to support the life of the flowers. They can be kept moist by inserting them in a plastic bag and tying it tight to prevent moisture from escaping. It is possible to use a piece of foam several times providing it is kept moist and is in good enough condition to hold flowers. When reusing the materials, to avoid holes created by the previous arrangement it is best to use the opposite side from that used before. It is possible to make an arrangement using foam as a holder without securing it in any way. However, for best results the foam should be taped to the container with waterproof tape as shown in Figure 4-10.

Flower stems should be cut at an angle and pushed into the foam, making sure that the flower is in the correct position. The cut end of the stem should remain in contact with the material and should not be retracted creating a space between the stem and the foam. These spaces normally do not fill with water and flowers will wilt within a short time. If necessary to change its position, remove completely and insert it again. If handled correctly, most flowers will last as long or longer in these foam materials as they will in clear water providing a reservoir of water is available to give a continuous supply to the foam and flowers.

Now, having become acquainted with the various tools and equipment to be used and the theory involved in the art, the designer is ready to begin the construction of an arrangement. The prospective designer is confronted with a vase, some

FIGURE 4–10. Floral foam can be held firmly in the container by use of waterproof tape.

flowers, foliage—and the problem of what to do with them! Rather than just dropping the flowers and foliage into the container and hoping for the best, an idea, a mental picture, or the general design should be clearly developed before the first flower is placed in position. With the general design in mind, it is now possible to proceed with the arrangement. The procedure usually involves a series of trials, errors, and corrections, and a step by step type of construction.

The first step is the construction of the main line or "backbone." Construction steps are shown in Figures 4–11 and 4–12. This is the foundation upon which the whole arrangement is built. It is important that this foundation be held securely in place and that it does not tend to move when other materials are inserted. It can be made with flowers, foliage, or a combination of both. Before cutting the stems, hold the flower or foliage in the desired position and cut the stem to the correct length. It is better to cut it a little long and make a second cut than to cut it too short in an effort to save time. Details on construction of the main line are described in Chapter 3.

When establishing the main line, it is sometimes desirable to select branches that are naturally curved or can be shaped to form lines that will add interest to the arrangement. To affect the desired curves or lines in an arrangement, it will be necessary to bend stems occasionally. Solid stems such as pussy willows, sweet peas, and heather can be bent easily by placing the

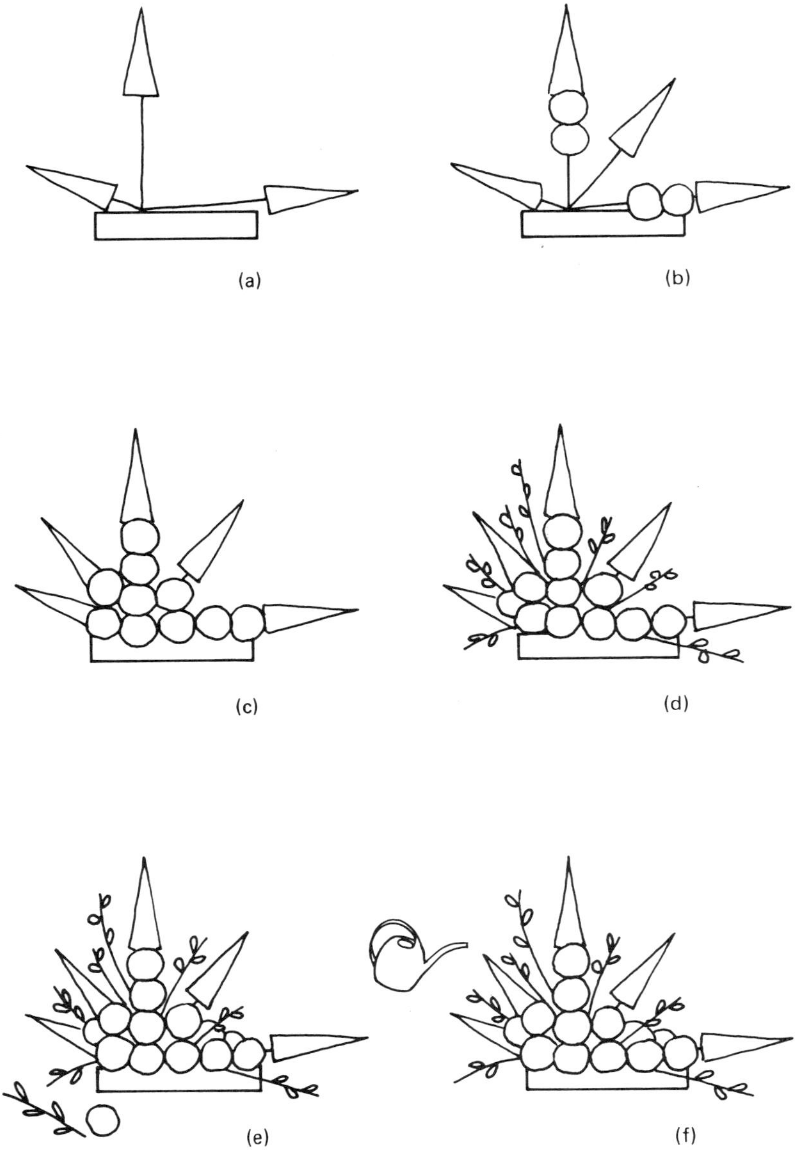

FIGURE 4-11. Steps in construction: Combination of round and spike-type flowers. Left to right Top Row: (a) Establish main line with spike type flowers. (b) Fill in with round and spike types. Middle row: (c) Fill in and establish focal area. (d) Add foliage. Bottom row: (e) Take out unnecessary material; add more if necessary. (f) Add water.

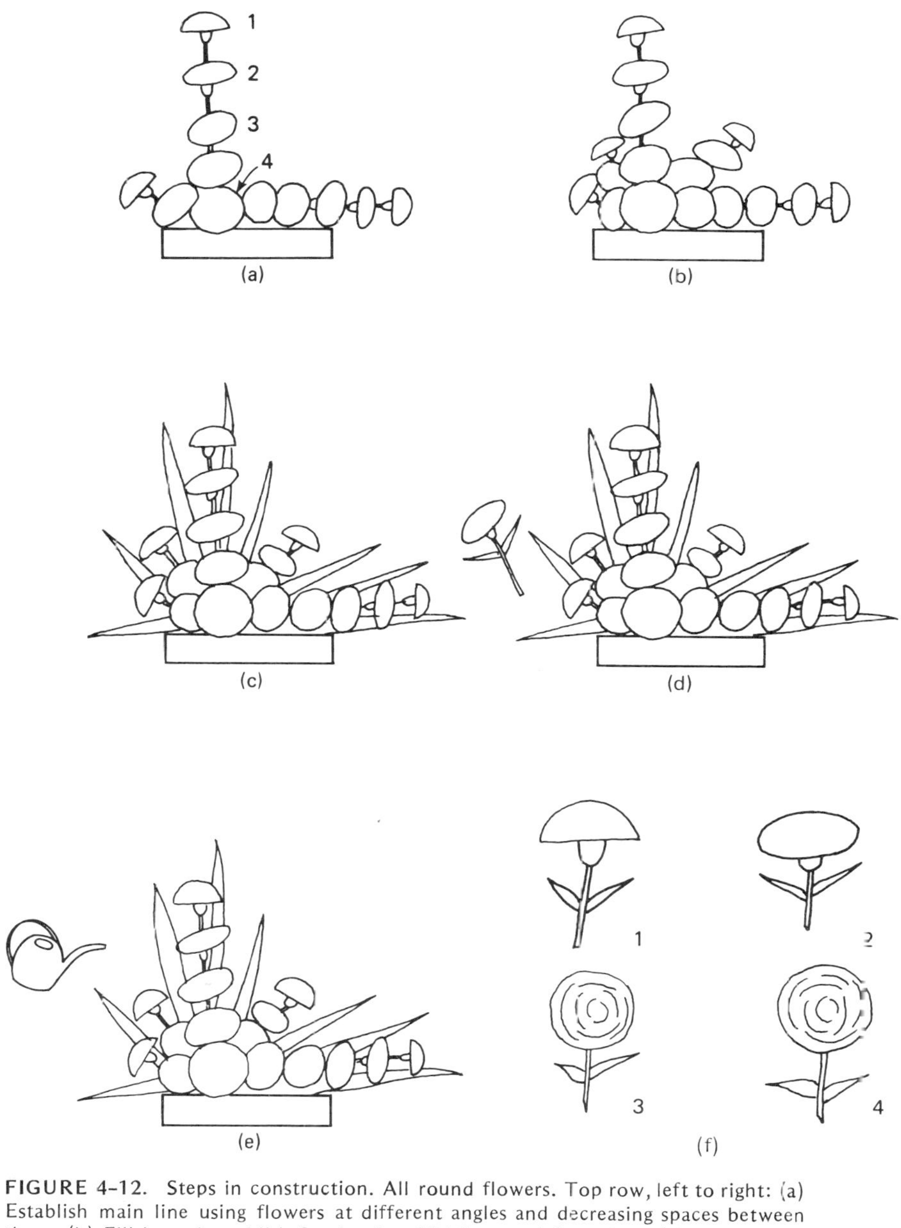

FIGURE 4-12. Steps in construction. All round flowers. Top row, left to right: (a) Establish main line using flowers at different angles and decreasing spaces between them. (b) Fill in and establish focal point. Middle row, left to right: (c) Add foliage. (d) Take out unnecessary material; add where necessary. Bottom row: (e) Add water. (f) Round flowers at various angles as indicated in (a).

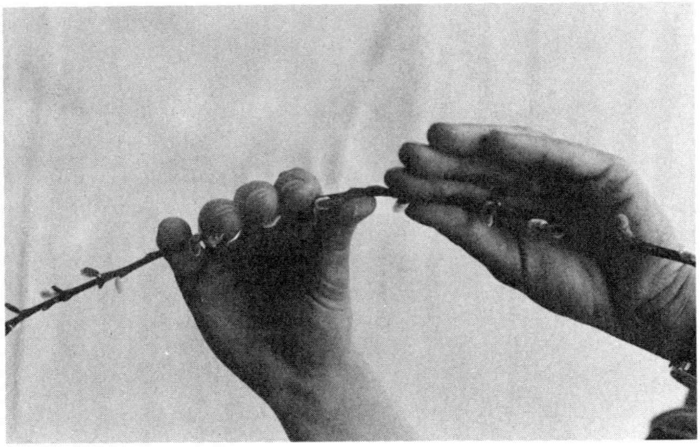

FIGURE 4-13. Bending stems of pussy willow or other flexible-stemmed flowers or foliage. Place thumb on underside and fingers on top.

thumbs of both hands on the underside of the stems and the fingers on top, as shown in Figure 4-13. By pushing up with the thumbs, down with the fingers, and gradually moving along the stem, the desired curve can be made. It will probably be necessary to go along the stem several times since too much bending in one place at the same time may break it. Curves can be made in scotch broom, juniper, daffodil foliage, or similar materials by pulling the material between the fingers of one hand. Each time it is pulled through the hand a more pronounced curve is made.

With hollow stems it might be necessary to insert a wire through the hollow part of the stem and then bend it to the desired curve. The wire should be heavy enough to support the curve: Fine wires are useless for this purpose on most flowers.

After the main line has been established, the next step is to insert secondary lines. Again, see Figures 4-11 and 4-12. These are important lines in the arrangement and help to fill in the voids between the main lines; however, they should not compete with the main lines for dominance. They are used at various angles to help to secure depth, the characteristic that gives the arrangement its three-dimensional quality rather than the two-dimensional—height *and* width found in some other forms of art. All lines in the arrangement should create the illusion of radiating from a single point of origin and crossing of lines should be avoided whenever possible.

Secondary lines, similar to the main lines, should appear lighter at the extremities and should create the impression of

FIGURE 4-14. Flowers of equal size are placed at angles to give the impression of increasing size toward the base.

weight or heaviness at the base. This is easily accomplished with spiky-type flowers such as gladioli and snapdragons, which have buds at the extremities, flowers in various stages of maturity along the stem, and fully opened flowers at the base. When flowers of varying size are used, buds or small flowers are used at the extremities and the size of the flowers gradually increased toward the focal point. If flowers of equal size are used, they are placed at different angles to give the appearance of being larger or smaller. These two concepts are illustrated in Figures 4-14 and 4-15.

FIGURE 4-15. When using flowers of different sizes have the smaller flowers at the top and larger ones at or near the focal point.

Spacing of flowers is also an important factor—indicated in Figures 4-14 and 4-15. Greater distances should be left between flowers at the outer parts of the arrangement and these spaces gradually decreased so that flowers are overlapping each other at the focal point.

With the completion of secondary lines, the next step will be the addition of other flowers and foliage throughout the arrangement to help to give it body and depth (see Figures 4-11 and 4-12). Care should be taken to avoid layering of flowers or having them at the same height. For layering, see Figure 4-16. At this stage, the various mechanics that have been employed should be hidden. The holder should not be visible in the finished arrangement and can be camouflaged with flowers and/or foliage. Flowers should be placed at different levels to create depth and avoid flatness at the surface. Placing some flowers deep inside the arrangement and others in a forward position, this third dimension is easily obtained. Color can also be used effectively in creating depth as discussed in Chapter 6.

The focal point can now be inserted. Some designers prefer to establish the focal point directly after construction of the main line. However, the less experienced designer will find this cumbersome when placing other flowers in the arrangement.

FIGURE 4-16. Lines of flowers, especially when different colors are used, create a layered situation with little unity between layers.

FIGURE 4-17. A well-done early American-type arrangement using several kinds of spring flowers. Too much material has been used for present-day arrangements.

Methods of establishing a focal point are described in Chapter 2. The focal point should fit well into the arrangement and tie in with the other materials being used. Care must be taken that the focal point does not detract from or dominate the overall design.

The arrangement is now complete except for a few finishing adjustments. At this point, it should be carefully scrutinized for the minor details that can make a difference between a good and a passable arrangement. A small piece of foliage added at some point might be just the thing needed. Perhaps the removal of a single flower or even a few flowers might be necessary to avoid bulkiness or overcrowding. Refer to Figure 4-17. If a flower or piece of foliage can be removed and not be missed, it should *not* be used at that point in the arrangement. Knowing what and how much to take out are factors that lead to award-winning designs.

Taking out or adjusting material might lead to voids in some areas. Do not hesitate to add flowers or foliage to fill them. It might also be necessary to add material to emphasize the line, to tie in the focal area with the rest of the arrangement, or to have the arrangement fit better with the container.

Be careful with these final adjustments. Too much emphasis on them might be the downfall of a perfectly satisfactory arrangement.

One final step is to check the water supply in the container to make certain that sufficient water is available for the flowers. When pinpoint holders are used, the water level should be well above the top of the holder. When foam is being used, an ample reservoir of water should be in the container to ensure a constant water supply to the flowers. The completed arrangement, no matter how well constructed, will last only as long as water is available; without it, the whole effort of making the arrangement is lost.

5 Containers, Bases, Backgrounds, and Accessories

Selection of the correct container is a significant part of any flower arrangement. It plays an important part in any design and is considered subordinate only to the flowers inserted into it. A container may be defined as "anything that will hold flowers." It may be a discarded tin can or a fine piece of porcelain, pewter, or silver. Monetary value alone does not enhance its significance when incorporated into the arrangement. In fact, some of the more expensive containers may distract from the arrangement and be a source of conflict within the composition.

It is not necessary that all containers for floral designs hold water. However, some method of providing water to fresh flowers is necessary. Auxiliary containers are often used for this purpose. For dried arrangements, water is not a consideration, and containers should be selected accordingly.

When selecting containers, several factors should be taken into consideration. The type of arrangement, its use, space available, and the kinds of flowers to be used are prime considerations. These in turn will have effects upon the design of the container, material from which it is made, color, texture, and overall size.

As one begins making flower arrangements, the basic designs shown in Figure 4-4 will serve well. However, as one progresses to more elaborate designs, a greater variety of vases will be desired. At this time, a separate hobby of collecting containers can be started. The only limitations on a collection of this kind would be the space and money available. When collecting containers, the purpose for which they are to be used should be of utmost consideration. Some vases serve best as decorative features by themselves and should be used accordingly; see Figure 5-1. Other types, shown in Figure 5-2, will work well only with specific plant material. The highly decorated vases shown in Figure 5-3 *rarely* contribute to the overall floral design.

FIGURE 5-1 A Chinese vase that is highly decorative in itself *without* the use of cut flowers.

FIGURE 5-2 A vase decorated with iris blossoms and one in the shape of a football have limited use.

FIGURE 5-3 Decorations on containers often detract from otherwise good arrangements.

The general design or shape of the container may be classified as vertical, horizontal, round, rectangular, symmetrical, or asymmetrical. Figure 5-4 shows various shapes. The container shape should fit the overall shape of the arrangement. For example, a vertical container would be best for a vertical type arrangement and a low, flat container best for a horizontal one. However, there will be circumstances where this will not always hold true, and a low, flat dish might be the best choice for a vertical arrangement.

FIGURE 5-4. Design or shape of containers. Back row, left to right: Vertical, horizontal, rectangular. Front row: Symmetrical, asymmetrical, round.

Symmetrical containers can be used for most types of arrangements. Asymmetrical ones, however, are best suited for asymmetrical designs, and difficulty will be encountered when trying to make symmetrical arrangements in them.

Containers may be classified as bowls, vases, pedestals, baskets, and "miscellaneous" types. *Bowls* are generally considered those containers where width exceeds height. They may be rectangular, round, oval, or irregular in shape, made of various materials, and can be plain or highly decorated. This type exceeds all others in usefulness in floral design.

If height exceeds width, the container is usually referred to as a *vase.* Vases may be cylindrical, triangular, or rectangular; sides may be straight or curved; and they may have small or wide openings. These are used primarily for arrangements where height predominates.

The *pedestal container* is one of the more popular types and includes urns, compotes, and the most elaborate—the epergne. See Figure 5-5. These containers have a fixed base. The urn is distinguished from the compote by having a shorter pedestal and usually a greater water-holding capacity. The epergne, an ornate type from the Victorian era, is a combination of containers holding flowers, fruit, or a combination of both.

The pedestal types are excellent for table use where space is limited, but a floral display in scale with the surroundings is desired. By being elevated on the pedestal, the arrangement is high enough to allow space for trays of food, dishes, and other necessary items to be placed on the table under it.

Baskets come in a variety of sizes and shapes, some made of waterproof material, some provided with metal liners to hold

FIGURE 5-5 Pedestal-type containers. Left to right: Vase (not a pedestal), urn, and compote.

water, and others for which the designer must provide some means of holding water for fresh flowers. Figures 5-6 and 5-7 show some arrangements in baskets. Inserting some kind of

FIGURE 5-6 Basket of garden flowers. All flowers are arranged low in the basket and within the confines of the handle.

FIGURE 5-7 Arrangement of snapdragons in a pottery basket. Note how the handle tends to split the arrangement into two sections.

bowl or wrapping water-holding foam materials in aluminum foil or plastic will serve this purpose. Baskets come with and without handles; those with handles deserve serious consideration when making an arrangement. Should the handle be covered or should it split the arrangement into two sections? This is for the designer to decide, but much care and thought should be given to this situation.

The *novelty* or *miscellaneous containers* shown in Figure 5-8 are used extensively by florists and by many other designers. More often in these arrangements the container becomes the center of attraction, and the flowers subordinate to it. When used they should harmonize with the surroundings or the specific occasion for the arrangement. Household items including teapots, pitchers, and gravy boats (see Figure 5-9) can serve as containers for flowers. Care must be taken that these odd-shaped items do not detract from but add to the overall arrangement and setting.

Containers can be made of most any material. Pottery, china, metal, wood, plastic, paper, and glass are all satisfactory, and each will fit well in a specific situation. The choice of material is dependent upon the occasion, the types of flowers being used, and the placement of the completed arrangement.

Pottery containers come in a variety of sizes, shapes,

FIGURE 5-8 Novelty containers are used for specific occasions. Many times they become the center of attention and the flowers become subordinate to them.

FIGURE 5-9. Household items such as this tureen are useful for many arrangements. A symmetrical arrangement seem from all sides includes the correct placement of the accessories—cover and ladle.

textures and colors. They may be dull or highly glazed, plain or extensively patterned. Most have a heavy appearance, and flowers and arrangements should fit accordingly. Zinnias, marigolds, chrysanthemums, and similar coarse-textured flowers work well in them as shown in Figure 5-10. However, roses, lily of the valley, and other delicate materials would be out of harmony in these containers.

FIGURE 5-10 One arrangement using several pottery containers makes an interesting corner piece for a small table. Coarse-textured marigolds, zinnias, and pearly everlasting are in harmony with the texture of the containers.

FIGURE 5-11 The use of marigolds, tansy, and goldenrod fit together well in a monochromatic arrangement in an inexpensive gold metal container.

Fine china bowls and dishes are useful for many flower arrangements designed for specific occasions. A container of this material might be just the thing for a dinner party or afternoon tea. Care must be used in picking up the delicate patterns of the container with the plant material, which should coincide with the texture of the china.

Metal containers vary—from discarded tin cans to prized pewter and silver; from dull wrought iron to highly polished chrome and brass; from heavy bronze to light aluminum. See Figures 5-11 and 5-12. All have a definite place in flower arrangement, and there are plant materials which are suitable for each.

Plant material should harmonize with the container. A highly prized rose is out of place when placed in a tin can. Instead, this might be just the right container for an arrangement of garden or wild flowers. The rose would be more attractive and in better harmony if placed in a pewter or a silver container. The tin can is best for an informal situation, a kitchen arrangement, or one in a recreation room. The silver is best reserved for formal occasions, dining table, or buffet table arrangements.

Wrought iron is a good sturdy material to use for informal party arrangements. Its dull appearance does not detract from the flowers, and its rugged and heavy appearance lends a feeling of stability to the arrangement. Figure 5-12 illustrates this. Iris, bird of paradise, and other heavy-appearing flowers used in wrought iron containers will be given the stability they need by the heavy appearance of the container. One must be careful when using highly polished brass or chrome containers—they can easily become the center of attraction and the flowers appear subordinate to them. Yellow and bronze pompon chrysanthemums harmonize with highly polished brass, and sweetheart roses will do well in chrome.

Heavy bronze is seldom used for containers in American flower arrangements. It does have limited use in contemporary arrangements, and as the number of these increases, more bronze containers will be used. They were used extensively for some early styles of Japanese arrangements and are still in use

FIGURE 5-12 Wrought iron containers give the impression of heaviness, stability, and strength.

today for some of these. Bronze, with its heavy appearance, will support large, heavy plant material without detracting from the overall design. Aluminum containers are used to some extent; most are light in weight and will fall over easily unless carefully balanced. In tall aluminum containers, some weight placed in the bottom will counteract this situation.

Tarnished metal containers are sometimes more desirable than the highly polished ones. Copper, with its dull, bluish-green effect, harmonizes well with many garden flowers. It lends stability to the arrangement but does not compete with the flowers for dominance. Aluminum and some pieces of silver will conform to some situations better if the bright, shiny appearance is allowed to become dull. This would not be desirable for a formal dining table but would harmonize well in living room arrangements.

Highly prized or expensive metal containers should be protected when used for arrangements. Some materials used to secure pinpoint holders will react with the metal and damage it; chicken wire, if used, will scratch it. There appears to be no reaction between the foam products and metal. For these expensive containers, it might be well to employ auxiliary containers; these are smaller containers placed inside or beside the container that is visible and holds the flowers, holder, and water. The original container then is used only as a "front" or outer shell hiding the auxiliary one from view. When used in a silver bowl, it is a good idea to place a paper towel between the silver and the auxiliary container to prevent scratching. Since auxiliary containers do not show in the completed arrangement, they can be made of any material. Plastic ice cream containers or similar items can be used successfully.

There are many wooden containers available to the floral designer. Small boxes of various sizes and shapes, chopping bowls, driftwood, and many homemade units will be a welcomed addition to one's collection. These containers must be properly handled or disasterous results will occur. For boxes, some kind of a waterproof liner should be provided; if metal or plastic liners will not fit, the inside can be protected with aluminum foil.

Mixing bowls and many homemade containers will split when water is put into them unless the wood is treated. Wooden bowls or vases should be waterproofed with a good coating of shellac or varnish and then waxed to be sure water does not come in contact with the wood. Even when the wood has been treated, however, the use of an auxiliary container is desirable.

FIGURE 5-13 Driftwood or weathered wood make attractive containers. Chrysanthemums in this arrangement are inserted into floral foam in an auxiliary container hidden by the weathered wood.

There is nothing more discouraging than to spend time making a nice wooden bowl and constructing an arrangement in it, only to find the bowl split, the flowers wilted, and all the water on the table and floor the next morning!

Driftwood arrangements are popular. The wood is used either as an accessory in the arrangement or as a container for flowers. When used as a container, it is normally only for effect, and the plant material is placed in an auxiliary container hidden by the wood. Figure 5-13 shows the use of driftwood or weathered wood. For large arrangements, holes are sometimes drilled into the wood, and test tubes or small plastic vials inserted into them. See Figure 5-14. These are filled with water and flowers are placed in them. Arrangements using a piece of driftwood can be attractive. However, one of the greatest faults is letting the driftwood predominate and become the center of attention in the design.

Plastic containers have been gaining in popularity. Reproductions of metal and pottery are made with plastic, and from a short distance it is difficult to distinguish them from the real thing. While some designers have thought of them as inexpensive, some plastic containers do command relatively high prices. Plastic does have advantages over some other materials: If dropped it will not shatter, most plastics will not chip, and

FIGURE 5-14 Holes are sometimes drilled into large pieces of driftwood or weathered wood to hold vials of water. Flowers are placed into these so they will receive the necessary water.

it is easy to keep clean. One disadvantage is the relatively light weight of plastic containers which allows many of them to tip easily.

Clear glass is difficult to use. Containers made of this material can be light and delicate or heavy and course. However, they all have the clear characteristic of glass, making both stems and holders visible. To complicate the situation, not only will stems and holders be visible, but they will be magnified at the same time. This can detract from the arrangement and become a disturbing influence. In some arrangements consisting of only a few flowers, however, showing of the stems can be an important asset to the overall effect. A few well-placed magnified stems will have a stabilizing effect and can contribute considerably to the overall theme.

Colored glass or colored water can help to reduce the visibility of stems but most of the time they do not completely mask them. Colored water may detract from the arrangement of floral material if the color is not carefully chosen.

One way to use crystal containers is to construct a frame using heavy florist wire as shown in Figure 5-15, which is used to support a piece of plastic foam inserted about an inch into the container. A small opening must be left on one side of the foam to allow addition of water, which should be in contact with the foam at all times. As the arrangement is constructed, the flower stems are inserted into but not through the foam. Upon completion, flowers or foliage should overlap the container enough to hide the mechanics and leave only the water showing in the container.

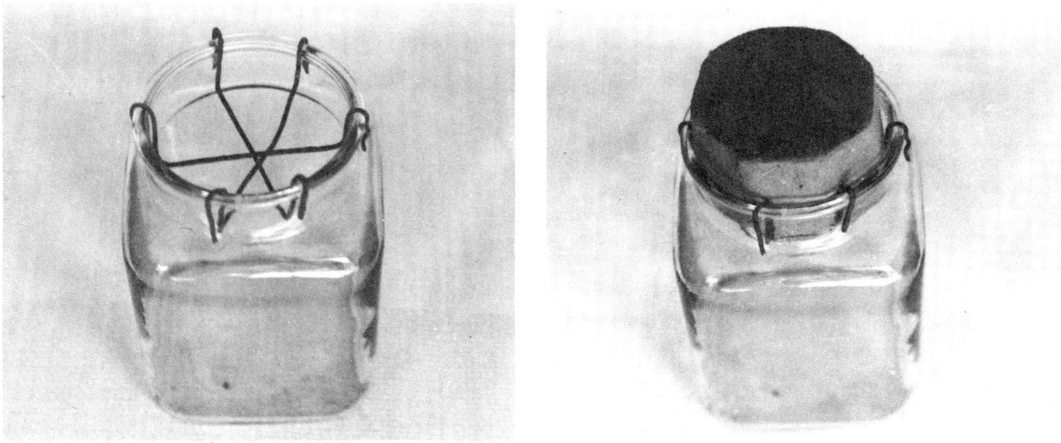

FIGURE 5-15 A wire frame is made to fit an inch or two into the opening of the container. A piece of foam is fitted onto this frame with an opening left on one side to allow water to be added.

Fruits and vegetables are sometimes used as floral containers. Pumpkins at halloween (shown in Figure 5-16) and squash at Thanksgiving give good effects for these occasions. If the arrangement is to be used for only one day, the seeds can be removed, an auxiliary container inserted, and the arrangement constructed. Once cut, fruits and vegetables deteriorate quickly and will last for only one or two days. To prolong their usefulness as a floral container, the insides can be covered with melted parafin wax after the seeds have been removed. If treated in this way, they should last for a week or longer.

FIGURE 5-16 Pumpkins are often used as containers for Halloween arrangements. Because of their heavy appearance, they can support relatively large arrangements of plant material. This container can support a larger arrangement of plant material.

The color of a container must be in harmony with its surroundings. This includes backgrounds, furnishings, and the flowers. Neutral colors are generally best, but there are times when strong, contrasting colors may be used. Because green compliments most flowers, it is sometimes thought that "when in doubt use a green container." This is far from being true. There are many different greens; and unless selected carefully, a green container may conflict drastically with the plant material being used in it.

White, black, and pastels most often will compliment or harmonize with the plant material. Black and white, when added to a basic color, will produce shades or tints of that color. When used as containers, they tend to produce the same effect with the plant material and in doing so fit in well with the overall design.

Silver, bronze, aluminum, and pewter are considered neutral colors. Grey, natural pottery colors, and most browns fit into this same category; they can generally be used successfully, but one must be aware that conflicts do not occur.

Muted tones are desirable. Bright colors can cause trouble and may ruin an otherwise good arrangement.

Texture is another important factor to be considered when selecting containers. The visual weight of the container, which to some degree is determined by its texture, will have an influence upon the size of the arrangement that can be placed in it. Coarse-textured containers have a feeling of heaviness associated with them and can support larger arrangements than can delicate or fine textured ones of the same size.

The texture of the container should fit or harmonize and have the correct relationship with its surroundings. Pine-panelled walls and heavy appearing furnishings call for a heavy or coarse textured one while a room with a delicate appearance should have a more fragile or lighter appearing container. Pottery containers with their heavy appearance and coarse texture are put to good use in a den or an informal setting, while a formal dinner with fine lace, linen, and an abundance of silver and crystal would need a container similar to the delicate nature of the setting.

The relationship between the plant material and the texture of the container is an important consideration. Both should have similar textures and have a good relationship with each other. Fine, delicate baby's breath, lily of the valley, and small sweetheart roses, arranged together in a fragile or delicate container of crystal, porcelain, or silver, have the same texture and harmonize well. Flowers with coarse petals and heavy stems are best suited for heavier, more sturdy containers. Often the designer gives little thought to the foliage being used. All plant material, flowers *and* foliage, should have a good relationship to the texture of the container and the surroundings.

The size of the container should be compatible with that of the arrangement of plant material and the space it is to occupy. The relationship between the size of the container and the arrangement is discussed in Chapter 2. It can be interpreted to indicate that the height of the container should be one-third to two-fifths of the height of the arrangement or one-quarter to two-thirds of the total length of the arrangement. Since these are not definite rules, as found in Oriental arrangements, but only are guidelines, they may be varied depending upon the plant material used and the space to be occupied. Quite often the arrangement of plant material will exceed two times the height of the container and still be in proportion to it. If the plant material is about the same height or less than the height of the container, it is usually out of scale, and the container can be overpowering and dominate the arrangement.

In determining the size of the container to be used, the allotted space plays an important role. In a flower show, the size of the background may be given, and then the container must be selected accordingly. Often an arrangement is made in a favorite vase, squeezed into the allotted space, and found to be too big for it. If the container had been chosen according to the available space, this situation would not develop.

Containers are often selected for special places or uses. Sometimes flower show schedules will be specific in the type of container to be used for each class or a few classes in the show. If the designer does not follow the schedule, the arrangement will be disqualified. Where containers are not specified, for best results they should be selected according to the theme of the show.

Vases for church arrangements should harmonize with the furnishings and architecture of the church. Tall brass or gold vases are commonly used, but many times these are not compatible with available flowers or the architecture of the surroundings. Pottery or glass containers are in keeping with the furnishings of some churches but would be completely out of place in others.

Home arrangements can be made in almost any type of container. However, consideration should be given to the kinds of plant material available, the furnishings of the room, and the place the arrangement is to occupy. The container should be the correct size, color, texture, and shape for the room and flowers.

Bases, blocks, or stands are often used in conjunction with a flower arrangement. They are placed under the vase and become an integral part of the overall design. When used, they should be considered a part of the container when determining the overall height of the arrangement.

Not all arrangements need some type of base or stand, but many times a stand will help to give the necessary height or to present a stabilizing force to help balance the design. Bases or stands should be selected carefully and be the correct color, size, and texture to harmonize with the rest of the composition.

Many ready-made bases and stands are available to the floral designer. Some examples are shown in Figure 5-17. These will vary from the complicated wood carvings used with oriental designs to some of the plain contemporary ones found in florist or supply shops. Tiles, bamboo mats, and mirrors are often used, and each presents a special problem to the designer.

FIGURE 5–17 Commercially made bases in a variety of sizes and shapes are available at florist shops, garden centers, and arrangement supply shops.

Tiles with ornate designs or highly glazed finishes often compete with the rest of the arrangement for attention. If they must be used, select those with a minimum of artwork and distracting color. Mirrors require that special attention be given to the reflected part of the design: A good arrangement can have its whole effect destroyed by placing it on a mirror which reflects some of the mechanics in it. The use of mirrors as bases should be discouraged. However, if a class in a flower show calls for such a base, the mirror should be available during construction, and reflections from the arrangement observed and any errors corrected at that time. Bamboo mats are often out of unity with the type of plant material in the arrangement and should be used only when they contribute to the overall composition.

Homemade bases, blocks, or stands work well with many arrangements. They can be easily made by cutting pieces of wood or metal or by molding clay or plaster into various shapes. They can be given a natural finish or painted and polished to have a more formal appearance. Dishes or containers turned upside down often work well; doilies and textiles are satisfactory.

Placement of the arrangement on the base is an important consideration. Improper placement can result in a good arrangement becoming out of balance. A symmetrically balanced arrangement is normally placed in the center of the base, an asymmetrical one to one side. It might be necessary to place the arrangement toward the front or back of the base depending upon the circumstances. Only a little experience and trial and

FIGURE 5-18 Placement of the arrangement on the base is important, especially for balance. This arrangement is in good position. If placed nearer to the center, the overall composition would be out of balance.

error will determine the proper placement. Figure 5-18 illustrates a well-balanced arrangement.

Backgrounds play a vital role in the overall effect of a flower arrangement. A fussy or confusing background will destroy the lines in the arrangement as well as its overall design. Figured wallpaper, windows, bamboo or shutter type screens, pictures, and mirrors all lead to confusion in the arrangement. Wallpaper with intricate designs, large swirling outlines, and intense colors will completely dominate the area, and flower arrangements placed in front of such background material will be lost in the confusion as seen in Figure 5-19. Placing arrangements on window sills as shown in Figure 5-20 is often seen at flower shows and in the home. Light coming through the window, as well as the window frame and the outside area, will detract from the arrangement. Unless the arrangement is a solid mass or consists of flowers and other plant material with strong, bold silhouettes, light will penetrate through the arrangement emphasizing stems and individual flowers and will detract from

FIGURE 5-19 A well-designed arrangement of peonies and scotch broom. The wallpaper and shadows in the background detract from and confuse the lines in the arrangement.

FIGURE 5-20 A window is usually a poor place to display a flower arrangement.

FIGURE 5-21 Prominent horizontal lines of the background interfere with the vertical lines of the arrangement.

the overall design. The light will also reduce the color effectiveness of it.

Lines formed either vertically or horizontally by background screens will interfere with the design of an arrangement. A shutter with its horizontal lines will appear to continually cut the lines of a vertical arrangement; the same situation exists when an arrangement with a predominantly horizontal line is placed in front of a screen with vertical lines. See Figure 5-21.

Pictures placed behind arrangements usually predominate, and the floral designs become secondary to them. If it is desirable to place an arrangement in such an area—a picture above a mantel—it should be made to keep its uppermost part below the picture frame.

Mirrors create difficult situations for the floral designer. Arrangements placed in front of them will be reflected, oftentimes resulting in confusion. Figure 5-22 shows the confusion that may be created. One way to help reduce the difficulty is to place arrangements on either side of the mirror and either a low arrangement or nothing directly in front of it.

To emphasize flower arrangements, plain backgrounds are best. The color and texture of the background material should harmonize with that of the plant material. This should be kept in mind when entering flower shows if the designer is to supply background material.

Accessories are objects or materials added to an arrangement, either within the container of plant material or separated from it, which contribute to the overall theme of the composition. They include such items as figurines, ceramic figures, fruit, covers of containers, and background fabrics. At no time should the accessory compete for dominance with the plant material; instead, it should be a vital part of the whole composition and should blend in with all of the material used.

FIGURE 5-22 Pink rubrum lilies, snapdragons, and roses combined into an interesting symmetrical arrangement. Placing it in front of a mirror causes confusion.

Accessories should not be used just for the sake of using them. Unless they contribute to the overall design or theme, they should be eliminated. Many good arrangements have been downgraded at flower shows, and home arrangements have looked completely out of place because of them. A good rule to follow is "When in doubt, leave it out."

Flower show schedules often call for accessories to be used to carry out the theme of the show or class. A theme is shown

FIGURE 5-23 In a flower show, the theme of the class often calls for an accessory. Without knowing the theme, the accessory might appear out of place. This class suggested "Transportation of the Past." Everything ties together well including the vase (track clamps), base (a piece of railroad tie and a steel track supporter), plant materials (railroad grass, briers, sweet fern, and goldenrod), with chrysanthemums used for overall effect and old railroad spikes used as accessories. All materials except the chrysanthemums were collected along an abandoned railroad track.

in Figure 5-23. In such situations be sure the accessory does the job that is expected of it. Does it fit the theme? Does it contribute to the design? Does it harmonize with the rest of the composition? Is it the correct color, size, and shape? If all of these questions can be answered in the affirmative, the accessory is probably satisfactory to use. If only one has a negative answer, do not use it.

It is best to select an accessory when the composition is being planned. The whole composition can be designed around it, and it can then be tied in appropriately with the rest of the material. It is a mistake to make an arrangement and then select an accessory to use with it. Most often it will look as though it was an afterthought and will detract from the composition, a situation shown in Figure 5-24.

All accessories should be in scale with other parts of the

composition. There are no set rules regarding size, but the size of the accessory must be appropriate with the other materials. Too small an object will lose its effectiveness while a large accessory will tend to dominate. See Figures 5-24 and 5-25.

FIGURE 5-24 The accessory seems to have been added to satisfy the desire for an accessory. It appears too large for the arrangement.

FIGURE 5-25 Birds used as an accessory harmonize in color and texture with all parts of the composition. Their size is a bit too small when compared with that of the box and dishes, however.

Color and texture of accessories should harmonize with the rest of the material. Neutral colors, pastels, or tints or shades of the plant material or container are satisfactory. A dominant or contrasting color is difficult to use. The texture should be appropriate to the rest of the composition. A highly glazed pottery object would be out of place with a dull container and subdued colors of plant material but might fit in well where bright colors are used.

The shape of an accessory must be appropriate to that of the design. Its lines should follow those in the arrangement and not conflict with or suggest crossing or cutting them. Tall accessories incorporated within the arrangement of plant material will suggest vertical lines and help to accentuate them. Low ones will help to stress horizontal lines.

Placement of accessories can help to balance or destroy the balance of the composition. In a situation where they are separated from the arrangement of plant material, a pair of accessories placed on either side of a symmetrical arrangement would provide stability; however, with a similar arrangement accessories placed on *one* side would destroy balance unless other measures were taken to counteract the effect. A single accessory would be appropriate for use with an asymmetrical arrangement to provide balance. It must be the correct distance away from the vase; otherwise it will be ineffective. Placing accessories forward or toward the rear can be effective in helping to create depth. Those placed toward the rear will help this effect without competing with the rest of the composition. If the accessory is placed in a forward position, there is always the possibility of its detracting from the rest of the material.

It is important that the accessory harmonize with the season of the year as well as with the plant material. Ceramic frogs or butterflies would be inappropriate with winter arrangements but might harmonize well in late spring or summer compositions.

Containers, bases, backgrounds, and accessories all play a vital part in arrangements. They should harmonize with each other and with the plant material in the composition. The failure of any one can lead to disasterous results.

6

Color

One of the more important factors in the art of flower arrangement is *color.* It adds life to the arrangement; it gives each floral piece a personality of its own. Without color, the arrangement lacks that certain quality that attracts one's eyes to it. No matter how closely the principles of this art are followed, how precisely construction details are adhered to, and how perfect the plant material may be, because of the improper use of color, the arrangement can be a dismal failure. Color harmony within the arrangement itself and with the area in which it is to be placed is an important consideration. Just as a new home is incomplete until the final finishing touch of color, the same situation exists in flower arrangements. Harmonies and differences occur in color just as they do in music; in many situations they are closely related to the individual's likes and dislikes. A close observation of nature will help one to understand color to some extent. Color combinations seen in individual flowers can be helpful; the dark brown center and yellow petals of the black-eyed Susan (*Rudbeckia hirta*) and the combinations often found in pansies (*Viola tricolor*) are interesting and can often be used as guides. However, an understanding of a few basic principles regarding color will assist the floral designer to do better work and to appreciate and comprehend those arrangements made by others.

Before proceeding with the various principles and uses of color, it is best that the term be defined. *What is color?* The physicist identifies color according to radiant energy, light, and wavelengths. The colors we *see* are reflected light with wavelengths included in the visible spectrum.

The chemist describes color according to pigments. The mixing of these pigments in various amounts along with black and white can be used to make up any desired color. Psychologists study color according to human response and reaction. The responses of individuals to certain colors or combinations of colors are important considerations to the psychologist as well as to the floral designer. Most artists, including floral designers, consider all of the above in their response to color. A detailed study of each is not necessary for one working with flowers, but some background knowledge is helpful.

When light waves of various lengths hit the retina of the eye, they are interpreted by the brain as different colors. The human eye can see only those wavelengths in the visible spectrum which is a small part of the entire light ray. Infrared with wavelengths longer than red, and ultra violet with wavelengths shorter than violet are at either end of this area but are not visible. Figure 6–1 illustrates the visible spectrum. (A parallel situation exists with light and sound. With sound only certain vibrations are heard by the human ear, whereas those of higher or lower pitch are not audible.)

As a ray of light is passed through a prism onto a sheet of white paper, a band of color known as the visible spectrum is produced as shown in Figure 6–1. These colors—red, orange, yellow, green, blue, and violet—are not divided by distinct lines among them; but there is a gradual blending of one into the next resulting from the different wavelengths of each. If a second prism is used and the band of light passing through the first is focused on this, the spectrum hues will again merge and will be seen as white light. From this demonstration, it can be concluded that white is the combination of all colors.

Colors seen by the human eye are reflected light. A blue or a yellow object as one sees it is the result of the color effects

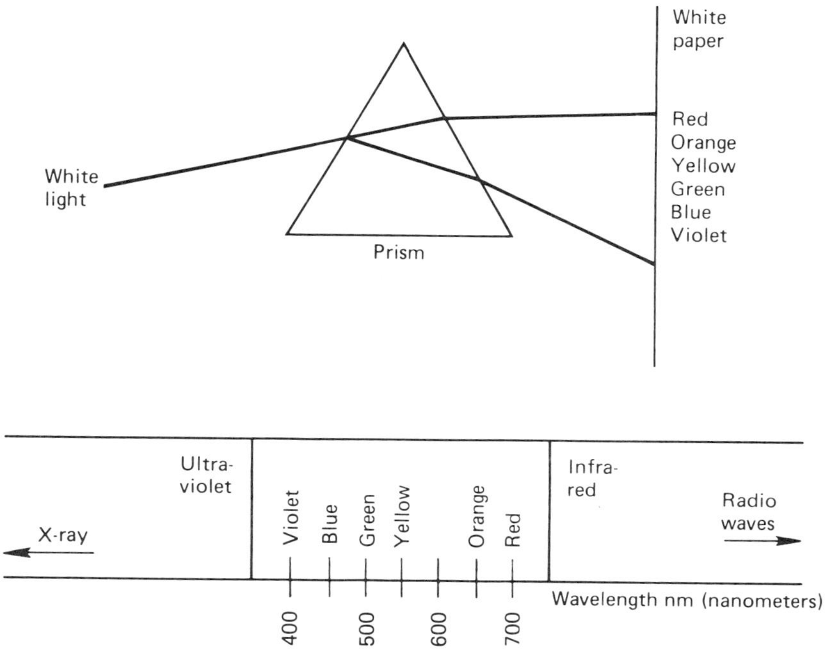

FIGURE 6–1 Top: A beam of white light passed through a prism results in the formation of the visible spectrum. (Newton's theory of color). Bottom: The visible spectrum and it's relationship to other kinds of radiation.

produced by light waves reflected from the surface. A blue delphinium is that particular color because blue wavelengths are reflected, and all those of other dimensions are absorbed by the surface. When the surface absorbs all wavelengths, the resulting effect is black; if all are reflected, the surface is white.

The source of light as well as its quantity and quality has an effect upon the color that one observes. A red rose in sunlight will be seen as a brilliant red. Under incandescent light the color will be more intense. However, if this same flower is placed under fluorescent lights, it will appear bluish and will not have the same radiance as seen under natural or incandescent sources. An interesting phenomenon can be observed by taking a red rose into a room lighted with fluorescent light. Stand at the end farthest from the window, where the bulk of the light on the rose is from the fluorescent tubes. Walk slowly toward the window where bright sunlight is entering and observe the color changes taking place in the rose. It will gradually change from a dull, bluish red to a brillant red at the window.

Even though the quantity of light (measured in foot candles) remains the same, the quality of it has reflected the changes that occurred.

It is important when selecting flowers to know the type of light in which they will be displayed. If the light intensity (quantity) will be relatively low, bright colors should be used. Under such conditions, darker colored flowers tend to fade into the background and sometimes will even appear as empty spaces in the arrangement when observed from some distance away.

Texture of the plant material is also a factor in color response. Some plant tissues possess a fine, delicate, velvety texture which are color absorbing and do not have the reflecting qualities of tissues with a hard, waxy appearance. Compare the petals of a rose with those of a camellia or tuberous begonia. The latter two usually provide more the vivid color related to their smooth texture.

Texture of the foliage used should not be overlooked when planning arrangements. Some foliage has an appearance almost like patent leather which will reflect color to the point of overpowering the other parts of the arrangements. Other types of foliage with a soft, delicate appearance are color absorbing and may be difficult to see under some light conditions.

From the chemist's point of view, there are three primary colors—red, yellow, and blue. By mixing these pigments in various proportions along with black and white, all colors can be obtained. Mixing two primary colors results in a secondary color. A combination of red and yellow results in orange; blue and yellow give green; and blue and red produce violet. A secondary color mixed with a primary color produces those colors known as tertiary colors. There are six of these: Red mixed with orange gives red-orange; orange and yellow produce yellow-orange. Other tertiary colors are yellow-green, blue-green, blue-violet, and red-violet. It is with these twelve fundamental colors that the designer must work.

White added to the above colors will produce a *tint.* The degree of tint will depend upon the amount of white added. By adding black, a *shade* is produced. Grey, a combination of black and white, produces *tones.* Figure 6–2 shows tints, shades, and tones. Tones can also be achieved by mixing two complimentary colors. This greying effort is easily obtained by mixing pigments but is difficult to visualize in flower combinations.

In a discussion of color there are several terms that are often used. The words "color" and "hue" are often used inter-

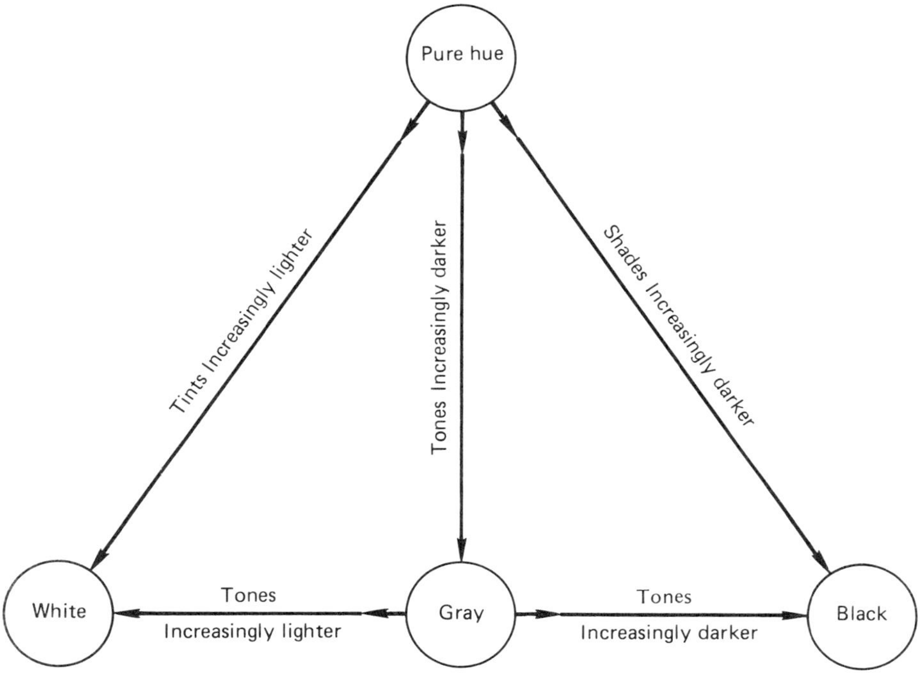

FIGURE 6-2 Shades, tints, and tones. The pure hue is at the top of the triangle. White added in increasing amounts on the left results in tints; black added on the right produces shades. Gray, a combination of black and white, results in tones in the middle.

changeably. However, color is most often used as a general term encompassing the whole wide range of the subject, including hues, values, and chromas. Hue is more specific and is recognized as a pure color with no addition of white, grey, or black which would alter its effectiveness or purity. It is that special attribute of a particular color that differentiates it from other colors of the same intensity. Red, red-violet, and red-orange are all considered as hues.

Value is the relative, or degree of, lightness or darkness of a hue. It is the amount of color distinguished between light, medium and dark of that particular hue. Pink is considered a light value of red; burgundy, a dark value of it. The addition of white and/or black affects the value of a color.

Chroma or intensity is the brightness or dullness of a hue. It is often referred to as the purity of a color determined by the degree of absence of white or grey. The spectrum colors are those that have maximum intensity.

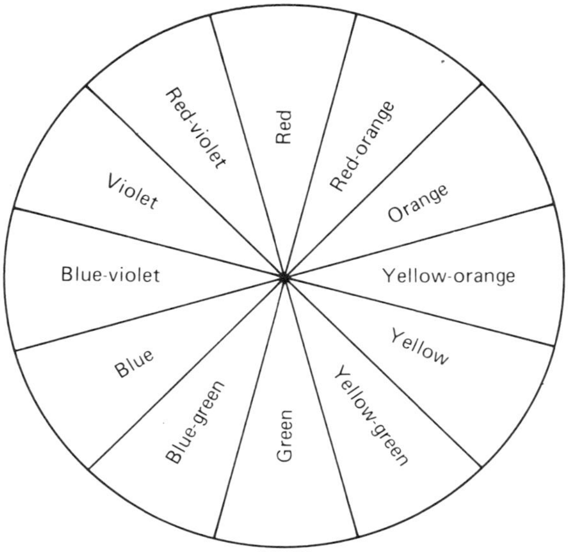

FIGURE 6–3 A color wheel composed of three primary, three secondary, and six tertiary hues.

The color wheel can be a useful tool for the floral designer. Although most designers do have a fairly good understanding of color and color combinations, the color wheel can be used in doubtful situations.

The color wheel most often used consists of the three primary, three secondary, and six tertiary colors arranged in a circle. Some have only primary and secondary colors while others have eighteen or more of them. Basically, the color wheel can be described as the visible spectrum bent so that both ends meet to form a circle . Figure 6–3 is a color wheel. They are readily available at artist supply shops and should be a part of every designer's kit.

The color wheel is used to determine combinations of color which go together or harmonize with each other. One of the easiest to use is called the monochromatic color scheme shown in Figure 6–4. This consists of the use of a single hue along with tints, tones, and shades of it. An arrangement of rose, pink, and red carnations would fit this category. In this situation, the red would be the pure *hue,* pink the *tint,* and rose the *shade* of it.

In any color combination, it is necessary to avoid equal amounts of color. This usually causes competition for interest and is a disturbing factor in any arrangement. One color should

FIGURE 6–4 Monochromatic color scheme using light pink snapdragons, medium pink carnations, and deep pink roses arranged in a pale pink shell. [See also Color Plate.]

predominate and others be subservient to it. In the above combination, if red is to be the dominant color, the pink and rose should add support to it but not be in a position to overpower it.

Analogous color schemes consist of one primary hue along with those that are adjacent to it. See Figure 6–5. This combination can involve those hues making up to one-third of the color

FIGURE 6–5 Analogous color scheme of yellow, yellow-orange, orange, and red-orange chrysanthemums. [See also Color Plate.]

wheel, but no more than one primary color can be involved. Many varieties of annual flowers work together well in this color harmony. Yellow, yellow-orange, and orange zinnias using a combination of the so-called "Cut and Come Again" variety and the larger flowering types can be effective. Marigolds, calendulas, snapdragons, and arctotis can be used together to secure analogous color harmony.

Complimentary colors are those directly opposite each other on the color wheel. Figures 6-3 and 6-6 deal with complimentary colors. Red and green, blue and orange, yellow and violet—all are examples of this color harmony. These combinations can be used to create rather sensational effects especially in contemporary arrangements. Full chromas of each hue are rarely used, except for these arrangements. A combination of a light value (tint) of one and a dark value (shade) of the other usually creates the most interesting effect. Pale blue delphinium and orange marigolds can be used together as an interesting color combination. The use of these two values tends to emphasize both, and each color is used to its best advantage. If a different delphinium was used which had a value similar or equal to that of the marigold, the two colors would tend to neutralize each other and the overall effect would not be as striking as the first example.

The triad or triadic color harmony consists of three colors equidistant on the color wheel. See Figures 6-3 and 6-7. Orange, green, and violet, and red, blue, and yellow are examples of this color harmony. When using these color combinations, shades, tints, and tones should be used rather than the full chroma of each. It is also important that unequal amounts of each be used to create proper balance in the arrangement. Pink snapdragons, blue delphiniums, and yellow marguerites combined into a light, airy, spring arrangement is an effective use of the triad combination.

In the above color harmonies, no mention has been made of white, grey, and black. In most color schemes these, along with green, the natural color of most foliage, are considered neutral and can be used for containers or backgrounds. However, if the arrangement is for a flower show, the schedule or show committee should be consulted to be sure their use is not prohibited.

The use of color in floral designs is often referred to as "an arrangement within an arrangement." In the construction of the overall arrangement, one is concerned with lines, balance, and

FIGURE 6-6 Complimentary color scheme using yellow snapdragons and violet stocks. The darker colored stocks might appear as empty spaces in a dimly lighted area. [See also Color Plate.]

FIGURE 6-7 A painter's palette is the base for this triad color combination. Red and yellow gladioli and blue delphinium make up the triad. The white can be considered neutral. [See also Color Plate.]

other factors. For effective use of color, the same factors must be taken into consideration. However, there should be an interrelationship between the construction details and the use of color.

The design of the arrangement and the use of color must be considered simultaneously and constructed accordingly. Just as the lines of the arrangement flow toward the focal area, color should move in the same direction, with the heavier colors concentrated there. The focal point of both flower size and color should coincide to ensure unity and to avoid competition for attention among the different parts of the arrangement.

Balance can be achieved by careful placement of hues, their values, and chroma. The use of full chroma should be limited to a small area, and unequal values of the same or different hues should be used throughout the arrangement. If the full chroma is used in different areas, a spotty appearance results, creating competition for dominance in these areas. Light values are used at the extremities and those of darker value used toward the base. Darker values appear heavier than their lighter counterparts and when concentrated toward the base will lend weight to this area and will help to support the rest of the arrangement. Figure 6–8 contrasts darker and lighter values.

FIGURE 6–8 Darker values appear heavier than lighter ones. The use of the red roses at the base focuses the visual weight on that area. [See also Color Plate.]

FIGURE 6-9 Colors should flow together with no dividing line between them. Pink roses and snapdragons are concentrated at the top and bottom of this arrangement separated by white chrysanthemums in the center. [See also Color Plate.]

FIGURE 6-10 Layering of colors tends to cause divisions in an otherwise good Hogarth curve. The heavy bowl, pedestal, and mat give good support to the arrangement of plant material. [See also Color Plate.]

Shades, tints, and tones of the various hues in the arrangement can be used effectively to create the principle of *rhythm.* Starting with tints at the extremities, followed by tones and shades toward the focal area where the full chroma can be used, movement can be easily obtained. Because shades appear heavier than tones and tones heavier than tints, movement in the arrangement can be controlled by their use.

There should be no sharp dividing line between colors. See Figures 6-9 and 6-10. Instead they should flow together and create the feeling of oneness rather than the effect that each is going its own separate way. This can be accomplished by a gradual intermingling of the colors at the point of junction and flowing toward the single hues in each direction. It should be remembered that when two or more hues are used, only one should predominate, and the others should be secondary to it.

Darker colors appear heavier than lighter ones and are usually used in a low position. However, because of their size, there are occasions when lighter colored flowers appear heavier than their darker counterparts and will be used in the lower areas. A guideline to follow is: if two flowers are of equal size, the darker appears heavier and should be used low in the arrangement; if the darker flowers are smaller and appear lighter in weight than the light colored ones, they should be used toward the extremities of the arrangement.

For good balance in an arrangement of red and white carnations, for example, the red would be placed low and toward the center whereas the white would predominate at the extremities. A combination of blue salvia and white carnations would have the darker colored salvia outward with the white concentrated at the base. This situation exists because of the size relationship between the two flowers. In both of these examples, it should not be interpreted that only one color is at the base but rather that a predominance of that color is there and color values lessen as they move away from the focal area.

Background colors are important considerations when an arrangement is put in place. To be more effective, arrangements of light-colored flowers should have dark backgrounds, and those with dark flowers are more pronounced when light backgrounds are used. If the background color is similar to that of the arrangement, background and arrangement will tend to blend together to such an extent that it may be difficult to distinguish the outline of the arrangement. Too sharp a contrast may also cause difficulty by exaggerating lines or materials at the perimeter at the expense of those within. For flower shows, neutral backgrounds are best; black, white, or grey are all good; pastels are usually satisfactory; brightly colored backgrounds will overpower some arrangements and should be avoided if possible.

Although the chemical and physical reactions are quite fixed and rigid, the psychological response to color is often more flexible and variable. Colors do have an effect upon human reaction and response, but these vary considerably among individuals and under different conditions. Some colors have the effect of creating a feeling of warmth; others, coolness; some cheerful and others depressing. There is a group of colors that give the feeling of coming forward; these are called "advancing colors" while others tend to move away and are known as "receding colors." Each of these factors should be kept in mind when making floral arrangements.

Warm colors are those involving red, orange, and yellow. If red is placed at the top of the color wheel, those colors between the eleven and five o'clock positions going clockwise are known as warm colors. These include red-violet, red, etc., through yellow-green. This group of colors has a warming effect upon most individuals. The degree of warmth is greatest at the red position and gradually decreases as one moves farther away from it. Those colors proceeding through green, blue, and violet are known as cool colors with blue having the greatest degree of coolness.

This effect can have an influence upon the types and color of flowers used at different times of the year. On a hot summer day, red flowers conveying the impression of warmth would tend to make the atmosphere feel hotter; whereas blue flowers would have a cooling effect upon those present and provide for a more comfortable condition. The reverse of this would be appropriate for a cold, snowy day. Red, conveying the feeling of warmth, would help to counteract the coolness associated with the blustery, wintery conditions. Blue flowers would only add to the unpleasant conditions outdoors and have an additional cooling effect within the room. The greater the chroma of the hue, the more intense will be the feeling of warmness or coolness of it.

Tints have a cheerful effect upon most individuals. Pastels fit into this category and create the feeling of well being or happiness. Many of the flowers used by designers are tints; few have full chroma or the degree of intensity that can be obtained from pigments; some flowers have colors which are considered as tones; fewer would be shades of a color.

Tones are known as quieting, shades as depressing. Care must be taken when selecting these values because of the reaction of individuals to them under certain conditions. When used together with tints and hues of full intensity in a monochromatic arrangement, they can be quite effective in brightening the general atmosphere.

Shades and tones make good backgrounds for flower arrangements. Because of their subdued nature, arrangements of flowers of other hues can be more effectively displayed against shades or tones.

The psychological effect of some colors protruding forward and others moving backward can be used to some degree in floral design. The theory of advancing and receding colors involves the idea that bright colors are advancing or moving for-

FIGURE 6-11 Two similar arrangements. The one on the left has bright colors forward and dark colors deep, creating the impression of depth. The arrangement on the right, with dark colors forward and light ones deep, appears to have less depth. [See also Color Plate.]

ward and that darker colors are receding or moving away. A room with bright colored walls appears smaller than one of similar dimensions with the darker hues. The visual dimensions of a long, narrow room can be changed by having the wall at one end of a different color from the others.

In flower arranging, the theory of advancing and receding colors can be used to obtain depth; this theory is shown in Figure 6-11. By placing darker colors deep within the arrangement and the brighter colors forward, a feeling of greater depth can be obtained. It is necessary that placement and lighting be considered when using these hues. From distances or under conditions of low light intensity, darker hues may appear as open spaces or voids in the arrangement. If the darker colors are forward and the bright hues placed within, depth will appear to be completely lacking or at best, less than the real depth in the arrangement. Under most conditions, this situation should be avoided.

The choice of color reflects the personality of the designer and should reflect that of the one receiving the flowers. Some designers tend to use bright colors in most of their designs—these may not be appropriate for a subdued or quiet individual or for some situations. Bright colors or those of full chroma can be depressing for one who is seriously ill but can be cheerful and stimulating for a patient well on the way to recovery.

The designer's choice of color can be as important as the choice of flowers. Oftentimes a relatively poor arrangement catches the eye of admirers strictly because of the way the colors have been combined or manipulated. Color is often misleading and often can cover errors that could downgrade the arrangement. It can also work the other way by detracting from arrangements that are well done with regard to construction details but lack the well-balanced or correct combinations of hues.

The time that the designer can devote to color scheme is unfortunately limited; also, color schemes are defined by the availability of flowers. It is important that the designer have enough knowledge of color use so he can diagnose and interpret color combinations quickly and arrive at harmonious groupings with the floral materials available.

FIGURE 1–25

FIGURE 2-21

FIGURE 2-25

FIGURE 3-2

FIGURE 3-13

FIGURE 6-4

FIGURE 6-5

FIGURE 6-6

FIGURE 6-7

FIGURE 6-8

FIGURE 6-9

FIGURE 6-10

FIGURE 6–11a

FIGURE 6–11b

FIGURE 10-8

FIGURE 10-10

FIGURE 10-16

Cutting, Buying, and Keeping Flowers

7

The floral designer has many sources of cut flowers. These include retail florists, street vendors, garden centers, nearby greenhouses, local gardeners, and the designer's own garden. Since flowers can be an expensive item, many designers grow their own when facilities are available. By proper selection of varieties, one can be assured of an ample supply of flowers during the entire growing season.

A garden which is planted primarily as a source of cut flowers should be well planned and flowers should be selected not only for their beauty but for their keeping qualities as well. Daylilies and gazania, while beautiful in the garden during the day, close up at night, much to the disappointment of the designer who uses them. Asters, snapdragons, and marigolds are easy to grow, have excellent keeping qualities, and will last for several days in arrangements. Some flowers such as large dahlias wilt rapidly and many times will not recover even when given the special treatment described later in this chapter.

The garden should be planned in such a way that there is a continuous supply of flowers rather than many at certain times and none at others. Many daffodils and tulips, along with iris and violets, may be a designer's utopia or may be a source of frustration in the spring, but then grown at the sacrifice of other flowers later in the season. Before planting, one should decide on the types of arrangements to be made, colors that will be compatible, and when flowers will be needed. A little time spent planning ahead will be well rewarded during the growing season.

The designer-gardener will encounter many of the problems faced by the commercial grower of cut flowers. These include the cultural practices that must be followed to get the best quality flowers possible and for the harvesting and caring of them. Even with top quality flowers in the garden, if they are not handled properly as cut flowers, their lasting qualities can be poor.

The length of time cut flowers will remain in satisfactory condition is influenced by many factors. These include various environmental conditions, how they are treated after cutting, and to some extent the time of day they are harvested. Should flowers be cut in early morning, mid-day, late afternoon, or evening? In this regard, some growth factors such as photosynthesis, respiration, and water relations must be considered.

Photosynthesis, the manufacture of plant food (carbohydrates) by the green plant, is carried on only in the presence of light, whereas respiration, the breaking down or use of this material, is a continuous process. If flowers are picked during the morning hours, their supply of reserve food is at a minimum. If picked in the late afternnon or early evening, the food supply is greater. This would indicate that late afternoon is the best time to harvest them. However, water relations must also be considered.

The water content of flowers is usually greatest during the early morning hours and least in late afternoon, the opposite of the manufactured food content. Therefore, the question arises, which is more important to the life span of cut flowers, the water content or the amount of stored food at the time of cutting? In reality, little difference is apparent in the life span of most cut flowers harvested in early morning or late afternoon. However, there is considerable difference between those cut at these times and those cut at mid-day when both water and carbohydrates are low. Therefore, early morning or late afternoon are the best times to harvest flowers.

When picking flowers, it is a good idea to know the type of design to be constructed and the approximate number of flowers needed to carry it out. It may be desirable to select flowers in various stages of maturity rather than only those fully opened. A few buds and partially opened flowers along with those at their peak of maturity will make a more interesting arrangement as well as reducing the difficulty of construction.

As flowers are picked, they should be placed in water as soon as possible to reduce the possibility of wilting. With many annuals and perennials, it is often recommended that a pail of water be carried into the garden and the stems placed in water as soon as they are cut. With a few flowers, it may be necessary to make a second cut under water to ensure an uninterrupted flow of water through the stem. Some flowers if allowed to wilt will never fully recover; others, such as tulips and snapdragons, will have crooked stems unless they are wrapped to keep them in an upright position. Figure 7-1 shows wrapping. Chrysanthemums, celosia, and gladioli will hold up well even if they are not placed in water for an hour or more after cutting. It is a standard practice among commercial growers who are shipping cut

FIGURE 7-1 Snapdragons wrapped in waxed paper hold spikes in an upright position to reduce bending.

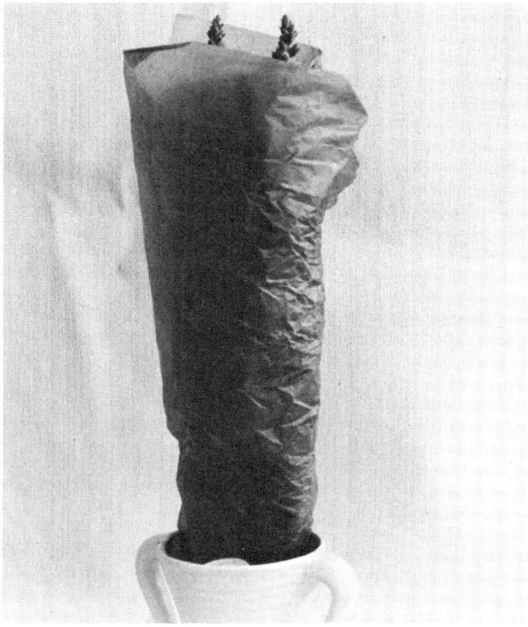

flowers long distances to ship them in a wilted or semi-wilted condition. Carnations, chrysanthemums, and gladioli are handled in this manner but are thoroughly conditioned by the wholesale or retail florist before being sold to the ultimate consumer. Figures 7-2 and 7-3 pertain to shipping procedures.

After flowers have been brought into the workroom, conditioning them should begin as soon as possible. With many, especially those that have wilted, it will be necessary to recut the stem. Only the lower inch or two need be removed. The foliage should be stripped from the lower third of the stems and the stems then placed in 110 degree (F) temperature water. Extremely soft foliage should be removed to a height where none will be immersed when the flowers are placed in water. Because of bacteria action, most foliage will decay rapidly under water, resulting in the clogging of the cut ends of the stems through which most of the water enters. Very little water actually enters through the surface of the stem and foliage. Water at 110 degrees (F) will be absorbed by the stems and flowers more rapidly than will colder water. This reduces the probability of wilting, and those that have already wilted will gain their turgidity more rapidly.

The flowers should be kept at room temperature for one to three hours before removing to a colder location. During this time they should be out of direct sunlight and away from drafts. The purpose of this procedure is to allow them to absorb water as rapidly as possible and at the same time to keep water loss at a minimum.

They should then be removed to a cool, dark location for 12 to 24 hours before using them in arrangements. Most florists keep their refrigerators between 38 degrees and 40 degrees (F). This is too cold for some flowers such as orchids but is a satisfactory temperature for most other flowers. If a home refrigerator is used, it is a good idea to use a thermometer and watch it closely. Do not let the the temperature go below 35 degrees (F). This will give some margin of safety so the flowers will not freeze or be damaged by low temperature. Above all, keep them away from the freezer compartment. The process of handling flowers described above is known as "conditioning" or "hardening." Proper hardening before use in arrangements will help to ensure a greater life span for the flowers and greater satisfaction from the arrangements made with them.

Even though handled in the prescribed manner, some flowers wilt quickly, perhaps even during the hardening process. These usually have some obstacle to water absorption and

FIGURE 7-2 Carnations packed tightly in special flower boxes as received by the wholesale florist via air freight.

FIGURE 7-3 Left: Carnations are removed from the shipping box and placed in warm water after cutting the ends of the stems. Right: The same flowers 24 hours later.

should receive special treatment before hardening. Stems of some flowers, such as poinsettias, excrete a milky latex when cut from the plant. This seals the end of the stem preventing water intake. To eliminate this condition, the ends of the stems should be burned or charred before placing in water. The charring will stop the flow of latex and allow water to pass through the charred areas into the flower. Immediately after charring, place the stems in water and continue the normal hardening process. After this treatment, the stems should not be recut unless the treatment is repeated after cutting.

Woody shrubs and many varieties of garden chrysanthemums often wilt a short time after harvest even though the stems are in water. With these, the stem is hard and the cut end may be small in proportion to the size and number of flowers per stem. This restricts the amount of water that can enter resulting in wilting and eventual death of the flowers. By splitting or crushing the end of the stem, more area is exposed and enough water can be absorbed during the normal hardening period to support the flowers. Removing a few of the leaves will help to reduce the water requirements and help to prevent wilting.

Flowers with hollow stems such as dahlias and oriental poppies which have large water conducting vessels often present problems in keeping quality. When cut from the plant, air enters these vessels, moves up through the stem, and forms a bubble preventing water from entering the flower, causing wilting or eventual death; this might be compared with a vapor lock in the fuel system of a gasoline engine. To reduce wilting, the air must be removed. A common method is to immerse the stem in hot water [160 to 180 degrees (F)] for a few seconds, leaving only the flower head exposed. This will help to force the air out of the stem. It should then be placed in warm [110 degree (F)] water immediately to begin the hardening process. It is a good idea to protect the flower head with a paper or cardboard shield during the hot water treatment. This is especially true with lilies and spring flowering bulbs.

For those who do not grow their own flowers, it is necessary to secure them from other sources. The local florist is always a good place to visit. See Figure 7–4. In addition to roses, carnations, gladioli, and chrysanthemums, which are available throughout the year, he will have some seasonal and sometimes unusual flowers which might be ideal for a specific arrangement. Seasonal flowers such as daffodils, tulips, and

FIGURE 7-4 Inside a florist's refrigerator. Most florists carry a good variety of flowers.

stocks are available in abundant numbers only at certain times of the year. It might be possible for the florist to supply some of these varieties at other times, but they will be expensive. If a specific or unusual item is needed, there is a possibility he can locate it through his sources of supply. It is always a good idea for the designer to visit the florist shop rather than using the telephone. It is not only an exciting place but is a source of new ideas, new equipment, and exotic flowers, which might probably be overlooked or unknown of without personal contact. Get to know the florist and listen to what he has to say. Most florists enjoy talking about their product, will make suggestions regarding flowers and equipment, and in general will prove most helpful.

It is possible that the designer will find the street vendor and supermarket satisfactory sources of cut flowers. The flowers obtained are usually of good quality, but the varieties sold by these retailers are somewhat limited. Many may be prepackaged, and therefore it is not possible to purchase the exact number wanted. Flowers that are in surplus supply in the wholesale market are sometimes purchased by the street vendor in large quantities at reduced prices, and he is able to sell them to the ultimate consumer at a reduced price. Because of the popularity of chrysanthemums and the small demand for roses in the fall, one may be able to get a good buy on roses from this dealer. The same situation with other flowers can take place at other times throughout the year.

The local greenhouse, garden center, or gardener may have flowers available at times throughout the year. Most large greenhouses are wholesale growers and do not encourage retail sales. Many of the smaller units feature a combination of wholesale/retail operation and can be an excellent source of flowers. Because of their size, they may grow only one specific crop (carnations) or limit themselves to three or four kinds of flowers.

The local gardener will have a wide variety of flowers throughout the growing season; but this supply, of course, is limited by weather conditions. He will have some flowers, generally not available from other sources, as well as many of the common ones such as gladioli.

When buying flowers, there are several things that should be considered. Costs seem to be the utmost concern of many designers. Although many florists try to stabilize prices and keep them constant throughout the year, there sometimes are special sales on flowers that are in abundant supply and occasionally there are cash-and-carry sales on other items. The best buys are those flowers that are in season or those that are in plentiful supply with low demand.

Red flowers are in great demand at Christmas and Valentines Day. Pink, blue, yellow, and white are the colors for Easter and Mother's Day. If other colors can be substituted in arrangements at these times, the buyer will find ample quantities and reasonable prices. Pink roses or carnations mixed with holly might be desirable for a Christmas season arrangement and would probably be less expensive than if red flowers were used.

Many popular florist flowers are graded according to length of stem—the longer the stem, the higher the price. Figure 7-5 lists rose prices by stem length. Since different lengths of stems are used in arrangements, it is less expensive to buy a few longer stems for the extremities of the design and shorter ones for filling in near the base. Crooked stemmed or crooked spiked flowers are sometimes available from the local gardener at a reduced price. These will probably make for a more interesting design and at the same time reduce the overall cost of the arrangement.

The local florist is a good source for foliage to use in arrangements. Most have such greens as laurel, huckleberry, salal, and leatherleaf fern. These have been used in such quantities

Roses*

Per Bloom

Stem Length	Each
26" and longer	60 — 70¢
22 — 26"	50 — 65¢
18 — 22"	40 — 60¢
14 — 18"	30 — 45¢
10 — 14"	20 — 30¢
6 — 10"	12 — 16¢

*Prices from Flower Market Report.

FIGURE 7-5 Price of roses varies according to stem length. These wholesale prices will also vary according to time of year and available supply.

that they now seem to lack interest in arrangements. By visiting the flower shops, one can find other kinds of foliage that will compliment the flowers being used and add interest to the designs. Multicolored croton leaves used with chrysanthemums or ti leaves with anthurium or bird-of-paradise make interesting combinations. The foliage from the flowers themselves—gladiolus leaves and flowers— is often times the best material to use. The foliage arrangement shown in Figure 7-6 using several kinds of leaves make interesting pieces to use for decoration and can be colorful and long lasting.

FIGURE 7-6 An arrangement using only foliage. A cut flower can be used as a focal point to vary the appearance of this long-lasting background.

When buying flowers, it is important that they be fresh and properly hardened. Roses that have been picked for several days develop black ends on the stems, and red roses develop a bluish color similar to that seen when they are viewed under fluorescent light. Carnations develop a soft calyx while many varieties of chrysanthemums, especially whites and yellows, have a purplish coloring of the lower petals. These flowers will not last as long as freshly cut ones and should be avoided if possible.

When the florist receives flowers from the wholesaler, he prepares and conditions them for sale. The designer can be assured that this has been done by the reputable florist. However, it is always a good idea to remove the lower inch or two from the stem which might have dried out in transit, and to place the flowers in water for a short time before arranging them.

Most designers prefer to cut flower stems on a slant with a sharp knife prior to inserting them into an arrangement. This exposes more surface at the cut end of the stem, resulting in better water-absorbing qualities for the flower. For those flowers where the rate of absorption is slow, yet the demand for water to prevent wilting is great, this has some merit. For other flowers, cutting on a slant for this purpose is questionable. A slanted cut does make it easier to insert stems into foam materials and does reduce the possibility of a stem being flat against the bottom of the container and unable to absorb water; but when pinpoint holders are used, a slanted cut stem may not fasten securely in the holder. For this type of flower holder, it is best to cut stems straight across. A knife is preferred because a clean cut can be made without the crushing effect obtained with scissors or pruning shears.

After arranging freshly cut and properly hardened flowers, there are still several things that must be considered if satisfactory results are to be obtained. Environmental conditions such as temperature, sunlight, humidity, air movement, and water supply play an important role in their life span. Food supply and bacteria are also important factors.

As temperature increases, the rate of respiration increases. This depletes the supply of stored food within the cut flower at an increased rate, resulting in a shorter life span. Temperature also has an effect on the water loss from the cut flower. At higher temperatures, the water loss may be at a rate faster than it can be absorbed by the cut end of the stem, resulting in wilting and death of the flower.

Sunlight is necessary for *plant* growth. However, once the flower is removed from the plant, direct sunlight is probably more detrimental than beneficial. Since an increase in temperature is associated with sunlight, the life span of the flowers can be reduced considerably. A common error made by the homemaker is to place an arrangement in a sunny window or next to a heating element—either a radiator or baseboard heating unit. Under such conditions, the arrangement can be expected to last for only a short time. If this is the only area where it can be used, removing it to a cool room at night will help to improve its lasting qualities.

In areas of high humidity, water loss from the flower will be at a slower rate than where humidity is low. Anything that one can do to increase the humidity will help to prolong the life span of the flowers. Misting several times a day will help. A vase with a wide opening and a large water surface exposed will increase the humidity somewhat. Avoid drafts: Rapid air movement will decrease humidity around the flowers resulting in greater water loss from them.

To reduce the possibility of wilting, an ample supply of water should be available to the cut flowers at all times. Since most water is absorbed through the cut end, it is not necessary that the stems be deeply immersed in it. It should be of sufficient depth to keep the end of the stem always covered. It is not necessary for the water to be changed in the arrangement every day. However, it is desirable that water be added daily to replace that taken up and lost by the flowers. This procedure is necessary regardless of the type of holder being used to keep flowers in place. Where foam materials are used, even though they appear moist, it is necessary for water to be added each day. Without this addition, there may be a rapid dehydration and resulting death of the flowers.

It is possible to increase the life span of cut flowers by adding materials to the water. Most designers have special "home" remedies which are supposed to have special virtues in prolonging the life of cut flowers. Some of these do work, while others are questionable. Aspirin has been used for years by many, but most research indicates that flowers will last as long or longer in fresh water without aspirin. A small amount of sugar will help to increase the life span of many flowers; vinegar or other acids added to the water will help to improve keeping quality; a few drops of a bactericide may also be effective. Figure 7-7 shows a few materials used to increase life span.

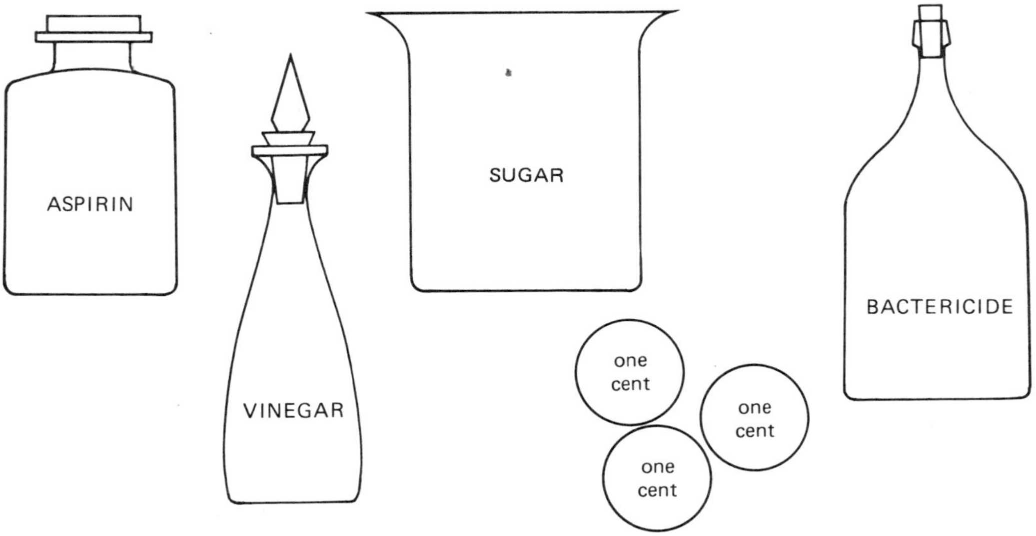

FIGURE 7-7 Many materials around the home have been used with varying degrees of success to prolong the life span of cut flowers.

Before adding materials to the water, we should first consider what we are trying to do and the factors in the water that will affect the life span of the flowers. The greatest problem is the bacteria in the water which rapidly multiply, clogging the cut ends of the stems and preventing water uptake. Anything that can be done to decrease bacterial population will help to increase the life span of the flowers. Most of these bacteria will not multiply as rapidly in an acid solution as in a neutral or alkaline one. Therefore, anything added that will increase the acidity of the water will help to reduce the bacteria. The idea of adding a penny to water, thinking that the copper from the penny will kill the bacteria has merit, but a penny is not enough copper. A handful of pennies or a copper container will help. There is probably enough copper in the water of today's homes with copper water lines to lower the bacteria population. This is especially true if there is a dripping faucet which leaves a blue ring in the bath tub!

Sugar added to the water at the rate of one teaspoon per quart of water will serve as a source of additional food for cut flowers. It will go into solution and be absorbed along with the water and eventually be used in the process of respiration. Too much sugar added to the water will cause dehydration and rapid death of the flowers.

For years, many scientists have been involved in seeking methods or materials that will prolong the life span of cut flowers. From this research have evolved several cut flower preservatives that are sold commercially. Some are specific and are used only for certain flowers while others are suitable to use with a wide range of plant material. Most are patented, and it is difficult to ascertain their ingredients. However, most contain sugar, acidifying agents, and bactericides along with other materials.

Most cut flower preservatives are packaged in solid or crystal form and must be dissolved in water before becoming available to the flowers. It is important that directions on their packages be followed closely and proper dilutions be made; otherwise, they may do more harm than good. When used according to directions, these so-called preservatives may increase the life span of flowers several days over what would normally be expected in clear water.

When preservatives are used, it is still necessary to add water to the arrangement on a daily basis. Under no circumstances should the water level be allowed to reach a point where it can no longer be absorbed by the plant material.

8

Drying and Dried Arrangements

When the first frost hits the flower garden in early or late fall, it should not signal the end of the season for flower arranging. Of course, fresh flowers are always available at the florist shop; but because of costs and other limitations, the designer must limit the amount of materials obtained from this source.

With proper planning throughout the growing season, the designer can collect an abundance of materials for use during the winter months. This involves growing and collecting materials suitable for drying and preservation practices.

Drying and preservation of plant material is nothing new. It has been practiced for centuries, as indicated by discoveries in Egyptian tombs. As one follows the history of gardening and flower arranging, references to the use of dried material for medicine, flavoring, and essence will be observed. It is interesting to note the use of sweet-smelling herbs to freshen the air and the use of dried plant material, flower petals, and herbs worn around the neck to ward off evil spirits.

Some of the early books on gardening refer to the use of dried plant material for use in home decoration. The methods described in this early literature include the hanging, pressing, and sand methods similar to those in use today. However, modern-day techniques have improved upon the earlier systems, giving us a better quality product for our arrangements.

For those seriously interested in drying and pressing plant material for use in arrangements, planning should begin with the arrival of the seed catalogs. Some companies have a special section devoted to those plants suitable for drying purposes. These involve such plants as strawflowers, statice, pearly everlasting, and globe amaranth. Although these are excellent for drying and failures are uncommon, the choice should not be limited to this list. Most flowers can be dried or preserved successfully if one is willing to do some experimentation employing various methods of preservation. Many failures will be encountered along the way; but with persistance and determination, a successful way will be found to dry most flowers. Select seeds of a few different species of plants each year; keep records of the methods used, the time necessary for drying, and other factors involved. Within a relatively short period of time a long list of plant material with a successful method of preserving each will be recorded.

Annuals which are grown from seed each year, shrubs, perennials, and bulbs are good sources of plant material for drying purposes. In addition to the cultivated plants, wild flowers should not be overlooked. When collecting these, be sure to follow good conservation practices; do not harvest those on restricted lists, receive permission from the property owner, and beware of poisonous plants. Collecting wild plant material need not be restricted only to the spring and summer months; berries and seed pods can be collected continuously. In fact, some seed pods can be more readily observed when the ground is covered with snow.

In recent years another source of dried plant material has been imported from distant lands. Much of this material has been prepared prior to being shipped and most is ready for the designer to use. It is excellent for the commercial designer or florist, but for the amateur is not only expensive but leaves a gap in the satisfaction of preparing one's own material.

Flowers in various stages of maturity should be harvested for drying purposes. Buds and partially and fully opened flowers can be used. Even parts of flowers are desirable and make welcome additions to dried arrangements. Do not overlook the possibilities of withered flowers. Daisy centers with petals removed will fit well in many arrangements. When carnations wilt, pull the petals from the calyx. Each section can be split back a short way and when dried will give the appearance of a flower. Many other flowers or parts of flowers can be used in similar fashion.

When harvesting flowers, it should be remembered that the drying process will never improve their quality. Therefore, only those of the highest quality should be collected. Those with blemishes, poor color, insect damage, etc., should be discarded unless a specific arrangement or design calls for this type of material.

Most flowers should be gathered at the peak of their maturity. Strawflowers and a few similar everlastings are exceptions since they will continue to open during the drying process. These exceptions are usually harvested when two or three rows of petals have opened and the center is still tight. With others such as honesty (*Lunaria annua*), the seed pod is the desirable part and the plant must not be picked until the seeds have ripened. However, they must be harvested before the cool, wet autumn days to prevent discoloration of the tissue.

The garden planted for a source of drying material should not be planned for its beauty in the overall landscape plan of the home. Instead, it should be in an isolated area where one will not hesitate to cut flowers as they mature. Since the bulk of the flowers will be cut as soon as they open, this type of garden will not produce an abundance of color.

Flowers should be picked on a dry sunny day, preferably in early or late afternoon after the morning dew has dried but before condensation forms in the evening. They should never be picked immediately following a rain. It is best to wait at least one day after a storm to allow them to dry. If overhead irrigation is used, water the garden after the flowers have been picked and wait a day before harvesting again.

Only a few flowers should be picked at one time, the limiting factor being the number that can be processed immediately. If they are to be dried by hanging upside down, a greater number can be handled at one time than if some of the other techniques are used. If it is necessary to harvest more flowers than can be treated immediately, such as before an approaching storm or predicted frost, place them in water as soon as possible to prevent wilting. This will help to keep them for a few days, but they should not be allowed to go past their peak of maturity before drying.

The main objective in drying plant material is to remove the moisture from it as rapidly as possible without damaging the plant and retaining as much of its color as possible. To achieve this, several methods of drying can be employed, each having advantages and disadvantages for specific plants. Several of these methods are described in detail later.

After harvesting, all foliage should be stripped from the stems of most flowers. This is easily accomplished by pulling the stem through the thumb and fingers from the flower head toward the base of the stem or by sliding the thumb and fingers down the stem from the flower head. Watch out for thorns or bristles on some stems. It might be desirable to bend some stems, especially those of spiky flowers (blue salvia, veronica) or foliage (scotch broom, eucalyptis) to desired curves before drying. (See Chapter 4 for bending techniques.) Flowers that are to be buried in sand, silica gel, or borax and strawflowers that are to be air-dried should be wired at this time. No wires are necessary for most of those dried by hanging upside down or pressing or for foliage prepared by the glycerin process.

Wiring is desirable for several reasons. It allows for flexibility of stems of dried flowers when arranging them; it reduces the amount of material (sand, silica gel, etc.) necessary for drying purposes; since stems and flower heads dry at a different rate, it allows for more uniformity in the drying process; and because of the brittleness and breakage of stems, less material needs to be prepared to allow for shrinkage.

The wire gauge used depends upon the size or weight of the flower. A supply of gauge 18, 22, 26, and 30 wire will serve well. The 18 is used on the heavy material, 30 on that of a delicate nature, and 22 and 26 on those materials of intermediate weights.

There are several methods of wiring flowers. The method used is dependent upon the flower being prepared. The first step is to remove the stem, leaving about an inch attached to the calyx. Insert a wire through the stem into the calyx. Care should be taken to be sure the wire does not protrude through the flower and be exposed. As the stem dries, this wire will become firmly anchored, and it will be difficult to remove it without damaging the flower. Strawflowers are prepared this way before hanging upside down. Others such as roses and daisies are wired in similar fashion before placing in the drying medium. Figure 8-1 illustrates wiring methods used before drying.

A modification of the above method is useful for many disc-type flowers, but extreme care must be taken to avoid ex-

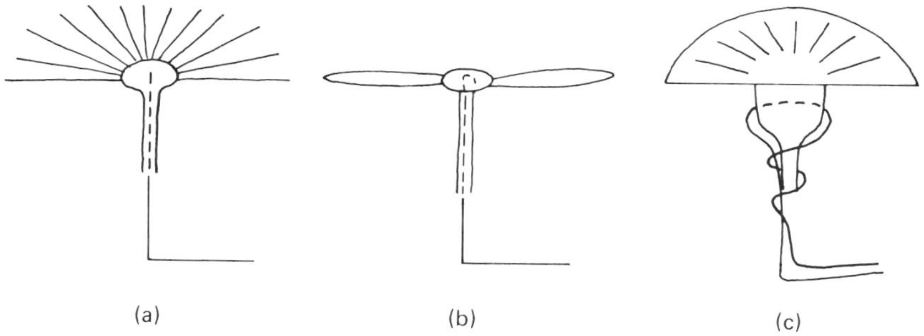

FIGURE 8-1 Methods of wiring before drying. Left to right: (a) Wire pushed through stem into the base of flower (example, strawflower). (b) Hook method for chrysanthemums and daisies. (c) Wire pushed through large calyx.

cessive damage. This involves pushing the wire through the stem and completely through the flower head. A small hook is made at the top of the wire, and it is retracted so the hook is imbedded in the flower head without being exposed. (See Chapter 14, "Methods of Wiring.") This method is useful with hollow-stemmed flowers such as zinnias, marigolds, and some varieties of chrysanthemums. Damage is most likely to occur when the wire is pushed through the flower head or if the wire is twisted causing the hook to move after being retracted into the flower. Both of these cause a shattering of the floral disc.

Carnations and similar flowers with a large prominent calyx can be wired by pushing a wire through the calyx at right angles to the stem. Both ends of the wire are then bent down parallel to the stem and twisted a couple of times around it. This is a good method to use when stems are hard and it is difficult to insert wires into them.

The most common technique in drying flowers is hanging them upside down, as shown in Figure 8-2. This practice, while not the best for most flowers, has been used for centuries and does work well with many kinds of plant material.

The first requirement for this procedure is a suitable location to hang the material. A dry attic with good warm air circulation and not too much light will serve well. Most basements are too damp, and much of the material will mold under such conditions. Closets lacking good air circulation will produce the same results. A room with too much light, especially direct sunlight, will cause excessive fading during the drying process.

String, wire, or wooden strips can be assembled parallel to each other leaving ample room between them for air circulation when material is hung. The material used will depend upon the

FIGURE 8-2 Hanging upside down is a common method of drying plant material. Those flowers to be used in arrangements should have the foliage removed before drying. For those to be used as herbs, the foliage is left on as it might be the primary material wanted.

permanence of the installation. Each strip should be of sufficient strength to hold the weight of the plant material.

Flowers should be harvested and foliage stripped as described earlier. Smaller flowers are tied in small bunches using string, twistems, or rubber bands. It is necessary that the stems be tied tightly because the shrinkage which occurs during the drying process will allow loosely tied bunches to fall apart. Stems should be of varying lengths so flowers are not touching each other; the greater the spacing between them, the faster the drying process will take place.

Large flowers should be prepared and tied individually for drying. Celosia with its thick stem and bulky flower head will mold if several are tied together.

Strawflowers should be wired before drying. After wiring they can be tied into small bunches of about a dozen flowers. It should be remembered that these flowers will continue to open during the drying period, and ample room should be allowed for this expansion. Figure 8-3 shows strawflowers drying.

The bunches of flowers or the individual flowers should be tied to the stringers, leaving enough room between them so they do not touch each other. It is a good idea to place them in groups. Those that dry quickly can be placed in one area, and those that take longer can be grouped together in another area. Experience will be the best guide in establishing groupings.

FIGURE 8-3 Left: Strawflowers harvested before fully opened, wired, and hung upside down to dry Right: The same flowers a few days later have opened during the drying process.

Most flowers will be dried and ready for use or storage in two to three weeks. Some of the fine and delicate materials may be ready within a week, and it may take as long as five to six weeks for some of the heavy, compact materials.

After flowers have dried, they can be used immediately, can be packed in containers and stored, or can be left hanging until needed. If left hanging there is always the possibility that they may be damaged by mold during periods of high humidity; they may fade because of light exposure; or they may be damaged by insects or even mice.

Drying flowers by burying them in some water-absorbing material is a method employed by many individuals. Dried sand, borax, corn meal, and silica gel are among the materials used for this purpose. All employ the same principles, and procedures vary only slightly. The lengths of time necessary for drying vary considerably among the materials, and final results will differ among them also.

Silica gel has been used by industry for years because of its moisture-absorbing qualities. A small packet placed in a package will absorb moisture within the package, thus preventing rusting or other deterioration of the product through moisture. Because of this feature, silica gel was tried for drying flowers and met with immediate success. It is now available with a special blue crystal that turns pink when moisture is absorbed by it and is sold by florist shops, garden centers, and other flower supply outlets under various trade names.

Because silica gel will absorb large amounts of moisture from the air, it is necessary that moisture-tight containers be used when drying flowers in it; plastic containers work well. For small flowers, half-gallon ice cream containers are satisfactory, and plastic containers found in department stores are also excellent. For larger flowers such as lilies that are to be dried individually, coffee or juice cans are useful. The size and depth of the container will depend upon the size and shape of the flower and the number of flowers to be processed at one time. Spikey flowers will require a long, narrow container with some cross partitions to support the weight and reduce the possibility of crushing. If cardboard boxes are used, it is a good idea to line them with polyethylene.

The bottom of the container should be covered with a layer of silica gel to a depth of two inches or more depending upon the flower being dried. Flower stems are removed, leaving only about an inch of stem attached to the flower, and the heads are wired as described earlier. After wiring, the wires are bent 90 degrees to the stem and the wired stem is inserted into the bed of silica gel with the flower head facing upward, as demonstrated in Figure 8-4. The silica gel is then worked under and between the petals, being careful that all parts are in contact with it. An artist's small brush will prove helpful during this operation to ensure that the petals are not bent or distorted in any way. Each flower placed in the container is handled as a separate unit and does not come in contact with other flowers. When the container is full of flowers, about an inch of the silica gel is carefully poured over the entire surface (see Figure 8-5). The cover is put in place and is often times sealed with cellophane tape. The container should be labeled with the types of flowers and the date they were buried. Because of differences in lengths of time required for drying, it is best to use only one kind of flower in each container.

Daffodils, lilies, and other trumpet-shaped flowers are placed in silica gel with the trumpet facing upward as shown in Figure 8-6. The silica gel is gradually built up inside and outside of the trumpet at the same time to hold the flower's shape and to prevent distortion. As seen in Figure 8-7, spikey flowers such as snapdragons are placed horizontally on cross partitions in a long, narrow container. Silica gel is worked around all parts of the flower with care being taken not to crush the underside. As

FIGURE 8-4 After wiring, the wired stems are pushed into silica gel and the lower petals of the flower lie flat on it. Chrysanthemums and black-eyed Susans are similar in texture and dry at the same rate.

FIGURE 8-5 When all flowers are in place, they are covered uniformly.

FIGURE 8-6 The insides of trumpet-type flowers such as petunia or lily are filled at the same rate as the outside to retain their shapes.

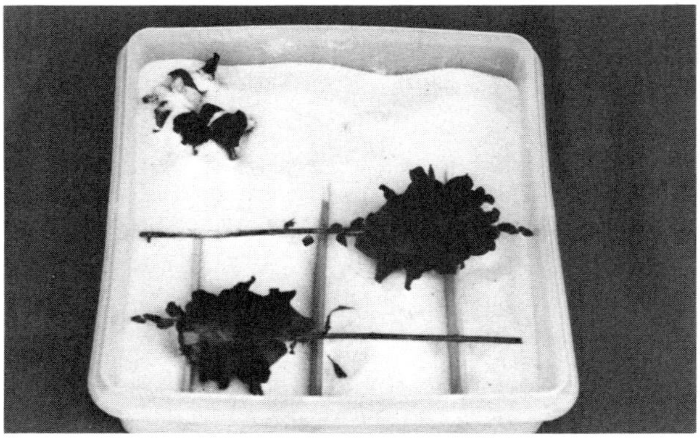

FIGURE 8-7 Spikey-type flowers such as snapdragons are laid horizontally on cross pieces and uniformly covered.

FIGURE 8-8 To remove flowers, place fingers carefully under them and remove slowly.

soon as the flowers are covered, the procedures described in the preceding paragraph should be followed.

Drying time for flowers in silica gel will vary from two or three days to two weeks or more, depending upon the bulkiness or size of the flower. Light, delicate-textured material should be removed in about three days; zinnias and stocks will take five to seven days; and lilies and orchids require seven to ten days. Experience will be the best guide in determining the length of time to leave flowers in the medium.

Removal of flowers from the silica gel requires care and patience. When the flowers are dry, they are brittle and will break easily. By tilting the container to one side, the excess covering on the top can be poured off into another container or tray. When the flowers are exposed, check for dryness. The calyx takes the longest time to dry and if it is found to be moist, cover the flowers for another two or three days. If they are dry, they can be removed by gently working the fingers under them and lifting them from the medium. Figure 8–8 shows flowers being removed from the gel. Excess silica gel is removed by holding the flower upside down, rotating, and tapping it gently. If some gel tends to stick, it can be removed with an artist's small camel-hair brush.

Damaged flowers should be repaired or disgarded before storage. A broken petal can be put in place with a drop of glue. Sometimes it might be necessary to add a little glue at the base of each petal for reinforcement. As soon as the glue is dry, the flowers are ready for storage.

Borax is also used for drying, following the same procedure as that for silica gel. Flowers dry more quickly in it, and damaged flowers are common. Some of the finer-textured material should be removed within a day. Most others will be ready at the end of two days. If allowed to remain in the borax too long, brown spots will appear on the petals and the flowers will be useless. Borax is sometimes difficult to remove from petals, especially petals with a velvety texture. The use of a camel-hair brush will help to clean the petals of excess material. If any borax is left on them, it will absorb water from the atmosphere and damage the flowers.

The use of sand is one of the oldest methods of drying flowers. Fine beach sand, free of organic material and salt, is best, although some other grades of sand work well. Sand obtained from saltwater beaches should be washed several times before using to leach out all the salt which causes burning of plant material. Place the sand on trays in a warm oven to thoroughly dry it before burying flowers in it.

The procedure explained for silica gel can be followed, although it is not necessary to place a cover over the box. Drying time, however, is considerably longer than it is with either silica gel or borax. Most flowers require two weeks, and some may take as long as three to four weeks.

It is possible to dry some flowers in sand without removal of the stems. This requires placing the flowers face down, working the sand between the petals, and then covering with two or three inches of sand, leaving the stems exposed vertically. It is difficult to bury flowers this way without flattening or damaging them.

Sand, borax, and silica gel can be reused several times, provided that it is thoroughly dried each time. The indicator crystals in silica gel are blue when dry and pink when moisture is

FIGURE 8-9 A homemade botanical press. Note the layers of blotters and corrugated cardboard.

present. If the crystals indicate that the material is moist, place it in an oven at about 250 degrees F until they turn blue. Sand and borax can also be dried in the oven at the same temperature. The length of time for drying in the oven will depend upon the amount of material being dried and the amount of moisture in it.

Preserving plant materials by pressing has resulted in many dismal failures. How many times has that first corsage or rose been placed between the pages of a book with great expectations of keeping it, only to become a moldy, discolored mass at the end of two weeks?

It is possible to preserve some plant material by pressing. Ferns and leaves dry well by this method. However, some do change color during the drying period. The use of a large telephone book, with plant material placed flat between every seven or eight pages, will prove satisfactory for ferns, leaves, and thin, delicate flowers. For other materials, a botanical press like the one shown in Figure 8-9 works well. These presses can be purchased at botanical supply houses or can be easily constructed. Newspaper, blotting paper, corrugated cardboard, wooden side panels, and straps are used. The plant material is placed in a folded sheet of newspaper, a blotter is placed on either side, followed by the corrugated cardboard. Several of these units are placed together with the wooden rack on either side and tied together tightly with straps. If placed on a radiator, air flowing through the corrugated cardboard removes the moisture quickly, material will be well dried in a few days, and most will retain much of its color. Flowers dried by pressing are not suitable for typical flower arrangements but are satisfactory for trays, plaques, lampshades, collages, etc. Foliage can be used in these as well as in dried floral arrangements.

Some flowers and many foliages respond well to the glycerin method of preservation. Statice retains its shape, remains quite flexible, and holds good color when treated with glycerin. Berries treated with this material hold their shape rather than becoming shriveled, stay on the branches well, and retain their color. However, the glycerin method does take longer and is more expensive than the hanging method.

Many leaves will change color when treated with glycerin. Beech will remain green if harvested in the spring but will turn yellow later in the season. Barberry will turn red in the spring and brown if gathered in the fall. Elaeagnus leaves will retain their green color if left in the glycerin solution only a couple of weeks, but will turn a bright yellow if allowed to remain longer. Only experience and research will assure what can be expected from the glycerin treatment.

Foliage to be treated by this method should be clean and in good condition. Wiping with a moist cloth will remove dust and other foreign material. The ends of the stems should be split or crushed to allow more rapid absorption and placed into a solution of one part glycerin and two parts water. They should remain in the solution about two weeks or until maximum absorption has taken place. The leaves that do not change color will have an oily texture, and sometimes droplets of the glycerin will be exuded from the tips. This excess material should be wiped from the surface before storage.

Some leaves such as galyx, and lily of the valley absorb moisture through their surface more readily than from the cut ends. These should be immersed into a one-to-one glycerin–water solution for five to seven days or until they feel soft and pliable. Upon removal they should be wiped dry before storage. Foliage treated with glycerin will remain soft and pliable for years if stored in a dark, dry place.

Most floral arrangers involved in drying and preserving plant material do not use all the dried material immediately but do plan to use it in the months to come. There is little value in spending a great amount of time in this processing activity unless the material is stored properly for future use.

Some materials can be stored by hanging upside down in a warm, dry, dark location. This is the most unsatisfactory method of storage since it allows for the possibility of insect and rodent damage, for fluctuations in humidity, and, in some situations, for light penetration. Insect eggs that have been deposited prior to harvest might hatch, the resulting larvae destroying the dried material. Mice can destroy a tremendous amount of dried flowers in a single night by ripping them apart to gather seeds. The bulk of the stored material may be destroyed before the presence of a mouse is detected. Periods of high humidity will cause molding of dried flowers, especially if there is little air circulation; several days of damp weather in late fall or early spring almost always causes damage; even small amounts of light will cause colors to fade. Although not as serious as the other problems, fading does detract from the flowers.

Best results are obtained by storing dried materials in sealed plastic or metal containers. Cardboard containers under some conditions will absorb moisture, resulting in molding and the destruction of the flowers in them.

The first step in storing plant material is to be sure the container is absolutely dry. The bottom can be lined with shredded wax paper similar to that used by the florist for packing orchids and corsages. This will form a soft base, and there will be less tendency for the brittle flowers to break. Flowers should be well spaced, and none should overlap. It is best if only a single layer is placed in each container; but often times because of numbers of flowers and amount of space involved, this is impossible. If a second layer is necessary, it is a good idea to separate the layers with a thin sheet of waxed tissue. If space permits, only one kind of flower should be placed in each container. It might even be desirable to store a few outstanding blooms separately.

Some of the more fragile flowers can be stuck into blocks of dry floral foam, then the entire block placed into the plastic container. This foam must be absolutely dry before use; otherwise, disasterous results will occur.

It is always a good idea to place a small cloth bag of silica gel into each container as a precaution against moisture when storing dried plant material. Some experts also recommend placing moth balls or crystals in the container as a protection against mice and insects.

All containers should be labeled with the kinds of flowers in them and the date of storage. They should be stored in a

FIGURE 8-10 An interesting symmetrical arrangement consisting of several kinds of dried material.

cool, dry, dark place. Attics or cupboards are best; storage in most basements is unsatisfactory. Easy access without having to remove or disturb all the boxes will result in less overall damage to the stored flowers.

There are many uses for dried plant materials. First and foremost is the typical flower arrangement normally created with fresh flowers, an example of which is shown in Figure 8-10. Other uses for dried material are wall plaques, framed pictures, trays, pressed flower pictures, lampshades, tabletop designs, Christmas decorations, and many other creations.

The same principles that are used in designs created with fresh flowers apply to those using dried materials. Although more difficult to construct because of the fragile nature of the material, once made, the arrangement of dried material is not subject to a constant change as is the one using fresh flowers. Buds do not open, flowers do not wither, and foliage does not wilt. Instead, the arrangement remains as constructed; and one has ample time to correct mistakes, make improvements, and rearrange material where necessary.

Dried arrangements need not be dull and drab in appearance. Refer back to Figure 3-2 and to the color plate. The methods previously described for drying flowers will help flowers to retain their colors, and it will be difficult to distinguish dried from fresh arrangements from only a few feet away. Of course, the arrangements will tend to accumulate dust and become dull after being exposed for some time, but this can be corrected by carefully brushing each piece of material. Some arrangers recommend placing the arrangement in a bathroom filled with steam for a couple of hours to help freshen the material, but this can do more harm than good. Some flowers will absorb moisture and be destroyed. Sunlight also has a deleterious effect upon dried arrangements; flowers will lose their effectiveness within a short time when exposed to it.

Containers used for dried arrangements need not be dull or be of dark colors but should compliment the plant material placed in them. If the arrangement is made primarily of seedpods having a general brown or grey effect, the container should be in the same general texture and tone. If bright, colorful flowers are used, a container complimenting these flowers should be used.

Flower holders vary considerably for dried materials. Chicken wire, pinpoint holders, floral foam, and styrofoam all serve well, but difficulties are encountered with some materials. Care must be taken that the floral foam is dry before using. In this condition it will tend to crumble when heavy stems are inserted. Delicate stems will shatter when pushed into styrofoam.

Products similar to those used for fresh flowers have been introduced especially for holding stems in dried arrangements. One is a dry material which does not crumble as readily as those materials used for fresh flowers. It remains in this dry condition, and flowers can be rearranged at any time. Another type is moist when used and hardens into a solid brick when dry; this holds flowers firmly in place, and it is difficult to remove the flowers without damage once the brick hardens. This, however, is an advantage for arrangements that are to be stored or moved around several times.

One of the major differences between construction of dried and fresh arrangements is that many of the flowers used in dried arrangements are on artificial stems. Most materials prepared by hanging upside down are on their own stems, but most other material has been wired prior to drying. These wired stems must be rewired or restemmed prior to arranging.

There are several ways of adding artificial stems to dried flowers. The first step is to add floral tape to the wire protruding from the flower as described in Chapter 14. After these short stems have been taped, a separate wire of sufficient strength to hold the flower is covered with tape and the two joined together with tape. Another method is to tape the short wired stem directly to another piece of dried stem. The former method is preferred because it allows for more flexibility of the stem and ease in securing desired curves in the arrangement.

With all material ready, the actual construction of the arrangement can begin. Construction details described in Chapter 4 should be followed.

Some dried floral material is suitable for wall plaques, framed pictures, wall hangings, and other designs. Figures 8-11 through 8-14 show some interesting uses for dried material. Pressed material is useful for floral pictures, trays, lampshades,

FIGURE 8-11 An interesting wall plaque made on a piece of plywood. Seedpods of various kinds, sweet fern foliage, and a cut pine cone have been used in a contemporary manner.

FIGURE 8-12 Dried flowers and foliage in a picture frame.

FIGURE 8-13 Pressed flowers and foliage along with a butterfly have been incorporated into an interesting arrangement in a lampshade.

FIGURE 8-14 Wall hanging of dried plant material attached to a strip of burlap.

and tabletop designs. For most of these designs, the plant material is held in place with white glue which is not visible in the finished product.

Since the material is glued in place and is impossible to move without destroying it or damaging the background material, it is always a good idea to either sketch the design before putting the flowers in place or to make the design with the plant material on a separate background before gluing. If the later method is followed, remove each piece separately and glue it in place on the permanent background.

9

Flower Shows

After studying the art of flower arranging, and making arrangements for the home, church, and festive occasions, the next logical step is arrangements for competition. To be successful in this new endeavor, the designer must be aware of many rules, regulations, and practices that were not necessarily followed in previous arrangements. Careful attention must be given to details and, above all, the flower show schedule must be closely followed.

Small local flower shows are always a good place to start. These can be followed by the larger ones, and eventually those by invitation only. One of the leaders in the flower show movement is the National Council of State Garden Clubs. This organization has been responsible for incorporating classes into the shows today rather than having shows like those of only a few years ago that consisted primarily of horticulture classes.

There are several types of flower shows staged in various parts of the world. There are those large shows usually in late winter or early spring staged in city coliseums. These involve forcing many plants and shrubs into bloom to be used in landscape plantings. Construction of many of the gardens is done by professional landscape architects or gardeners, although some sections are reserved for amateurs. The emphasis in most of these shows is toward elaborate gardens, and floral design occupies only a small section. The designs are usually made by those with considerable experience and many times are by invitation only.

Open shows conducted by various civic organizations are always good places for the novice to begin showing. Small local fairs, agricultural exhibits, church socials, and grange activities may have some flower arrangement classes open to anyone who wishes to enter. See Figure 9-1.

The most common type of flower show is that staged by the local garden club. In many of these shows, competiton is keen, and the beginner who is eligible will do best by showing in the novice classes for the first two or three times. These are classes open only to those who have never entered a flower show or who have never won a blue ribbon. The next step is to enter the major classes which are open to everyone.

Many times shows sponsored by garden clubs are limited to arrangements made only by its members. Others have some open classes available to members as well as nonmembers, and some have invitational classes where other garden clubs can

FIGURE 9-1 Flower arrangement classes at local fairs and amateur shows are always good places for the novice designer to begin.

FIGURE 9-2 Flower show in a public building. All classes may be set up in one large room or several rooms may be involved. At this show, horticulture classes are set up on tables in the center and arrangement classes along the walls.

each enter one arrangement in competition with those of other clubs. To avoid disappointment, if there is any question regarding who may enter an arrangement, be sure to contact the show secretary for guidance.

Flower shows are staged in various ways. The most common is where all exhibits are in a hall, classes are set up, and after judging, the show is open to the public. Figure 9-2 shows a flower show given in a public hall. Another type of show is where several homes are opened; arrangements are placed in these houses, and guests move from house to house. Figure 9-3 illustrates this type of show. A similar type of show is the

FIGURE 9-3 Homes are often opened for flower shows. Arrangements are made to fit specific locations. Here, the effective use of foliage helps to unite all parts of the composition.

house-and-garden show where private gardens as well as homes are open to those attending.

Many garden clubs have practice shows for its members. Classes are set up; the arrangements judged and placed while the members hold their business meeting. Upon adjournment, the judges discuss each arrangement and its placing with the group. This is a good learning experience, and every beginner should participate if the opportunity becomes available.

Shows sponsored by garden clubs, which are affiliated with the National Council of State Garden Clubs, follow the regulations set forth by the National Council for a standard flower show. These regulations call for two major divisions in the show—artistic and horticulture. There should be a balance between these to help ensure interest for all members as well as visitors. Junior sections in each of these divisions is desirable. Other divisions that should be considered are educational and commercial.

When considering these divisions, one should not lose sight of the main objectives of a flower show. These are (1) to stimulate an interest in horticulture, (2) to educate the public, and (3) to develop an aesthetic sense.[1]

Each flower show should be developed around a theme. Although it might be difficult to have all horticulture classes evolve around this theme, the artistic classes should follow it closely. The theme might be a particular season, a historic location or situation, or perhaps following styles of great artists. The possibilities are unlimited; and with a little thought and effort, excellent ideas can be put together to form the basis for a good show. Figure 9-4 shows an "idea" well carried out.

The show schedule is one of the most important considerations in any flower show. It should contain all the information regarding the show that any exhibitor might need. Each class should be clearly stated, all rules and regulations should be included, and all information regarding the show including a listing of the show committee should be available.

The first step when considering entering a flower show is to obtain a show schedule. It should be read over carefully to determine what classes are available and which ones the individual would like to enter. If the main interest is in the artistic classes, there are a few questions that one must ask himself; he must have affirmative answers for each question.

---

[1] *Handbook for Flower Shows,* National Council of State Garden Clubs, Inc., 1971.

FIGURE 9–4 The idea for a show arrangement can come from many sources. This class called for strength and flexibility. The rigidity of the cattails and the curvature of the fasciated willow in a wrought iron container conform well with the schedule.

The first and most important question is, "Do I interpret the class correctly?" If there is any doubt, no matter how insignificant one feels it might be, the flower show chairperson or the one responsible for the specific class should be contacted to get the exact interpretation. Do not guess. Most chairpersons encourage contestants to contact them to straighten out details.

After determining the correct interpretation of the class, other questions arise, such as "Do I have a suitable container?" "Can I secure plant material appropriate for the class?" "Do I have background material that will harmonize?" "Are bases or accessories required; and if they are, can I procure those that will be suitable?" "What is the correct size?" If there is any doubt in mind regarding any of these questions, it might be better to enter another class.

When selecting a container, be sure it ties in well with the theme of the class as well as with the plant material and background. The class might call for a specific container such as a teapot, a silver bowl, or a container of oriental design. Do not be misled and have the container predominate in these classes. Even though it is listed and is a requirement of the class, it should be subordinate to the arrangement of plant material.

Be sure the plant material that is needed will be available the day before the show. Nothing can be more frustrating than getting ready to make a show arrangement, only to find that one of the flowers needed is not available. If you plan to purchase flowers from a florist, place the order well in advance. By knowing the specific problem or requirement, the florist can usually get what is needed from one of his sources of supply, but lead time is necessary.

Some of the best plans go astray when planning to use garden flowers. Some may bloom a few days early or be only in bud stage at show time. Weather is always an important factor when considering flowers from the garden; heavy rains and winds can do considerable damage if they come just a few days before the flowers are needed. When making initial plans, it is a good idea to think of substitutes in the event that your first choice is not available. This will eliminate a lot of last-minute changes in plans.

In many flower shows, backgrounds are provided, and the use of fabrics, paintings, mirrors, and similar items are not allowed. If they are used, the arrangement may be disqualified. Be sure to consult the show schedule regarding use of these items.

If the background is provided by the show committee, be sure the arrangement is in harmony with it. Many times a perfectly good arrangement does not receive an award because the background detracted from it.

Space allocation is of prime importance. Where space is limited, the amount for each arrangement will be stated in the schedule, and the arrangement should be in proportion with it. If a niche or shadow box is used, there should be some space between the top of the arrangement and that of the background. Some space should also be left between the outer edges of the arrangement and the extremities of the background. Spacing is shown in Figure 9-5. Too often arrangements are found jammed into a niche with stems in contact with all sides of it.

Do not rely on guessing to determine how great the allocated space really is. Unless working with measurements every day, judgments on distance can be extremely poor. For best results and to avoid many disappointments, make a background having the measurements stated in the show schedule. Place this behind the arrangement as it is being made to ensure that the arrangement stays within its boundaries.

FIGURE 9-5 An arrangement of dried materials in good proportion to the allocated space. The arrangement is not jammed into a small space nor does it appear too small for it.

Obtaining and adding the right accessories to go with the arrangement of flowers can be the most difficult part of any flower show entry. If they do not fit the theme of the arrangement or contribute to the overall effect, they should not be used; however, some classes call for them. If this situation exists, much thought must be given to their selection. See Chapter 5.

To help to avoid disappointment, a pre-show rehearsal is always a good idea. This can be done anytime before the show, but ample time should be given to finding the materials that this practice session shows are lacking. It is recommended that this session take place as soon as possible after the class is chosen. Perhaps this rehearsal will indicate that the vase selected is out of proportion with the allocated space. Maybe its color does not harmonize with the flowers. Perhaps the flowers do not really fit the theme of the show after being arranged. By being alerted to these discrepancies several days in advance, changes can be made which will help to eliminate some glaring errors.

During the practice session, make a listing of all the materials needed which will be useful in the final arrangement. If the arrangement is to be made at the site of the show, be sure to include all working materials—scissors, knife, wire, etc.—on the checklist. It is quite discomforting to arrive at the show only to find that one or two important items have been left at home.

As the show time approaches, be sure that everything is ready the day before the show. Flowers should be picked up from the florist or gathered from the garden and properly hardened. Even those from the florist that have been handled properly by him, will hold up better with a little extra care.

Some designers prefer to make their arrangements the day before a show. This is normally a poor practice, especially when spikey flowers are used. Since the tips of these flowers curve upward within a relatively short time, an arrangement made several hours prior to show time will have a different appearance when seen by the judges. Figure 9-6 shows what can happen.

Make arrangements as late as possible, but allow enough time so that they can be in place in ample time for judging. Last minute rushing is not conducive to good workmanship. If the arrangement is in place an hour before the deadline, there will be time to make last minute adjustments.

Most arrangements can be made at home and transported to the show. This will help to avoid confusion at the show site and help to eliminate the possibilities of forgetting materials. Extra plant material should be taken along to the show for replacements made necessary because of movement or breakage during transportation.

Once at the show, put the arrangement in place, adjust the background and plant material if necessary, and then leave it alone until after all judging has taken place. Continued manipulation usually does more harm than good.

After the judges have completed their task, their decisions and comments should be accepted graciously. If taken as constructive criticism rather than as personal admonishment, arrangements should improve with each show.

In most horticulture classes, the flower show sponsors supply everything necessary to display the plant material. Bottles to hold specimen flowers and backgrounds to show them effectively are usually the responsibility of the show committee.

FIGURE 9-6 The tips of spikey flowers will bend upward within a few hours, changing the overall appearance of the arrangement.

Baskets for multiple-stem displays and saucers for pot plants are the responsibility of the exhibitor. However, for possible exceptions to the above, read the show schedule carefully.

Horticulture specimens are judged for perfection. When selecting material for the show this should be the prime consideration. Too often the exhibitor selects the largest or most colorful flower only to find it downgraded because it might be past maturity, have malformed or insect-damaged petals, or have other imperfections.

The exhibitor should know what constitutes a perfect flower and should strive to come as close to this requirement as possible. Each of the numerous plant societies has set qualifications for their specific interests; and if the exhibitor has any questions regarding these requirements, the standards for that particular society should be studied. These are available from the society or may be found in the *Handbook for Flower Shows.* (See footnote, page 158.)

FIGURE 9-7 The schedule should be closely followed. This class called for three stems. All were disqualified.

The flower show schedule sets specific requirements for each of the horticulture classes, and these should be followed closely to avoid disqualification. If the schedule calls for three blooms, only three should be entered. Two or four will be disqualified. See Figure 9-7. If three stems are called for in the schedule, this could mean three flowers on individual stems, or many flowers on only three stems depending upon the plant material being displayed. In the above classes, uniformity of plant material is important. Try to select specimens as nearly alike as possible. It is much better to display three flowers of equal size than to have two large and one small one in the grouping.

When displaying individual blooms, there are many things the exhibitor should observe when selecting them. Among these are maturity of the flower, color, number of florets, size and placement of florets, form, stem attachment, stem foliage, and overall condition. Figure 9-8 shows uniform specimens.

A popular horticulture class in flower shows is house plants shown either as individual specimens or as collections. Many schedules have classes for flowering plants and others for nonflowering ones. This may cause some confusion, and a call to the show chairman might be in order. Most nonflowering classes are for those plants that are normally grown for their foliage effect. However, many of these do sometimes bloom, and without clarification of the class they might be disqualified.

House plants that are exhibited should be in top condition. Proper grooming of the plant is necessary. This includes removal of all dead or dying flowers and foliage, as well as malformed or damaged plant parts. All foliage should be cleaned. Pots should be washed and be in good proportion to the size of the plant. When collections are exhibited, unformity is desirable. A display of African Violets would be much more attractive if all were of about equal size and in the same type pot rather than if they ranged in size from newly transplanted ones to large flowering plants in both clay and plastic pots.

Junior classes in both artistic and horticulture divisions should be encouraged. Many of these young people exhibit a considerable amount of talent for artistic arrangements, and special classes should be available for them. These classes should be quite easy to interpret and not involve the details found in other classes.

The horticulture classes for juniors can involve such things as terrariums, dish gardens, growing seedlings, or plants. Young people should be encouraged to grow and care for small gardens and exhibit the plant materials they have grown themselves.

FIGURE 9-8 Horticulture specimens displayed in containers as uniformly as possible. Judging is against a perfect specimen rather than against each other.

Judging junior exhibits should be done with as much care but not as much criticism as in other classes. The judging should be done to *encourage* these young folks because they will be the nucleus of the shows of the future.

Since one of the purposes of flower shows is to educate people and make them more aware of horticulture, exhibits specifically designed for this purpose should play an important role in shows. These exhibits should be well planned and designed and should lend support to the overall theme of the show. Those that do not coincide with the theme might be compared with an arrangement or a horticulture specimen placed in the wrong class. If they are not related to the rest of the show, it is better to leave them out.

The number of educational exhibits in any show should be limited; too many can cause confusion and burden the learning process.

When preparing an educational exhibit, the objectives should be well thought out and limited to only one or two. More can result in only superficial learning, which is readily forgotten. An educational display on the preservation of flowers and their use is too great an area to cover. By breaking down the subject and describing only one or two ways of preserving flowers will be much more effective.

With the objectives clearly in mind, displays which are clear and concise should be arranged. Avoid too many and too lengthy signs but have enough descriptive material to leave no doubts in the minds of the viewers. Arrange the material to conform with the flow of traffic and try to avoid "bottlenecks."

Handouts explaining the demonstration in more detail are effective ways to complete the exhibit. These serve as good methods to review what was seen at the show and help to complete the learning process for viewers, novices, and entrants.

Commercial exhibits can be a way of helping to support the show financially. A few well-planned and related exhibits of this type can be an asset and will help to support other divisions. See Figure 9-9 for a commercial exhibit. However, there is a tendency, especially in many of the larger shows, to have all types of unrelated commercial products exhibited; this takes away from or inhibits the effectiveness of the purpose of the show.

Some understanding of judging can be a tremendous help to any exhibitor. This does not mean that every exhibitor should be a judge, but some knowledge of how judges

FIGURE 9-9 Commercial exhibits should be related to parts of the show. Seeds, plants, containers, and accessories of various kinds have a close relationship to the display sections.

proceed and what they look for can help to improve the quality of arrangements.

It is not the job of the judge to determine that exhibits are in the correct location. They are judged in place, and should any not comply with the class, they are disqualified. Oftentimes a judge is severely criticized because a perfectly good arrangement or specimen is not placed. If one reads the schedule carefully, chances are it will be found that all the rules governing that specific class were not observed.

After eliminating this material, the next step is to closely examine each entry. Arrangements are usually judged against each other, although in some shows they are judged against perfection. Specimens are usually judged against perfection. In some small shows they might be judged against each other. At no time will the judge handle the arrangements but he/she may request the clerk to move them for closer scrutinization. However, it is permissible to move specimen material to check for quality and substance of flowers, stems, and foliage.

Preliminary judging using a rough scale of points either mentally or on paper follows. The experienced judge will scale each arrangement or specimen mentally and will eliminate several entries from further consideration. Wilted or poor quality material, poor design, or misinterpretation of the class are causes of elimination.

With the number of entries reduced, final judging takes place. In close competition it might be necessary to use a predetermined scale of points to determine final placement of arrangements. Most show schedules refer to the specific point system being used. If not in the schedule, the judges should agree prior to judging on the system they will follow. These can be found in the *Handbook for Flower Shows.* A typical point system is:

Point System for Arrangements

Design	40
Distinction	20
Originality	20
Suitability to placement	20
	100

Under most conditions the judge will not be required to use a scale of points except for close decisions. In the majority of classes, there are one or two outstanding arrangements which can be awarded first or second place without further consideration. Sometimes picking third place can be a difficult job, and here the judges might use the point system to advantage. Whether judged against each other or against perfection, only one first, one second, and one third place awards are normally given.

It should be noted that in the above scale of points most emphasis is placed on the arrangement itself and not on the plant material. Perfect horticulture specimens are not necessary for a top-quality arrangement. A crooked-stemmed gladiolus or a malformed flower might be just the right thing for an arrangement but would be eliminated in horticulture classes. Although condition is not stressed in this scale of points, it should be understood that any plant material that is not properly conditioned and is wilted at the time of judging provides grounds for elimination or severe downgrading.

Each plant society has its own scale of points for judging that particular plant or flower. Judges should be familiar with the rules of each society and make placements accordingly. Since judging specimen material is usually against perfection, it is possible to have *several* blue-ribbon awards or *none* of these in a class. The exhibitor will be able to improve the quality of both arrangements and specimen materials by studying the point system of his particular interest. Knowing where emphasis is placed on each will be rewarding in future shows.

10 Holiday Arrangements

Arranging flowers for the holidays can be an interesting and satisfying experience. It is a time when there are unlimited possibilities for the designer, a time to try out new ideas, and a chance to do that little special thing that one has wanted to do for a long time.

There are many holidays throughout the year when flowers can be used. Most are considered of minor importance to the flower industry, and little effort has been made to promote the use of flowers for them. Easter, Mother's Day, Thanksgiving, and Christmas are considered the major flower holidays, and most of us find the use of flowers on these occasions an essential part of the day or celebration.

The kinds of flowers and types of arrangements for each of these holidays vary considerably. Therefore, it is necessary to consider each separately and in some detail.

Easter is associated with the arrival of spring and heralds the season in with an abundance of flowers for the designer to

FIGURE 10–1 Forsythia branches force easily and quickly. Left: Cut branches placed in warm water and kept in a warm room. Right: One week later, all are in full bloom.

use. Spring flowering shrubs and spring bulbs are available in quantity, and after the long winter season when flowers are scarce or expensive for most people, the stage is set for unlimited numbers of arrangements.

This is a time when the avid flower arranger may try forcing some flowers into bloom. In the event of an early Easter, it may be necessary to resort to this tactic. Most shrubs have completed their rest period by this time, and it takes only a little heat to force them into flower. Cut the branches from the plant, place them in water in a warm room and within a few days most will begin to flower.

An example of a forced bloom, forsythia, is shown in Figure 10–1. Forsythia is one of the easiest shrubs to force into bloom. Peach, apple, flowering quince, and crabapple force equally as well. The lateness of the season will determine the length of time necessary to force the flower. The closer to normal flowering time forcing takes place, the shorter will be the time required to force shrubs into flower. At Easter most will bloom within a week.

Tulips and daffodils are flowers synonymous with the Easter season. These can be used in massive, colorful arrangements or can be used individually or in small groups. Daffodils are especially effective during the Easter season and lend themselves to most types of arrangements.

Easter lilies are thought of primarily as potted plants, but they can be used to make effective arrangements. See Figure 10-2 for an Easter lily arrangement. Some of the larger arrangements used in churches or hallways make good use of the lilies. They can be used alone or in conjunction with other flowers such as snapdragons and gladioli. Because of their size, it is important that the principle of scale be carefully applied when using them.

Easter is a time for subtle colors. Pastels predominate with only occasional use of the bright reds that predominated during the Christmas and New Year periods. Very little use is made of bronze and similar colors that are used in the fall.

Arrangements for the Easter season vary considerably. The typical line designs described in Chapter 3 are all appropriate, the line used depending upon the ultimate location of the arrangement. Mass arrangements with a generous use of spring flowers are also in vogue. See Figure 10-3. Baskets are excellent containers for the flowers, but the use of an auxiliary container in the basket will be necessary for those that do not hold water.

FIGURE 10-2 Easter lilies can be arranged effectively in large arrangements.

FIGURE 10-3 An arrangement of a few white daisy-type chrysanthemums and baby's breath in a silver candy dish can be a good addition to the Easter table. More elaborate arrangements are often used.

FIGURE 10-4 Colored eggs are often used during the Easter season. A mixture of white and pastel colors completes this table arrangement for the Easter holiday.

Multicolored Easter eggs are commonly used as accessories, sometimes incorporated within the arrangement of flowers as shown in Figure 10-4, and at other times are separated from the plant material.

Florists make good use of novelty arrangements during this season. Designs suggesting the Easter bunny or chick are common. The correct use of accessories is especially important in this type of arrangement.

Easter is a time for wearing flowers. More flowers are worn on this day than on any other day of the year. A single flower might be all that is necessary for the new Easter ensemble, or a more formal type corsage might be in order. The flowers should not be worn only for the fact of wearing them but should be appropriate for the dress and must be complimentary to it.

Fresh flowers for the Easter hat can lend support to the entire outfit. Many hats come with artificial flowers attached. These can be removed and replaced with fresh ones which will compliment those in the corsage. For future use, the artificial material can be resewn on the hat, or other fresh flowers can be substituted at any time.

Flowers are sometimes worn in the hair in place of a hat. A ring or band of them with nylon net or maline makes a suitable substitute; a few worked into the hair either in the back or on either side of the head are especially effective.

Flowers worn on the Easter ensemble should not be overpowering and should be selected with the same careful attention given to the selection of a fine piece of jewelry.

The use of potted plants is important during this holiday season. Most of the Easter plants should be treated as long-time "bouquets" and discarded after flowering. However, there are a few that can be planted in the garden, and they will produce flowers for many years.

In most areas, Easter lilies can be planted in the garden after the last bloom fades. The stalk will dry up and eventually can be cut off. Within a relatively short time a new shoot will appear and will produce flowers in early fall. With some winter protection in colder climates, the plant will survive the winter and produce flowers year after year. Spring bulbs can be planted in the garden immediately after flowering or held in storage until fall. They will bloom again in one or two years depending upon the kind of bulb and how hard they have been forced. Daffodils usually grow well; do not expect to get tulip flowers of the same quality as those from tulip bulbs on sale for fall planting.

Azaleas and hydrangeas used as Easter plants are not the hardy types grown in northern climates and will not survive the winters in these regions. Some success can be achieved with them in southern areas. Cinerarias, calceolarias and some species of begonia flower only once and should be discarded when the flowers fade.

Mother's Day is a time for cut flowers, arrangements, corsages, and potted plants. Red and pink roses and pink and white carnations are the most popular flowers at this time. Those flowers of a seasonal nature including violets and lily of the valley are available and are used to some extent. Orchids are in demand for corsages.

A gift of cut flowers is popular on Mother's Day. This gives the recipient a chance to arrange them as she sees fit. Flowers handled this way seem to have more meaning than do those already arranged by the florist. For those who have no artistic ability in arranging flowers, however, a box of loose cut flowers can be a source of frustration. For these individuals, the gift of a complete arrangement is much more appropriate. Many times the cut flowers are simply stuck into a container, and no attempt is made at arranging them according to prin-

FIGURE 10-5 The use of pink and white carnations is appropriate for Mother's Day.

ciples; there is actually nothing wrong with this as long as the recipient enjoys the gift and receives a certain amount of satisfaction from the flowers.

Arrangements using many kinds of spring flowers are popular for this holiday. A combination of sweet peas, heather, lily of the valley, and sweetheart roses or an arrangement using miniature carnations is a welcome addition to any home and will help create a bright and pleasant atmosphere. Figure 10-5 shows a Mother's Day creation. Violets and lily of the valley centered with a sweetheart rose clustered into a colonial type "bouquet" is easy to make. With the exception of the rose, it is possible in many areas to harvest these flowers from the fields and woodlands. This adds a more personal touch, especially when they are picked and arranged by children and given to their mother on this special day. See Figure 10-6.

The orchid is the most popular corsage flower for Mother's Day. Cattleyas predominate, but the paphiopedilums and cymbidiums shown in Figure 10-7 are also in demand. A common fault is to purchase the largest orchid possible with little regard to the size of the wearer. Flowers should always be kept in scale with the lady wearing them.

Potted plants are popular for Mother's Day gifts. Many of the same varieties of plants available during the Easter season are good for Mother's Day. Azaleas, cinerarias, miniature roses, and gardenias are among the numerous kinds found at florist

FIGURE 10-6 Violets picked by a child and given to mother on Mother's Day are appreciated as much as an expensive arrangement.

shops. Cinerarias should be considered a temporary or transient plant and thrown out after flowering. The others can be grown indoors and with proper care will be good house plants for many years.

FIGURE 10-7 Cymbidium orchids make effective and long-lasting corsages.

Thanksgiving can be called the "chrysanthemum holiday." Chrysanthemums in fall colors—yellow, bronze, and deep red—are in great demand for arrangements during this holiday season. They can be used alone, in combination with other flowers, and are especially useful in combinations with fruits and/or vegetables. Other flowers in fall shades are also used to some extent. Pastel shades that were in demand during the spring find little use at this time.

Arrangements during this season reflect the bountiful harvest that is celebrated on Thanksgiving day. Mass designs are in vogue, and little use is made of line arrangements. In fact, arrangements of this type are usually out of place and not in harmony with the surrounding atmosphere.

No home is complete without arrangements of flowers during the Thanksgiving season. They can be used in many places, including the dining room, living room, and hallways. Almost any table, sideboard, or mantel is an appropriate location. When used throughout the home, all arrangements should help unify the entire surroundings, should harmonize with each other, and must not be entities in themselves.

Most any type of container can be used for arrangements for this season. However, there are some that seem more appropriate than others. Footed containers, epergnes, baskets, and cornucopias are most adaptable. Baskets are excellent choices for arrangements of flowers and fruits or vegetables. They compliment the harvest season and will work well in most areas throughout the home. The cornucopia made of wooden reeds or ceramics is a good choice for the hallway or sideboard. Footed or pedestal containers and epergnes used on the dining room table will allow arrangements in this area without taking too much space and interfering with the dinner service.

Arrangements for the dining table made of flowers or combinations of flowers, fruits, and/or vegetables are part of the overall Thanksgiving festive activities. They should be in color harmony not only with themselves but with the overall table setting. Difficulty is sometimes encountered when using fruits and vegetables in combination with the fresh flowers. The yellow of a banana or the color of an orange or red pepper oftentimes conflicts with the fall shades of chrysanthemums. If there is any doubt about the color combination, do not use the flowers and fruits together. Instead, an arrangement of only fruits and/or vegetables or only flowers might be more desirable.

Any arrangement of chrysanthemums in fall colors is appropriate for the table. It should be viewed from all sides and should not be so high as to obstruct the views of those sitting opposite each other. By using the pedestal or footed container, it will be elevated enough to allow maximum use of the table during the dinner. Fresh fruits used with the flowers can be arranged attractively for their decorative effect and removed and eaten after dinner. For a more permanent type of arrangement, artificial fruits can be substituted for the fresh.

Epergnes filled with fruits and/or flowers make attractive arrangements for the dining table. Each of the dishes can be treated the same, or different arrangements can be made in each. An attractive way to use such a container is to use flowers and fruits in the center part and different arrangements of small fruits, such as grapes, cranberries, and nuts, in each of the other dishes. All dishes arranged in the same manner tend toward monotony and may actually take away from the overall effect.

Cornucopias or horns of plenty are typical Thanksgiving arrangements designating the bountiful harvest. These are mass arrangements with flowers, fruits, and vegetables flowing out of the containers as shown in Figure 10-8. To be most effective, the flowing effect should be considered seriously and must possess a natural appearance which can be obtained by tipping a full container and allowing the material to roll out.

It is best to use an auxiliary container when making an arrangement in a cornucopia. A small plastic dish or bowl can be

FIGURE 10-8 An attractive arrangement of chrysanthemums, fruit, bittersweet, and dock in a cornucopia. Note how the material seems to flow out of the container. [See also Color Plate.]

anchored inside and foam material inserted in it to hold the flowers. Some provision should be made for adding water. It is difficult to have all flowers in a position to receive water, but by careful manipulation most of them can be stuck into the moist foam. Sometimes it may be necessary to have a few of the flowers in tubes of water which can be camouflaged with other material. Flowers should be pushed into the foam to give the idea of spilling out of the container. Fruits and vegetables are added in similar fashion.

For ease of handling, a cornucopia can be placed on a board or a piece of heavy cardboard covered with a napkin or piece of cloth which will harmonize with the final placement of the completed arrangement.

An effective arrangement for a sideboard is to use two cornucopias placed back to back with the material flowing in opposite directions. Care should be taken that each is similar in size and shape to secure a balanced effect.

Arrangements in baskets, large or small, are excellent throughout the home during this holiday season. A basket arrangement is shown in Figure 10-9. Small baskets of various shapes are excellent for pompon chrysanthemums which can be arranged in many ways for each specific location. Dried material harmonizes well with baskets and can be used in them alone or in combination with berries, nuts, and small vegetables.

Larger baskets are more appropriate in hallways or in large areas which can support a big arrangement. Some of the large chrysanthemums can be used in these, along with pompons and other material.

Door decorations expressing a feeling of welcome are commonly used for the Thanksgiving holiday season. A cluster of ornamental corn gives a warm feeling. Three ears tied together is in scale with the average size door. A bow of ribbon of fall colors similar to those of the corn kernels contributes to the overall design. With a little care, the corn husk can be manipulated into a bow. If it has completely dried, it should be soaked in warm water for a few minutes to make it flexible and prevent breaking when bending it.

Della Robbia wreaths made with fruits, vegetables, nuts, cones, etc., are especially attractive for the door or above or under the mantel. The manufacture of plastic fruits and vegetables, with their life-like appearance, and the ease of construction of this type of arrangement has increased its popularity. It is possible to use fresh materials in these wreaths, but the

FIGURE 10-9 A mass arrangement of bronze and yellow chrysanthemums in a basket. Bittersweet and Scotch broom are used to complete the design.

length of time they can be kept in good condition is relatively short.

Gourds are often used in Thanksgiving arrangements. If used as they come from the garden, they will last for several days, but if treated properly, they can be used for several years. The first step in preserving gourds is to dry them thoroughly. With a nail, punch a small hole in one end and place them on a screen in a warm attic for several days. It is necessary to turn gourds every two or three days to prevent moisture from accumulating in the lower portion resulting in rotting. When they have completely dried (the seeds will rattle when shaken), they can be removed from the attic, wiped clean, and covered with a coating of varnish or shellac. When this has dried, they can be waxed for a more permanent finish.

Large numbers of potted chrysanthemums are used during the harvest season. These are greenhouse varieties; in most areas they should be considered long "bouquets" and thrown out after flowering. In some southern areas, potted chrysanthemums can be cut back and planted out of doors. Because of the nature of the plant which is dependent upon length of day for flowering, the results of planting out of doors are sometimes questionable and discouraging.

Festive decorations are as much a part of the *Christmas* holidays as are the wrapping and exchanging of gifts. Decorations can be rather simple consisting of only a few sprays of greens or they can be highly complex and extravagant with many expensive and elaborate items incorporated into them.

Decorations are used throughout the home during the Christmas season. As one approaches the home, a door decoration gives a warm welcome; when inside, the decorations present a feeling of warmth and good tidings.

The mantel, tables, hallways, open stairways, and even light fixtures are places where arrangements of various kinds, sizes, and shapes can be used effectively. In conjunction with the arrangements of Christmas greens, Christmas plants can be used to compliment them.

Many greens are used for Christmas decorations, and these vary considerably from one area to another. Balsam fir is the one most widely used, not only because of its availability but because of its lasting quality and little or no shedding of its needles. Greens can be obtained from the florist, from landscape plantings around the home, from the woodlands, and from extra branches at the base of the Christmas tree.

A variety of greens can be obtained from the local florist. Many of these are imported from different parts of the country and are obtainable only from this source. English holly, magnolia, mountain laurel, rhododendron, and boxwood are only a few of the greens sold by florists. These are relatively long-lasting materials and are excellent for use indoors in arrangements, as well as for outdoor decorations. For indoor use, stems should be recut and placed either in water or in one of the water-holding foam materials. Treat them the same as you do cut flowers for the maximum longevity. When outdoors, most will last for a considerable period out of water if they are not in direct sunlight.

Another source of Christmas greens is from shrubs and ornamental plantings around the home. It is possible to prune evergreens at this time of year and use the clippings in Christmas decorations. Taxus, boxwood, ilex, camellia, juniper, and many other plants are well suited for this dual purpose. They will last as long as material purchased from the florist and are satisfactory for both indoor and outdoor decorations.

The woodlands are still another source of greens. One must remember that these *do* belong to someone and are not there to be taken by anyone desiring to cut them. Many of these plants are protected by law, and written permission must be obtained from the property owner before they can be harvested and transported. When harvesting material from the wild, it is necessary that conservation laws and practices be carefully observed and that poisonous plants be avoided.

Laurel, American holly, fir, spruce, pine, and hemlock can all be used successfully. Some do last better than others: Holly tends to dry out rapidly unless placed in water, and spruce and hemlock will lose their needles in a short time if kept in a warm place.

The fresh cut Christmas tree can be the source of a limited number of greens. Often it is necessary to cut a section from its base for it to fit into the room. These cuttings should not be thrown out but used for their decorative effect somewhere in the home.

Decorations for Christmas arrangements are obtainable from the florist, gift and novelty stores, garden centers, Christmas shops, and from many other similar enterprises. It is possible to gather many materials from the fields and woodlands that make attractive additions to many arrangements. Pine cones and those from other evergreens can be manipulated in various ways to add interest. By cutting the cone into sections, flower-like structures are formed, which when painted or varnished are very attractive. Refer back to Figure 8-11 which shows a cut pine cone. For variation, pine cones can be used upside down. Seedpods gathered from gardens, fields, and woodlands can provide a wealth of materials. Milkweed pods can be wired and formed into the shape of a poinsettia or can be used individually; teasels, datura, Siberian iris, and gas plants (*dictamnus*) are others that can be used effectively. Seedpods and cones can be used in their natural state or painted. Cans of spray paint do an efficient job without using excess material. Dipping and hand painting are time consuming.

Door decorations play a major role during this holiday season. The wreath shown in Figure 10-10 is the most popular arrangement for the door and can be made in many ways. Before the actual construction of a wreath there are several things which must be taken into account; the size of the door, its color, location, the presence of a storm door, and a place to hang the wreath are all important. There is a general tendency toward selecting or making a wreath too large for the door on which it is to be hung. The wreath should be in proportion to the door and somewhat smaller than its width. Some space should be exposed on the outer edges somewhat in the same idea as an arrangement being placed in a niche or shadow box for a flower show. See Chapter 9.

FIGURE 10–10 A boxwood wreath with pine cones and a red ribbon is an attractive decoration for most doors during the Christmas season. [See also Color Plate.]

The color of the door should influence the selection of decorations and ribbon and sometimes even the selection of the greens. A red or a green door can present problems. Evergreens used on a green door should be compatible with it; they should not blend with the door to the extent that the wreath does not show and from a short distance only the bow and decorations stand out. Foliage with a pale green color might look anemic on a dark green door. Evergreens such as blue spruce, golden arborvitae, or juniper are worth consideration for these situations.

For a red door, selection of a red bow and decorations can be disastrous. There are many shades of red found in Christmas decorations and unless these are carefully selected, serious conflicts can result. To avoid troublesome combinations, it is better to select decorations of another color. Natural, silver, or gold cones with a green or contrasting-colored ribbon can be used successfully. Doors of other colors present few problems, and the traditional red and green of the Christmas season can be used on them.

A southern exposure will shorten the lifespan of the evergreens used in Christmas wreaths. Some will turn brown within a few days while others will remain green somewhat longer; under such conditions, one can delay hanging the wreath until just a few days before Christmas or expect to replace it if hung early. Most wreaths with other exposures will last for weeks, and many will still be in good condition when disposed of after the holidays.

If a storm door is present and it is necessary to hang the wreath between the doors, the distance between them is important. The wreath should be made with this space in mind to avoid crushing it when the doors are closed. Because of a heat buildup between the doors, especially in a southern exposure, the greens will dry out rapidly and will not last as long as those on the outside.

Wreaths can be made on a wire coat hanger, a single-wire frame made especially for them, a frame filled with moss, or a styrofoam ring. Figure 10–11 shows different wreath frames. The first step when using a coat hanger for a frame is to bend it into a circle. Then bunches of greens cut into about six-inch lengths are tied to this frame with string or wire, starting at the hook. Florist spool wire is preferred by most because of its flexibility, strength, and holding quality; string will often break when tightened and greens slip or fall out more easily when it is used. After the first bunch is wrapped in place, others are added

FIGURE 10–11 Wreaths can be made on a coat hanger, a styrofoam ring, or a florist-type box frame filled with moss or straw.

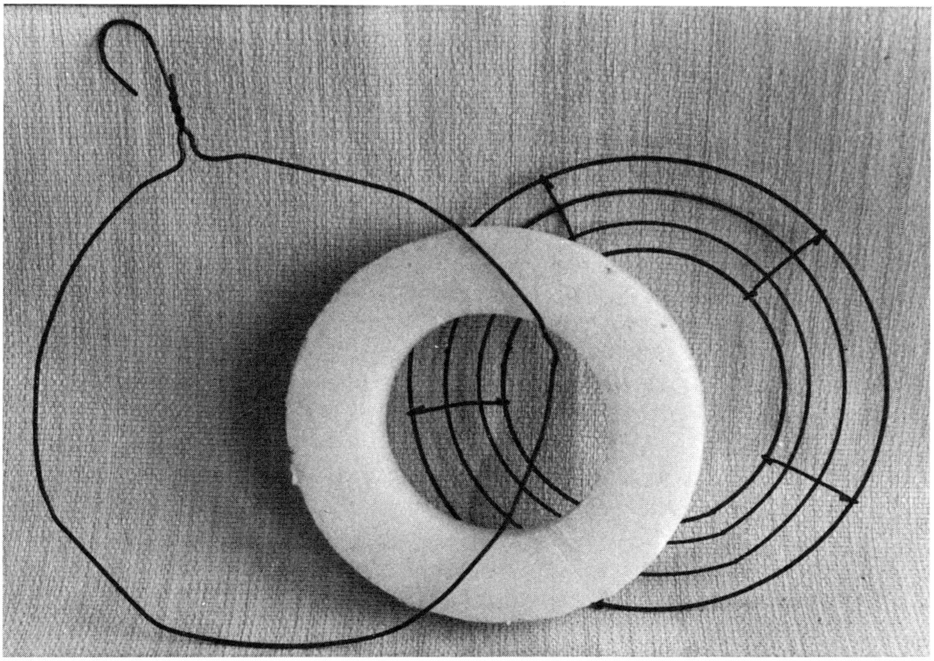

and wound by the continuous string or wire until the complete circle is covered. The end is tied firmly at the hook, and a bow of ribbon or decorations can be used where the ends meet.

The florist single-wire frame, although more sophisticated than the coat hanger, is made in similar fashion. These frames do come in various sizes and are made of wire heavier than the coat hanger. Because of this feature, they hold their shape better, and it is easier to make a perfectly round wreath on them.

The florist box-type wreath frame, available in many sizes, makes an excellent base for many types of wreaths. For most, the frame is filled with moist sphagnum moss, tied in place with string, and covered with waxed paper or thin plastic. A special florist wreath wrap is available for this purpose. Wrapping reduces moisture loss and ensures a neater and cleaner base. If sphagnum moss is not available, the frame can be filled with straw or similar materials, but the holding quality is not as good as the moss.

Greens are inserted directly into this base. Those with rigid, woody stems can be cut to the desired length and the end of the stem sharpened to a point and pushed through the covering into the moss. With materials having more flexible or thin stems, it will be necessary to bunch them using florist wired picks which are then pushed into the moss.

Actual construction begins by placing the filled frame on a table or bench and inserting greens of equal length completely around its perimeter. It is best to lay the piece of green flat on the table and push the stem into the base at an angle. When the perimeter is completed, all greens should lay flat on the table. This is a major step in securing stability of the wreath and ensuring that it will fit flat against the door where it is hung.

With the outside completed, the rest of the wreath is completed by filling it in with shorter pieces of greens. It may be necessary to place many of these shorter pieces on wired picks to hold them securely in place.

Upon completion of the greening, decorations are added. Cones of various types, seedpods, glass balls, and many other materials will prove useful. A bow of ribbon will add the finishing touch. See Figure 10–10 again.

The wreath described above is to be seen from one side only; therefore, it is not necessary that the back be finished with evergreen. However, if it is to be placed on a glass door or window, greens can be fastened to the back. It is best to use short pieces to avoid excessive thickness.

FIGURE 10–12 A combination of a wreath and doorspray made on a styrofoam ring or moss-filled wreath frame wrapped with ribbon.

A modification of the above wreath combines the features of a wreath and doorspray. The frame is mossed and wrapped as described above; then about three-quarters is wrapped with ribbon. Into the remainder greens are stuck, with long pieces at the top and bottom and reducing the length of each toward the midpoint. Decorations are put in place and a bow of ribbon of the same material used in wrapping completes the arrangement. Figure 10–12 shows this type of decoration.

The wreaths described above can be made on styrofoam frames instead of the mossed ones. These are lighter in weight, there is a possibility of breaking, and they do not hold the greens as firmly as the mossed base. However, they are easy to use, and the mossing and wrapping operations are eliminated. For wreaths to be used indoors or in areas where they will not be subjected to strong winds, these frames are satisfactory.

Wreaths made entirely of cones, or cones, nuts, and seed pods, can be made on the box-type frame. Instead of filling the frame with moss, long thin cones such as those of white pine are pushed through the wire frame to form a base. Soaking these cones in water overnight causes them to close and

FIGURE 10–13 A cone wreath made with a variety of cones. Nuts and seedpods are sometimes added for variety.

become pliable, making it easier to insert them into the frame. Upon drying, the cones will again open resulting in a tight base onto which other material can be attached.

All material used in making the wreath should be wired and attached to the cone base. It will be necessary to drill small holes through nuts and acorns to wire them securely. Wire should be placed between the bracts of the cones and not attached to the small stem at their base.

Larger cones are usually placed around the circumference of the wreath and the smaller ones inside. Care should be taken not to align the material in rows forming a series of circles. Upon completion, shown in Figure 10–13, the whole wreath can be sprayed with varnish or clear spray.

One of the easiest types of door decorations to make is the doorspray or swag. This can be just a couple of evergreen branches tied together and a bow of ribbon added for decoration, or it can be quite elaborate, as is the one in Figure 10–14, with greens, decorations, and a fancy bow. To begin this type, select two well-shaped branches of evergreen and tie them together with their tips going in opposite directions. More branches can be tied in to give a fuller appearance. Decorations such as pine cones, bells, etc., can be added, along with a bow of ribbon. The bow is attached where the branches meet to hide the mechanics used in construction.

Centerpieces and other Christmas arrangements can be very simple or very elaborate. A few sprigs of green and a candle can be effective in some situations. Other areas require considerably more material to provide the proper atmosphere.

Christmas arrangements, whether for the table, sideboard, or mantel, give one a chance to express individuality, creativity, and originality. The idea may arise from the setting, the general atmosphere, or from some of the decorations or accessories being used. Whatever the arrangement, it should be compatible with the surroundings and other arrangements.

Many arrangements are made on a styrofoam base. This is available in various thicknesses and colors. The white, two-inch material is almost universally used. It does not hold water, and most fresh greens will last only a few days in it. For longer lasting arrangements, one of the water-holding foams can be used in conjunction with the styrofoam or it can be used in a vase.

FIGURE 10-14 An elaborate door decoration using artificial fruits, bayberries, a mixture of greens, and a velvet ribbon, all incorporated into an old lantern.

FIGURE 10–15 An easy-to-make Christmas centerpiece consisting of a styrofoam base, candle, greens, and a few red Christmas balls.

A centerpiece involving a minimum of expense consists of one ten- or twelve-inch candle, a four-by-four-inch block of two-inch styrofoam, a few greens, and some artificial red berries. A hole smaller than the diameter of the base of the candle is cut in the center of the styrofoam and the candle forced into it by twisting the candle along with a downward motion. This should hold the candle firmly in place.

Evergreen branches are added, first completely around the base to establish the overall size, then toward the center completely covering the styrofoam. These should be kept quite low to avoid being out of scale with the candle. Artificial Christmas berries are wired onto florist picks and inserted to complete the arrangement. The completed arrangement can be seen in Figure 10–15.

Larger and more elaborate arrangements require more styrofoam, greens, and decorations. Flocked greens, treated to make them look as though covered with snow, are useful along with many Christmas novelties. These arrangements, used on end tables, buffets, and shelves, are the most versatile and most interesting of all those used during this season. They can be conversation pieces and will help to create the holiday atmosphere. See Figure 10–16.

Many beautiful and lavish arrangements can be made for the mantel. However, sometimes only a very simple arrangement is in order, depending upon the architecture and furnishings of the room. When making arrangements for this location, there are at least two things the designer should watch for—mirrors or pictures hung above the mantel. If a large mirror is above the mantel, it will reflect the back of the arrangement; therefore, the arrangement must be finished on both sides, just as one viewed from all sides on a table. If there is a picture hanging above the mantel, make it part of the overall scheme. It is advisable not to place any material from the arrangement across the frame or on the front of the picture itself, unless both the arrangement and picture fit together into one unit.

A few sprigs of English holly and a few candles placed on each end make an attractive yet simple mantel arrangement. The holly can be stuck in moist floral foam to increase its lasting qualities and to hold it in desired positions. Other pieces can be placed flat on the mantel. Placing large poinsettias on either side of the fireplace completes this simple but beautiful composition.

A few sprigs of evergreens or a few holly leaves along with a bow of ribbon and some berries can be made into a Christmas corsage with little time and effort. The evergreen and wired decorations are tied together with a piece of fine

FIGURE 10-16 A Christmas centerpiece with a large candle, pine cones, nuts, and artificial fruits. Greens are inserted into moist foam to keep them in good condition. [See also Color Plate.]

wire, and this area is then covered with floral tape. A small bow in proportion to the size of the arrangement completes the corsage.

If holly leaves are used, each leaf is wired and taped individually and the points on them cut off. They are assembled together into a desired shape. Decorations and a bow are then added. Details of corsage construction are discussed in Chapter 14.

Many house plants are used during this holiday season. The poinsettia exceeds all others in popularity at this time, and new cultivars of poinsettias have increased the length of time these plants can be kept in good condition in the home. It is not uncommon, to be able to keep the Christmas plant until Easter or later. After flowering, it is best to dispose of poinsettia plants. They *can* be kept for another season, but because of light and temperature requirements, most remain vegetative and fail to flower.

Christmas peppers, cherries, azaleas, begonias, and many other plants are popular at Christmas time. Like the poinsettias, it is possible to keep most of these growing in the home, but overall results are generally unsatisfactory, and many disappointments occur.

There are other holidays when flowers are used, and each does have a certain amount of significance. Valentine's Day is considered a time when flowers are appropriate. What greater gift could one receive than a box or arrangement of red roses with their understood message, "I love you"?

New Year's Day, Washington's Birthday, Memorial Day, and Independence Day are times when a limited number of flowers are used, but none of these are considered major flower holidays.

11 Miniatures and Small Arrangements

One of the more interesting attractions at flower shows is the class of *miniature* arrangements. One should not be led to believe, however, that the miniature is strictly a flower show arrangement. These arrangements fit nicely into several areas of the home, can be used as favors for parties, work well as individual place settings on a table, make excellent gifts for shut-ins, and are attractive on bedside trays or tables. Although they have been made for years, it is only recently that they have gained tremendous popularity.

There has been some confusion about exactly what constitutes a miniature arrangement. The miniature arrangement is a scaled-down regular size arrangement with all of the principles, rules and details found in its larger counterpart. A group of miniatures can be seen in Figure 11–1. A picture of a miniature arrangement would give the impression of a normal-sized one unless some object was used for size comparison. A single flower or two placed in a small container does not constitute

FIGURE 11–1 A group of floral miniatures, each with the maximum dimension of less than four inches. The arrangement on the left has flowers and foliage out of scale with the container as well as overpowering for the overall arrangement.

a miniature arrangement merely because of its size. Perhaps the most important thing to keep in mind when making miniatures is to visualize the arrangement "blown up" several times in the same manner that a photographer increases the size of a photo. If any part of the composition is out of scale, this is a sure way to see it.

There are many interpretations regarding overall size of miniature arangements. Some authorities regard three inches as the maximum height while others suggest four, five, or six inches. The National Council of State Garden Clubs' *Handbook for Flower Shows* (1977) lists the maximum size for a miniature arrangement as five inches in its greatest overall dimension. It also gives a maximum size of eight inches for small designs. Because of any confusion that might exist, each flower show schedule should indicate the maximum dimensions of miniature arrangements for that show. Usually, these smaller designs create much interest, and the viewers are intrigued at the intricate work necessary to make these fascinating works of art.

Collecting containers for miniature arrangements (see the grouping in Figure 11–2) can become an interesting hobby. Sources, almost limitless, include such places as department stores, hobby shops, beaches, and the home. It is surprising the things that can be adapted for use when a little thought and ingenuity are applied. The prime consideration in collecting containers for this purpose is size. It should be remembered that the arrangement should be one and one-half to two times the

FIGURE 11-2 Containers suitable for miniature arrangements. The opening in the pot on the far left is one and one-half inches.

height of the container. With this in mind, the container for a five-inch arrangement should not exceed a height or length of more than two inches.

A quick trip around the home will reveal many items that can be used as containers. Doll's dishes, lipstick tubes, perfume vials, thimbles, buttons, bottle caps (shown in Figure 11-3), and pill boxes can be useful. They should all hold water. The holes in buttons can be filled with clay or wax to make them waterproof.

FIGURE 11-3 A miniature arrangement using a bottle cap as a container.

The workshop will provide nuts and bolts, blocks of wood, or pieces of scrap metal which can be bent and shaped into suitable containers. The wood should be waterproofed with varnish and a coat of wax applied on the inside. The outside can be left natural or can be painted.

Many interesting shells can be found at the seashore. They come in a variety of sizes, shapes, and colors and with a little care will last indefinitely.

Care should be taken when purchasing miniature containers. Many interesting pieces are destroyed by the manufacturer by placing ornaments or decorations on them that are completely out of scale or not in keeping with the item or arrangement.

It is possible to make containers with potter's clay or modeling clay, which can be manipulated into interesting shapes, baked in an oven until hardened, and then painted and waterproofed. Blocks of soap can be carved into interesting designs. The hollowed out area should be sealed with paraffin before use as a container for arrangements. White soap will give the appearance of alabaster or marble, green might appear as jade, and other colors can give the appearance of gems or minerals.

Stones, seedpods, nutshells, and even small eggshells can be used as containers.

Flower holders vary according to the container and plant material being used. Small pinpoint holders are available, but vases must be of sufficient depth to hold enough water to reach the flower stems that are placed in them. Some are only about one-half inch in diameter; the points relatively short, thin, close together, and imbedded in a plastic base. It is possible to make holders using paraffin and pins. However, these are not too sturdy and care must be taken when working with them.

A toothbrush can be a substitute for a pinpoint holder. With a hacksaw, cut to the desired size and shape and place into the container. It can be anchored with floral clay to hold it in position and to add stability.

Steel wool is a good material for stuffing "tall" containers and is used in similar fashion to chicken wire in larger arrangements as described in Chaper 4. It should be placed in rather loosely and never compacted; if packed too tightly, it will be impossible for the stems to penetrate through it. The vase may also be loosely stuffed with thin stems or wooden toothpicks. The toothpicks will swell when water is added so room for expansion must be allowed. These materials should be placed vertically in the vase to allow the flower stems to be inserted among them.

Fine wire crumbled and pushed into the container will support and hold the stems in place. It is sometimes difficult to secure flowers in place with this method, but with careful attention and manipulation the arrangement can be successfully completed.

The water-holding plastic foam materials can be cut into small blocks and used successfully for miniature arrangements. In flat containers, the block will tend to slide around, but this can be overcome by glueing one or two thumb tacks to the bottom of the container and anchoring the foam onto them. Some difficulty may be encountered when trying to place thin, fragile stems into the foam. A hole made with a toothpick, a piece of wire, or a needle before inserting the stems into the foam will help.

Containers with thin necks and small openings need no holders. The plant material can be carefully placed in the container until the arrangement is completed. If the arrangement fits loosely, a short piece of stem can be used as a wedge to tighten the whole arrangement in place.

A few tools will prove useful for constructing miniatures. Tweezers are a good substitute for fingers. No matter how small fingers may be, they are cumbersome when working with these delicate materials. Manicure scissors should be used instead of florist shears. The latter are just too large for the job. Fine wire, either No. 30 or No. 32, will be useful; it can be used for wiring flowers or can be used to support them. An eye dropper can be used instead of a watering can. Florist clay, tape, pins, and fine thread will be valuable assets to aid in making these arrangements.

Plant material is limited only by the designer's imagination. Any small flower or piece of foliage can be used as long as it is in scale with the container and the overall size of the arrangement. A general rule to follow is that no flower should be more than one-third the size of the container. Figure 11–4 illustrates a well-scaled miniature arrangement. Of course, size alone should not be the only consideration—color, shape, and texture play important roles. A dark colored, coarse-textured flower appears heavier than a light colored, fragile one, and should be used accordingly. An inflorescence such as ageratum is usually considered as a whole unit when used; however, under some conditions the florets can be considered individually. This is

FIGURE 11-4 Flowers are in scale with the vase in this miniature arrangement of fall asters, goldenrod, and ragweed.

also true with such plants as lantana and heliotrope, where each individual floret is seen as a distinct unit rather than a cluster. Buds of flowers are often used—individual geranium buds may appear as miniature roses, and those of dogwood are very attractive. Parts of flowers or seed pods are interesting in dried arrangements: The pods of gas plant (*dictamnus*) are very attractive, but because of their size can only be used in the larger (five- to six-inch) arrangements. The calyx of a small carnation is equally useful.

Care should be taken when using so-called miniature flowers such as button chrysanthemums, miniature marigolds and zinnias, roses, geraniums, and pansies. Although these are small when compared with the "normal"-sized varieties, they are still too large for most miniature arrangements. Most of these, however, will prove satisfactory for the small arrangements described later.

Among sources of flowers for miniatures are woodlands, fields, home gardens, herb gardens, and even house plants. Tiny violets, bluets, anemonies, false lily of the valley, and bearberry can be obtained from the woodlands. Fields will yield such treasures as Joe-Pye weed, Queen Anne's lace, butterfly weed, steeple bush, and meadow-rue. When gathering wild material, conservation practices should be followed, and those plants or flowers on protected lists should not be harvested unless rules and regulations are observed.

The home flower garden will provide an ample supply of material during the growing season. A little planning before planting the garden will be helpful. Alyssum, forget-me-not, Johnny jump-up, campanula, sedum, and lobelia are only a few of the dozens of annual and perennial flowers available at home.

The herb garden is a source of foliage as well as flowers. Arrangements made only with the foliage of herbs are attractive and receive many favorable comments at flower shows. The foliage of rosemary, santolina, thyme, and lavender, as well as the flowers of fennel, dill, horehound, and lavender, are worthy of consideration.

During the winter months when flowers are scarce in most areas, one may turn to house plants for a few flowers for a miniature arrangement. An African violet, wax begonia, geranium, or oxalis may provide enough flowers for the designer to use.

All sorts of foliage are used in miniatures. For the smaller arrangements, pine needles, sprigs of Scotch broom, tiny geranium leaves, or blades of grass are satisfactory. Sprigs of fern, boxwood, heather, or evergreens work well in those arrangements which are four to six inches high. One of the greatest faults found in miniatures is the use of foliage that is out of scale with the flowers and overall arrangement. The designer should beware of this and not fall into the so-called "trap."

With all materials at hand, actual construction of the arrangement can begin. This will proceed in the same manner as described in Chapter 4 for a normal sized arrangement. The first and most important step is the establishment of the main line. If the arrangement is for a show, be sure of the dimensions listed in the show schedule; do not guess at the size. A good trick to follow to be sure the arrangement is within the size limitations is to cut a piece of cardboard having the same measurements as those listed in the show schedule, a procedure shown in Figure 11-5. Place this behind the arrangement during construction to eliminate guesswork. It is important that the main line be within the confines of this background. If this procedure is followed, all other material added will be within the prescribed dimensions.

The main line can be made with foliage or flowers. Tendrils from grapevines, sweet peas, or passion flowers make interesting lines. Scotch broom, twisted stems, or roots also work well. This line should be anchored securely so that there will be no tendency for it to move when other materials are being inserted into position. Filling in, establishing a focal

FIGURE 11-5 A piece of cardboard having the same dimensions as the maximum allowable space in the show can be used as a guide to ensure that the arrangement does not exceed the designated dimensions.

point, and final manipulations of plant materials are similar to the procedures described in Chapter 4 except that everything is on a smaller scale. See Figure 11-6.

When fresh flowers are being used, it is important that each stem be able to receive moisture. Since many flowers used in these arrangements are small and delicate, they will wilt and die quickly if water is unavailable to them. Even if wired, the stems should be in contact with the water supply.

Miniature arrangements are often made with dried materials such as those in Figures 11-7 and 11-8. These are interesting to make and will last for a considerable period of time. Construction procedures are basically the same as when fresh material is used.

Accessories and bases can be used, but it is especially important that they be in scale with the rest of the composition. If a base is used, as shown in Figure 11-4, it is included in the overall dimensions of the arrangement. Small pieces of wood carved into attractive shapes, painted, or stained make attractive bases. Buttons, poker chips, and small mirrors also serve well.

Gift, novelty, and hobby shops are good sources of tiny accessories. These should be selected with much thought because of the tendency to include material too large or too small for the arrangement.

FIGURE 11-6 Pine needles, thyme, and blue salvia flowers arranged in a miniature container.

FIGURE 11-7 Dried materials work well in miniatures; seedpods, dried flowers, and grasses are effective in these long-lasting arrangements.

FIGURE 11-8 An arrangement of dried material in a lipstick tube. The curvature of the twigs and santilina make up the lines of a Hogarth curve, and ageratum is used as the focal point.

FIGURE 11-9 A small arrangement on a bedside tray. Marigolds, herbs, and pea foliage have been used effectively in a wooden box.

Small arrangements, rather than actual *miniatures,* are those with maximum dimensions of eight inches. This added size gives the designer more working space, but the same intricate considerations that go into miniatures should be employed. Flowers should be somewhat larger than those used in the miniatures but should be in scale with the overall arrangement. Small zinnias, marigolds, and button chrysanthemums work well. Pussy willows, grape hyacinths, and varieties of small narcissus fit together to make an attractive small arrangement.

Small arrangements are suitable for use in several areas where the miniature is too small and inconspicuous or a regular sized arrangement is too large. As shown in Figure 11-9, bedside tables or trays, window sills, and even the kitchen table should be considered.

Although miniatures and small arrangements gain much attention at flower shows, neither is eligible for the tri-color award, award of distinction, or creativity award.

12 Modern Arrangements

One of the many types or styles of arrangements made by floral designers is the so-called "modern arrangement." The terms "modern" or "contemporary" are perhaps misnomers. They are used because of the lack of a general term that adequately describes many of today's arrangements. "Free form," "abstract," "nontraditional," "out of the ordinary"—all seem to fit the so-called modern arrangement of this era.

Not too many years ago when the American line-mass type of arrangement was developed, it was referred to by publications of that time as the modern type of flower arrangement. Prior to that there were other periods when arrangements were referred to as being "modern." In flower arranging, as in other forms of art, "modern" can be described as a breaking away from the traditional; therefore, when using this term, one must keep in mind the particular period being described by the writer.

There is a difference between *fads* and *modern design.* Fads are of a temporary nature and disappear almost as rapidly

FIGURE 12-1 Modern design, the breaking away from traditional types. An interesting use of twisted branches and carnations with foliage and skeletonized leaves tied together with a lamp at the base.

as they appear; modern is a more gradual and often times a more permanent type of change.

Modern arrangements in vogue today depict a breaking away from the typical American type of flower arrangement. Figures 12-1 and 12-2 show some attractive "modern" designs. Although the floral designer cannot go to the extremes used by the painter, it is possible to manipulate flowers, foliage, and accessories into abstract designs that are difficult for the layperson to understand. To make such designs, the artist, whether working with flowers or paints, must have a purpose in mind. In addition to a purpose, the design usually carries a message and also reflects the personality of the designer.

Floral art, as practiced by most designers today, follows certain basic rules or principles. This can lead to set patterns in designs, the same general type being made over and over with

FIGURE 12-2 The use of gladioli, bold foliage, and grape branches crossing the spikey gladiolus stem indicates a breaking away from the traditional American type of arrangement.

the only differences being in the placement and kinds of flowers and foliage used. Modern design is a breaking away from these standard forms but does continue to involve many of the earlier principles of design. This helps to create originality and to foster self-expression, key factors in this new form of floral art.

Originality, the act of creating something new, not something copied or imitated, can be achieved in various ways. The idea for the design might originate from the flowers, the container, or some accessories being used; it might evolve from an event or the use or placement of the arrangement. The true artist will be able to develop this through the manipulation of his materials, without being restrained by rules and regulations. Originality is individuality; it is the self-expression of ideas. To communicate his thoughts in modern arrangements, the artist is not limited to only fresh flowers but may use unusual combina-

FIGURE 12-3 Protea and fasciated (fan-tail) willow are combined into a modernistic arrangement having a distinct character of its own.

tions of these along with dried, man-made, and even parts of flowers. As in Figure 12-3, many innovative designs can be created.

Simplicity is one of the keynotes of modern flower arrangement. All unnecessary details are eliminated, and each part of the arrangement is considered a detail in itself rather than a grouping or mass for effect. See Figure 12-4. It is not necessary to hide stems or even disguise some mechanics. In fact, these can play an important role in the overall message carried by the arrangement. Heavy stems such as those of bird of paradise denote strength; those of pussy willow, flexibility. Exposure of a heavy flower holder suggests weight or stability. Each element can be an important factor in supporting the theme of the design.

Each flower and piece of foliage is an absolute necessity in this form of floral art. Most arrangements involve only a few

FIGURE 12-4 Simplicity is one of the keynotes to modern design. A minimum amount of material is suggestive of Japanese design.

flowers, but the objective of all is to secure the maximum effect from each piece of plant material used. Three large chrysanthemums in a heavy pottery container might be all that is needed for an effective design in an uncluttered contemporary living room. This piece would be out of place in many of our homes, but if several smaller pompons were added, the arrangement would then fit nicely into their general "busy" appearance.

Another characteristic of the modern floral design is boldness. Each part of the arrangement and the arrangement itself are designed to stand out and not to blend into the background as might be done with some other types of arrangements. To achieve this, oftentimes unusual or striking color combinations are employed—black and white, blue and orange, or red and brown are combinations that are often used. See again Figure 12-1. White chrysanthemums combined with palm fronds that have been cut into triangular form, painted black, and arranged in a heavy black container make an interesting combination for a specific location. In addition to color, boldness can be achieved by employing various geometric forms. In the above example, the chrysanthemums through proper spacing would each be seen as circles or spheres. The palm fronds are triangular. The proper combination of these two forms can lead toward the characteristic of boldness.

Materials that are unusual or eye-catching can be prime factors in modern floral art. The use of one or more of these can create an outstanding arrangement. An odd-shaped container, an out-of-the-ordinary accessory, or distinctive flowers or foliage can be the feature leading to an attractive and appealing design. However, any of these if not scrutinized carefully and used correctly can lead to deleterious results. A modern arrangement is more than just the use of an unusual item; it must be a closely knit organization of *all* design details.

In recent years with the aid of rapid air transportation, exotic flowers from the South Sea islands and other enchanting places have become available at a reasonable cost for all designers throughout the world. These flowers, through their unusual shapes, color characteristics, and overall fascinating nature, are excellent media for modernistic flower arrangements. Orchids have always possessed an exotic character. There are many species of orchids available, each having its own peculiar characteristics. The most popular are the large cattleya types. These relatively large flowers are available in a variety of colors with white, purple, and white with a purple lip the most popular and most readily available. Do not overlook other species: The paphiopedilums and cymbidiums are long lasting, come in a variety of colors, and have interesting shapes. The cymbidium is a spray-type orchid, and it is not unusual to have 20 or more flowers per stem; they can be picked off and used individually or entire sprays having a few or many flowers can be used effectively.

Bird of paradise has been grown in conservatories for many years, but only in recent times has it become readily available to the designer. The blue and orange coloration of its flowers is an interesting complimentary color combination which can be used effectively in modernistic arrangements; and its unusual shape can also be an important contributing factor.

Anthurium, often described as one of the world's most exotic flowers, has beautiful scarlet flowers which will last for several weeks. Their unusual heart-like spathe with large yellow-orange spadix is a structure conducive to modern design. The

FIGURE 12-5 Calla lilies and effectively arranged foliage in a marble container create the feeling of strength and purity.

texture, similar to patent leather, is another unusual feature of this flower. Spathiphyllum, bromeliad, and ginger are among the other unusual flowers available from throughout the world.

Some of the flowers grown in local greenhouses and gardens are excellent choices for modernistic design. Large chrysanthemums are quite effective when each bloom is seen by itself; fuji mums are also a good choice. Calla lilies seem to have a character of their own: Their thick strong stems denote a quality of strength, and the pure white flower signifies purity. This combination of strength and purity can easily be worked into an effective theme for an arrangement such as the one seen in Figure 12-5.

Tritoma, commonly called red hot poker, is available from many perennial gardens. Its golden yellow lower florets blending into a bright orange-red at the tip create an unusual color combination which readily lends itself to the modernistic approach. Most species of iris have fascinating structures that can form the basis for unusual or original ideas.

Most flowers that are readily available from flower shops can be used successfully by imaginative designers. Probably because we are more familiar with them than with those imported from foreign places, more difficulty is encountered with roses, carnations and similar flowers in the creation of innovative modern designs. Gladiolus, however, can be an excellent source of ideas. Top quality gladiolus spikes, straight and strong, denote rigidity and may carry out the theme perfectly. Those spikes that are crooked may suggest flexibility and the gracefulness of a ballerina.

As indicated above, almost any flower can be used in modern design. Massing or grouping them is seldom necessary. Most flowers are seen and used as individuals and are details in themselves, each having a specific part in the overall theme of the arrangement.

Foliage is used in modernistic-type arrangements but not in the same way as in the line-mass types. Its purpose is not to camouflage mechanics or to fill in holes; each leaf is as important as is each flower. Materials such as huckleberry, leatherleaf, and asparagus fern are seldom beneficial. Crotin, aspidistra, philodendron (monstera and others), birds of paradise, and palm fronds are used individually as grown, or can be trimmed into geometric forms, made into loops, or twisted in different ways to perform a specific function. See Figure 12-6 for a curved variation.

Driftwood or weathered wood plays an important role in many of the free form designs as shown in Figure 12-7. Natural pieces may, by their individual shapes or forms, suggest interesting ideas. Other pieces may be carved into suggestive shapes or objects to carry out a theme. Twisted branches of grape, bittersweet, and wisteria are well suited for these arrangements. The twisted nature can suggest movement or motion to help to carry out a certain motif.

Many of the principles set forth in Chapter 2 are involved in this modern type of floral design. Although not adhered to as closely as in the line-mass arrangement, the principles do have an important impact on the modernistic trend.

The principle of design is always present regardless of the type of floral arrangement. However, traditional design with its standard geometric patterns has been eliminated in favor of a more free style and a personal approach. Design is limited only by one's imagination and thoughts. See Figure 12-7.

Balance, obtained by the manipulation of the material within the arrangement, is always present. The precise balance

FIGURE 12-6 The use of trimmed and twisted cycad leaves creates a modernistic version of the Hogarth curve.

FIGURE 12-7 Weathered wood forms the bulk of this contemporary design. The flowing lines of the scotch broom and the twisted copper tubing are in direct contrast to the strength and rigidity of the bird of paradise. Shadows created from a light placed above the arrangement add to the effectiveness of the material.

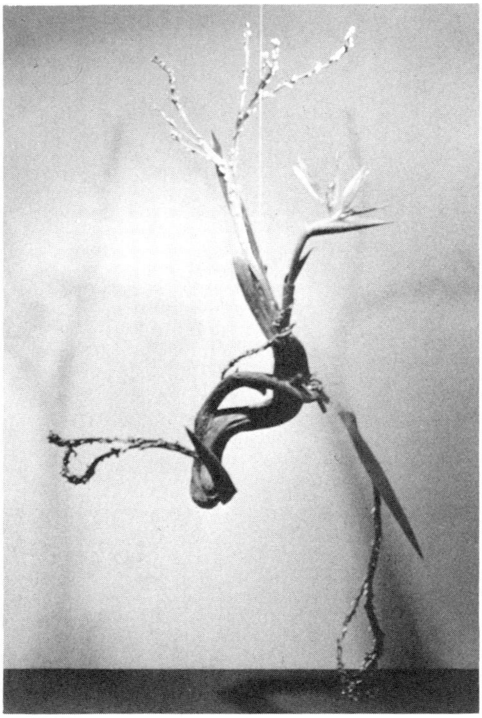

FIGURE 12-8 Precision balance is necessary in kinetic designs. This arrangement (a motorized design) suspended by a nylon line and continuously rotated by a concealed motor above is perfectly balanced. Weight and distance from the centerline are especially important.

of stabiles, mobiles, and other kinetic designs indicates the care needed and the awareness of this principle that must be incorporated into these designs. Balance is achieved by having equal weight on either side of an imaginary line, running vertically through the arrangement. Figures 12-8 and 12-9 show perfect balance in kinetic designs.

In modernistic design, space plays an important role in obtaining balance. The greater the distance between the flower or other material from the vertical axis, the greater the weight it possesses. With this in mind, a small flower placed some distance from the axis would balance a larger one close to it; balance can also be accomplished by proper handling of color, texture, and shapes of materials.

Scale and proportion are important factors in any design, whether traditional or modernistic. The importance of the size

FIGURE 12-9 Perfect balance is necessary in hanging arrangements. This arrangement hanging by a nylon line gives the impression of being a mobile (free movement by air currents), although it is in a stationary position.

relationship of the units within the arrangement cannot be overemphasized. Contemporary, free-form, or abstract designs do allow more leeway than do those designs of traditional nature, but with this freedom greater responsibilities also occur. Flowers and/or foliage that would be considered out of scale when used together in typical line-mass arrangements can be used successfully together in these new styles; however, problems concerning balance and other factors must be considered in greater detail.

The ultimate size of the arrangement must be compatible with its surroundings. In modern design, shape is an important consideration and will affect the size of the floral design to a much greater degree than it did with those of earlier designs.

In modernistic arrangements, it is permissible and in most, desirable, to use various combinations of materials. Man-made objects, natural materials, fresh flowers and foliage, and dried material are all used in these designs. The main objective is to be certain that all parts unite and work together to complete the overall theme. In this respect a combination of dried and fresh materials would not be out of unity as it would be in the case of traditional types of arrangements.

With the three-dimensional space aspect of many of these arrangements, the use of the traditional focal point has changed considerably. Instead of being at the lower part of the arrangement where lines converge and support the weight of the rest of the arrangement, areas of interest can be at any point or at several points throughout the design. These points of interest do not compete with each other but support the overall theme of the design. They tend to flow together and a direct relationship with each other exists throughout the three dimensional area occupied by the arrangement. See Figure 12–7.

Rhythm is an important principle in free-form or contemporary design. Flowing curves, space relationships, color contrasts, and blending—all aid in creating a flowing motion among the various parts, as can be seen in Figure 12–10. Although sometimes difficult to catch by the untrained eye, it is ever present in well thought out arrangements. This rhythm principle is often compared with music: When new styles are introduced, the rhythmic patterns are often difficult to understand; in time, however, these become understood as easily as those of the traditional types. The same situation exists with modernistic floral designs.

Accent and focal areas basically perform the same duties. Accenting certain areas may be accomplished with color, size, and shape, as well as by space relationships. Distances between parts along with certain emphasis on them (accent) can be important factors in overall stability. Repetition deserves consideration but is not a prime factor in modern design. In many designs, a single flower is all that is necessary to carry out the theme. Other similiar material reused (repetition) may destroy the whole effect.

In this type of arranging, construction details are difficult to describe because each arrangement is an entity in itself; no basic lines or placement of them can be given as guidelines. A thorough understanding of the mechanics of floral design (Chapter 4) is of utmost importance before attempting to get deeply involved in this art.

FIGURE 12-10 Rhythm is an important principle in free-form or contemporary design. The placement of flowers, branches, and the child's swing helps to create the rhythmic response.

Containers vary almost as much as do flowers. Almost anything can be used: Pottery, glass, metal, wood, and even paper can be effective. All are important factors in developing the theme. Bases are often used and camouflaged auxiliary containers placed on them may give the impression of the arrangement rising from the base. Flowers may be inserted into tubes of water which are put into holes drilled in inconspicuous places in driftwood or other wooden forms. In kinetic design, flowers are often placed in small tubes of water to keep them from wilting. Clear glass containers which allow stems to be seen can play important roles; these stems are magnified in clear water and become an integral part of the overall design.

Although types of containers are almost limitless they should be selected with much care. They can be as important as any other element in the arrangement and may be responsible for a blue ribbon award or elimination at a flower show.

The use of accessories plays an important part in modern floral art. They can be the inspiration for the theme of the design or strong supporters of it; in fact, many modernistic designs depend upon the accessories to interpret the theme. Accessories should be used with a specific purpose in mind and should not lead to a confused situation.

As an example of an unusual accessory, in some arrangements copper tubing may be used. If manipulated into forms such as a spiral or a series of different sized circles, the tubing can add tremendously to the arrangement, but if it is just twisted into an uncontrolled mass, it can be more of a detraction; the designer would then be wise to eliminate it.

It is not necessary for accessories to be used in all arrangements; if they do not add to the overall theme, do not use them. It is wise to experiment with them. Try them in different places. Use different ones in the same design to see how they compare. Some practice with accessories will help to increase confidence in their use.

Modernistic floral designs do have a place in today's living. In the contemporary homes and offices that are being built, they serve an important role; they make excellent conversation pieces and fit well with modern decor; and in flower shows they are always major attractions. This style of free-form, contemporary, or modernistic design is an important step in the evolution of floral design.

Floral Arrangements for the Home

13

Floral arrangements are an essential part of the home decor. They add charm, serve as conversation pieces, and add the finishing touch to complete the overall atmosphere. They can be used for accent and to accentuate certain architectural features or furnishings. It is not necessary for them to be made with all the care and precision that go into those created for flower shows. Instead, a single flower or stem of flowers placed in a container in an appropriate place might be more in keeping with the surroundings than a more stylized arrangement.

Flowers for everyday use are an important consideration for any home. In addition to helping create a cheerful atmosphere, they do have other therapeutic effects upon the occupants. Proper selection of color, as described in Chapter 6, is important in this respect: Bright colors on a hot day can be disturbing, whereas other colors can help to reduce the discomfort caused by the high temperatures. A feeling of hospitality or the thought that someone cares is created when flowers are attractively arranged and used effectively. They should not be used in such an abundance that they detract from the other furnishings; instead, each arrangement or vase of flowers should serve a definite purpose and contribute to but not dominate the overall theme; it may be an entity in itself or it may be used to emphasize other objects.

Several years ago the Society of American Florists adopted the slogan "Say It with Flowers." This can be interpreted in many ways including the reasons for the use of flowers in the home. As one steps through the front door into a hallway, an arrangement of flowers will suggest "Welcome"; other floral pieces throughout the home imply "Enjoy yourself—have a good time." Many times it is impossible to put thoughts into words, but flowers readily carry this unspoken message.

Almost all areas in the home can be brightened by the use of cut flowers arranged in a tasteful design. Hallways, dining room, den, kitchen, and even the bedrooms are all areas where flowers have a place.

Many types of arrangements are suitable for hallways or vestibules. Most of these will be seen from one side only and can be symmetrical or asymmetrical. Because of relatively inefficient lighting in many of these places when compared to lighting in other areas, bright colors should be used. They are more inviting and express the welcome feeling more than do the subdued darker colors, which tend to fade into the background and many times are expressionless. A combination of red and white gladioli might be just the right selection for such a situation depending, of course, upon the background, furnishings, carpeting, and the space available. Care should be taken to avoid color conflicts with surrounding materials whenever possible.

If the furnishings are antiques, arrangements should be in keeping with the particular era. Flowers should be selected carefully for these arrangements to ensure that they will fit in with the period. Contemporary furnishings, or those common to the present day, would require just as much attention in the selection of flowers and arrangements as furnishings common to other times.

Large hallways require equally large arrangements. However, they should not be of such a size that they interfere with passage through the area; these arrangements should also be in scale with the table or other furnishings on which they are placed.

Some areas in the hallway will require symmetrical arrangements. If placed in the center of a table, along with other things equally balanced, the symmetrically balanced arrangement is correct; if used on one end of the table, an asymmetrical arrangement should be used with the extended base flowing toward the center of the table. An arrangement beside an open stairway should have its lines flowing in the same direction as the stairway, because lines going in other directions would cause a certain amount of confusion and might destroy the overall effect.

For the dining room, there are all sorts of possibilities. Of course, the dining table is the main attraction, and flower arrangements should be used to enhance this setting. Arrangements placed in other areas of the room should harmonize with but not detract from the table setting itself.

The particular occasion will affect the type of arrangement and the kinds of flowers used. For a formal dinner, a centerpiece of roses in a silver container along with candles in silver candlesticks would be in order. The color of the roses should blend with the motif being carried out with the dinner setting. For settings with dimmed lights or candlelight, light colored flowers should be used; under such conditions darker colors are ineffective and sometimes will even appear as voids in the arrangement.

Centerpieces for the dining table are seen from all sides. This is one of the most difficult arrangements to make, especially when it must be balanced from all viewpoints. Such a centerpiece is shown in Figure 13-1. Establishment of the overall

FIGURE 13-1 A symmetrical arrangement of pompon chrysanthemums and baby's breath seen from all sides is suitable for many locations in the home.

dimension is the first consideration when arranging flowers for the dining table. The length should never be longer than one-third the overall length of the table. A more appropriate size for most is about one-sixth of its length. The width should not interfere with the place settings on either side. Height is an important consideration. The arrangement should be low enough so guests can converse freely across the table without interference or having to look around the flowers. A good guideline to follow is to place the elbow on the table with forearm upward and the fist clenched. This should establish the maximum height and under most conditions will allow guests to see each other across the table. Large banquet head tables, where large arrangements are necessary to keep in scale with the surroundings, and arrangements in pedestal containers are exceptions to this suggested guide.

The next consideration is the establishment of the lines for the piece. Each designer has a favorite way of inserting them. One method that seems to work well is to cut two stems of equal length and weight and place them into the holder 180 degrees to each other to establish the overall length. Two other stems of equal length but usually shorter than the first two are inserted 90 degrees to the longitudinal lines to establish width. One stem follows in the center for the overall height. Figure 13–2 illustrates the correct placement of these lines. With these lines in place, the remainder of the flowers and foliage can be used to fill in and complete the arrangement. For this type of centerpiece, a *focal area* is created rather than a *focal point* by concentrating darker or heavier appearing flowers low over the center of the container as shown in Figure 13–3.

Another version of this centerpiece is to create a focal point on either side. These are constructed by completing one side similar to an arrangement to be viewed from one side; then turning it 180 degrees and doing basically the same thing on the other side. However, the same vertical and horizontal lines will form the backbone for both sides, and flowers for these should be selected with this in mind.

Candlesticks may be incorporated into the arrangement or may be separated from it. If separate from it, a few flowers and greens similar to those used in the centerpiece can be placed around the base of the candleholder to help tie all parts together. Fragile flowers can be put into small vials of water to prevent wilting; others will last for several hours even if out of water. There are plastic flower holders available that hold water

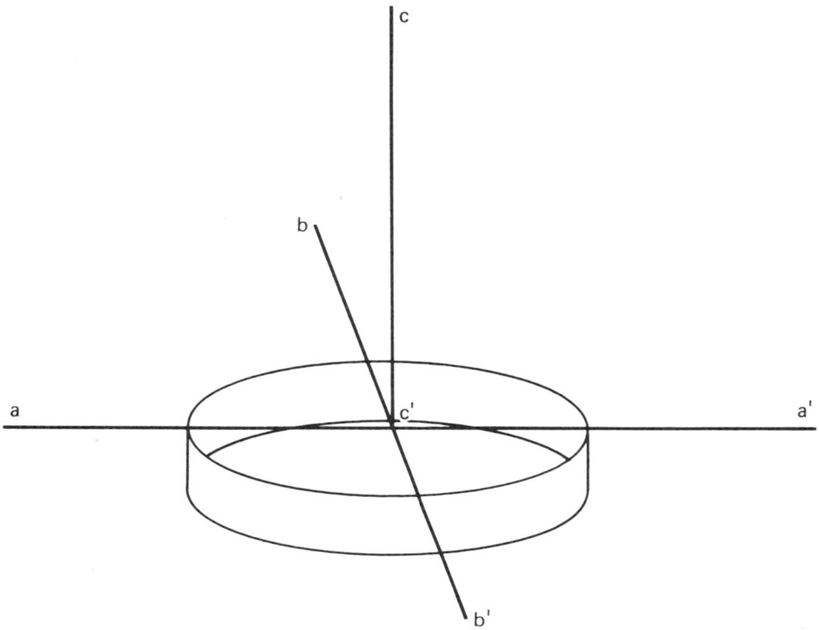

FIGURE 13-2 Correct placement of lines to establish length, width, and height of an arrangement to be seen from all sides. First, establish length a-a′; next, width b-b′; finally, height c-c′.

FIGURE 13-3 Pyracantha, Japanese lanterns, and varigated vinca in a symmetrical arrangement. Concentration of the weight directly over the container results in an effective focal area when seen from all sides.

FIGURE 13-4 Daisy-type chrysanthemums, baby's breath, and leatherleaf fern arranged in a plastic container that slips over the candle and rests on the candlestick.

and slip over the candles; small arrangements that harmonize with the centerpiece can be made in these containers as illustrated in Figure 13-4.

A buffet table presents the same problems as does the dining table if guests are to be served from both sides. However, if the table is against the wall or in a position where guests are served from only one side, a one-sided flower arrangement can be used. It can be a long, low arrangement or one considerably higher than that used on the dinner table. Symmetrical arrangements are commonly used if placed in the center; those of asymmetrical design are often used on each end.

The use of a pedestal-type container is a good choice for buffet table arrangements, especially in situations where space is limited. This allows an arrangement of maximum size to be used, yet does not interfere too much with the other items on the table. These can be placed beneath the flowers if necessary, without creating a crowded effect; Figure 13-5 gives an excellent example of this.

Buffet tables can be formal or informal, with the latter type predominating. The flowers, dinnerware, candle holders, etc., should fit the occasion and must harmonize with each other. For the informal table, chrysanthemums, carnations, snapdragons, or similar flowers used alone or in combination are

FIGURE 13-5 Roses, chrysanthemums, baby's breath, artemesia, and fern arranged in a candleabra are an excellent choice for a buffet or banquet table.

more appropriate than would be roses, which are better suited for more formal events.

In addition to the dining or buffet tables, there may be other places in the dining room where flowers can be used. These should be compatible with the other flowers, fit the occasion, and harmonize with the room and its furnishings.

The living room offers all sorts of possibilities for flower arrangements. End tables, mantel, coffee table, and miscellaneous stands throughout the room are all places where flowers can be used to enhance the overall setting. Furnishings, architecture, and general decor will all have an influence upon the type of arrangement to be used, its style, and the flowers chosen.

In homes of today, the architectural designs of this room vary considerably. It may have a high or low ceiling, perhaps even a cathedral type; it may be formal or informal, have painted walls or highly stylized wall coverings, and colonial or contemporary furnishings. Each has an effect upon the flower arrangements used.

As shown in Figure 13-6, mantel arrangements are commonly made with a horizontal line when used in the center of the mantel. The L line or asymmetrical triangle can be used on either side. The flow of the asymmetrical type will depend upon what is in the center of the mantel and the effect the designer is

FIGURE 13–6 A mantel arrangement of roses, carnations, chrysanthemums, statice, boxwood, and variegated pittosporum, a good combination of plant material that fits well with the marble mantel. Plant material crossing the picture frame should be avoided whenever possible.

trying to create. If the high line of the arrangement is on the outside with the low flowing toward the center, it has the effect of closing in the area and making it a separate unit in the room; whereas, if the lines flow in the opposite direction (outward), they will help to give the effect of added width and tie the fireplace-mantel unit in with the surroundings. Figure 13–7 shows the different effects of mantel arrangements. Mantel arrangements should not distract from mirrors, pictures, or other objects hung above them. As mentioned in Chapter 5, they should not cut across picture frames and should be attractively finished on all sides if a mirror is behind them.

End table arrangements should be kept in scale with the table and surrounding furnishings. Most require relatively small arrangements to avoid interference with lamps or other objects on them. If the table is against a wall, an arrangement viewed from one side is in order; but if the table is near a couch or chair, the arrangement will probably be seen from all sides. A small vase with a group of pansies or a bunch of violets is appropriate for many situations. (See Figures 10–6 and 13–9). They will provide that added touch of color and beauty to brighten an otherwise dull area.

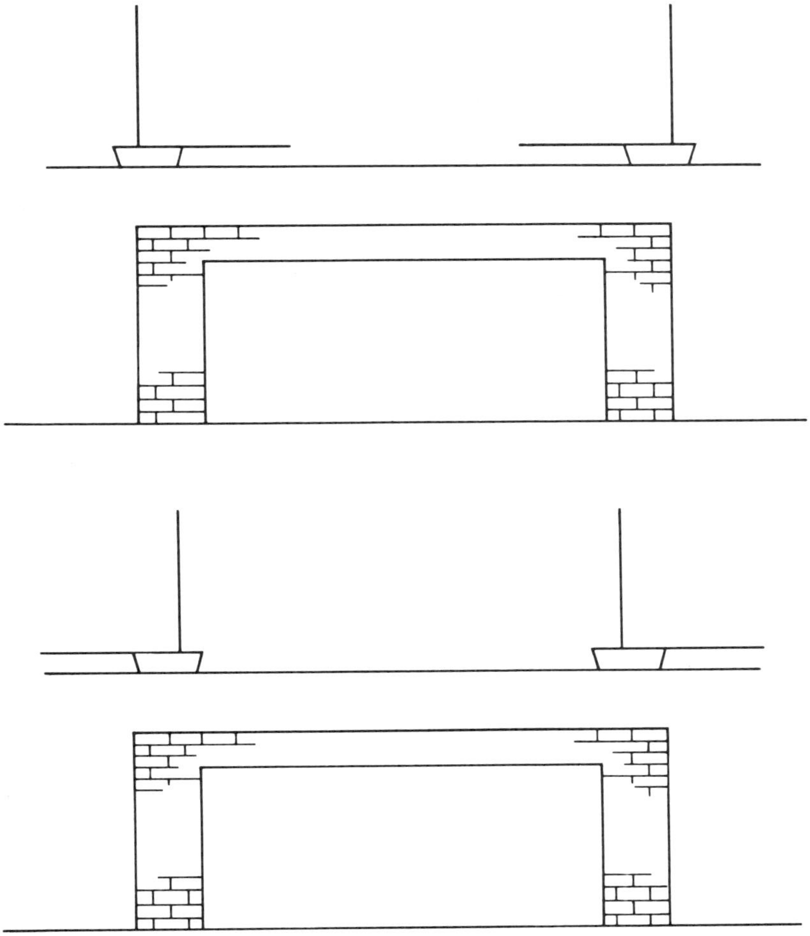

FIGURE 13-7 When the lines of mantel arrangements flow away from each other (bottom), they appear to tie the fireplace into the surrounding area. When they flow toward each other (top), the entire mantel unit appears as a separate entity in the room.

The coffee table is an area where activity is constantly taking place. Current magazines that are being used by the family are sometimes placed here as well as drinks and snacks. Because of this activity flower arrangements should be small and sturdy; a low flat container that is difficult to knock over is best for this situation. Flowers can be of any type as long as they tie in with other furnishings. These arrangements are seen from all sides, and most will be viewed from the top as well; in this situation, it is good practice to concentrate the bulk of the weight directly over the vase. Darker colors will help to give this impression; place them deep within the arrangement so that they can help to give a stabilizing effect as well as to create a feeling of depth and the three-dimensional aspect.

Many living rooms have a large picture window or bay window. This is a popular spot for arrangements, house plants, or lamps. If one of these items must be used, the best choice is house plants. Lamps obstruct the view and, in general, deteriorate from the purpose of such a window, and this is one of the most undesirable places in the home for flower arrangements. Not only does the arrangement interfere with the view out of the window, but the light penetrating through the arrangement many times destroys the effectiveness of it, as shown in Figure 13-8, and with a sunny exposure the lifespan of the flowers will be shortened. If there must be an arrangement in this location, it will probably be seen from outside as well as inside; therefore it should be attractively finished on all sides. Many times, a designer with little or no experience with flowers, will arrange them so they are attractive from the outside when viewed by passers-by with little regard to their appearance within the room. Sometimes the reverse situation exists.

Flowers in the den can be used to give warmth to the area, to create a quieting atmosphere, or solely for their decorative effect. Their use depends upon the main purpose of this room. If it is used primarily for reading or study, the quieting tones are most effective. Bright colors are more desirable if it is more of a family gathering area where television is watched, games played, and a general good time is had by everyone. A pottery bowl or dull metal container with marigolds or similar coarse-textured flowers might be just the right thing for this room. Roses or delicate flowers in a silver or crystal vase would be out of place and will not harmonize with the surroundings in most dens. Arrangements are informal and many times only a few flowers stuck into a container can be just enough to create the desired relaxed atmosphere. However, placing arrangements on the TV should be discouraged; because of a certain amount of heat generated by the television, flower life is shortened considerably. Moreover, a serious situation could develop if the arrangement were tipped and water spilled into the television unit. Short-circuiting and eventual fire might occur!

FIGURE 13-8 A well-balanced and symmetrical arrangement. Light penetrating through the arrangement and the outside area detracts from it.

Kitchen arrangements are usually small and should be placed in areas where they will not interfere with work or traffic. The window sill or knickknack shelves are ideal places for them. Small table arrangements usually seen from all sides will contribute to the overall pleasant atmosphere.

Arrangements on window sills should be small and should not obstruct the view to any appreciable degree. A miniature arrangement can be effective in this location; most, however, will be somewhat larger. Complicated arrangements taking much time and effort, even though the proportions are small, are out of place in this area. A few lilies of the valley in the spring, zinnias in the summer, and pompon chrysanthemums in the fall are all that is needed to create a cheerful mood. Again, avoid placing arrangements in direct sunlight.

The corner shelf is an area where two or three miniatures can be placed. They can be used in the same manner as collector's items which are commonly displayed in such places. Miniatures made with dried materials will last a long time, are attractive, and make good conversation pieces. Other small arrangements can be displayed in these areas, providing they are in scale with the shelf and do not give the impression of being too heavy for it.

FIGURE 13-9 Spring flowers, attractively arranged and placed on a bedside table at Colonial Williamsburg.

Kitchen utensils make attractive containers for arrangements on the table. A small bean pot with a few chrysanthemums attractively arranged in it is ideal. The weight of the pot will give stability to the arrangement and will reduce the possibility of it being knocked over in the busy kitchen. The container and flowers should blend with the tablecloth or place mats and other items that are on the table.

The small arrangement on a bedside table shown in Figure 13-9 is especially appropriate if guests are using the room. Any type of arrangement can be used, but it should harmonize with the surroundings. Some of the lighter colored flowers, especially white, pale blues, and lavenders are good to use on a warm summer day to help create a cooling effect, whereas warm colors are better to use during the cold days of winter. Delicate flowers giving a light, airy feeling, along with the sweeping lines of carefully selected foliage, give a dramatic effect yet are in keeping with the furnishings of the lady's bedroom. Flowers with strong odors such as gardenias should not be used in this room.

Porches, sun rooms, and patios are other places in and around the home where arrangements are used. Porches found on many of the older homes are good places to use mass arrangements of garden flowers in relatively heavy containers. Hanging arrangements are also attractive in open areas such as porches or patios. See Figure 13-10. Occasionally, contemporary arrangements are seen in such areas, but for the most part they are not compatible with the surroundings or architectural styling.

The sun room is more of an area for growing potted plants rather than for arrangements of cut flowers. Because of its location, the temperature may be considerably higher than in other parts of the home during the day. With this heat, the life span of cut flowers is shortened. Arrangements can be used for a party or other short-term purposes, but for longer periods, flowering house plants are a better choice.

Arrangements for the patio vary considerably. They can be large, massive, and colorful arrangements in urns or small ones in pottery containers placed on each table. Large urns with many flowers placed in strategic locations along the perimeter of a patio can be used to define its boundaries and at the same time provide a wealth of color for the occasion. Sometimes live plants are used in urns when more permanent settings are desired. See, for example, the urn in Figure 13–11. The arrangements on the tables should be in keeping with the occasion. Flowers, containers, and accessories should harmonize with the surroundings and be heavy enough to withstand wind con-

FIGURE 13–10 An interesting hanging arrangement of modern design suitable for use on a patio.

FIGURE 13-11 Urns filled with cut flowers or plants can be placed at strategic locations along the perimeter of a patio.

ditions. It can be embarrassing to the hostess to have arrangements fall over during a luncheon or tea and spill water on her guests!

This chapter has indicated where flowers can be used throughout the home. Many homemakers consider placing them in these locations only when they are having guests or for special occasions. If flowers last for several days after the guests leave, it is considered a bonus and flowers are not used again until another special occasion arises. The everyday use of flowers in the home is important. The more constant use of flowers is popular in some parts of the world but has been ignored in this country. Perhaps the prevailing but erroneous idea that one must purchase a dozen or more flowers when buying from a florist, spending a considerable amount of money for them, has been a major cause of this disinterest. It is possible to buy a few flowers at a reasonable cost from the local florist. A weekly or biweekly purchase of those flowers that are in season will ensure a continuous source of additional beauty in the home throughout the year.

14 Flowers to Wear

The use of flowers for personal adornment has been practiced for centuries. Figure 14-1 shows an 18th century portrait of a woman wearing flowers. Wearing them has been a custom throughout recorded history not only for their beautifying effect but for ceremonial purposes and as ways of expressing ideas or thoughts. Crowns of leaves or flowers were used by the Greeks and Romans as rewards for outstanding achievements; garlands of flowers were used in the hair and around the waists of young women in ancient Greece and at the time of the Pharaohs in Egypt. For centuries flowers have been worn by women in the South Pacific: Leis have been worn around the neck and individual flowers worn in the hair.

Flowers have been worn or carried by ladies on this continent since colonial times. The so-called "tussie-mussie," a round bouquet with flowers patterned in circles, was a popular item in the colonial period and is still one of the leading designs carried today. Flowers were also tied together and worn on

FIGURE 14–1 Flowers have been worn for centuries, as seen in the painting, "Duchesse de Chateavroux," by Jean Marc Nattier (1685–1766).

gowns for their beauty and fragrance. Most were bulky, heavy, and cumbersome and worn on the shoulder, waist, or wrist. Several flowers along with an abundance of greens, namely asparagus fern, were used. This type of arrangement was called a "corsage." Single flowers were also worn to compliment gowns and the ladies wearing them.

Today, "corsage" is a general term used for all flower arrangements that are worn. These include flowers for the hair, used as earrings, necklaces, or wristlets, as well as the traditional shoulder arrangement. Flowers on handbags, the waist, and even nosegays are also referred to this way.

Corsages may be worn at any time of the day, but they must fit the occasion and harmonize with the personality and attire of the individual. Informal arrangements consisting of a few garden flowers worn on a suit might be ideal for a luncheon (see Figure 14–2), whereas a large cattleya orchid would not be suitable for either the occasion or dress. A single gardenia or camellia can be worn informally during the day, but if arranged in a more formal manner will harmonize with formal attire.

Fresh flowers should be considered as an accessory when

FIGURE 14-2 An informal corsage of garden flowers with a plaid bow. Many garden flowers are suitable for this use.

being worn and should not compete with the clothing or the individual for dominance. They should be chosen with as much care as the lady uses when she selects her jewelry. The mere fact of pinning a large flower on a gown does not enhance the costume's beauty; the flowers should be chosen carefully, not only according to size but to color, durability, individual preference, and the reason for wearing them.

Some flowers are considered more formal than others. Some species of orchids, especially the cattleya, are most suitable with formal attire and often look out of place with casual dress. Gardenias, stephanotis, camellias, phalaenopsis orchids, and eucharis lilies are all considered formal. Most garden flowers have an informal appearance and are usually worn at such events. Recently, however, there has been a trend toward using these flowers for more formal occasions, and if they are arranged carefully and in a formal design, many can be used successfully for this purpose.

Durability or lasting quality is a prime factor in selecting corsage flowers. If one observes the most popular flowers used by florists, it will be found that most will hold up well for several hours out of water. This is one of the reasons why carnations, chrysanthemums, gardenias, orchids, and roses are so extensively used by them.

Some garden flowers, if hardened properly before using, will last several hours without water. Gladioli, delphiniums, dianthus, and small marigolds, as well as many others, are satisfactory for informal wear and will remain in good condition for some time. It is a waste of time, and many disappointments can occur, if garden flowers are not selected for hardiness as well as shape and color. Experiment with them at home several times before wearing them. Note how they must be handled and how long they last under specific conditions; some of the more fragile flowers are beautiful on the plant, hold up well in a vase of water, but wilt and die within an hour in a corsage. A wilted corsage can destroy the effect of the whole ensemble.

Color of flowers should be chosen carefully. It should harmonize with the gown and the personality of the individual wearing them. This is one time when a person making a corsage at home has an advantage over the florist, unless the florist knows the wearer and is able to see the attire. The color of the flowers should fit the complexion of the person: A person with pale skin should use bright colors as a source of radiance to her personality, whereas one who spends time at the beach or on the golf course and has developed a highly tanned, out-of-doors look will look better wearing pastels and paler colors. Vivid colors are more suited for brunettes, pastels are preferable for those with blonde or graying hair. It is difficult to match the color of a gown to flowers. Rather than trying to get the exact color, it is better to use a contrasting color or one that harmonizes well with the attire.

The size of the corsage should be appropriate to the size of the wearer. A small corsage will look even smaller on a large woman and a large one appear overpowering on a small person. Wristlets should be light and fit the arm well. Often these are made to extend almost to the elbow and down over the fingers, giving an extremely heavy appearance and a feeling of excessive weight attached to the arm. The size of the individual flowers should also be in scale with the size of the corsage and the person wearing them: A large orchid is completely out of place on a small person, whereas an individual of greater stature could carry it well. Small corsages are best when made with small flowers. Sweetheart roses are excellent for this type of piece,

FIGURE 14-3 Roses have always been popular corsage flowers. For a formal type of corsage, individual flowers are used at the top and the weight is concentrated at the base by using several flowers and ribbon. The arrangement should be worn with the single flower pointing upward.

but hybrid teas as shown in Figure 14-3 are too heavy for small, dainty arrangements.

If an individual prefers to wear a specific type of flower or has a particular fondness for one, there is no reason why she cannot wear it, unless it will not hold up under these adverse conditions. The flower may be manipulated in various ways to form an informal corsage for daytime wear or a more formal one for an evening affair. See Figures 14-4 and 14-5. There are some flowers that some ladies cannot wear well; they seem to result in a clash of personalities! The heavy fragrance of gardenias may cause discomfort to some women—under these circumstances, do not use them. If such situations exist, avoid the use of these flowers whenever possible.

The specific reason for wearing flowers can determine the type to be worn. Homecoming football games call for large chrysanthemums with a bow of ribbon, and little consideration is given to the lady's coat or jacket because school colors are in

FIGURE 14-4 An informal corsage using a single "glamellia" (gladioli arranged to resemble a camellia), suitable for daytime or informal evening wear. Camellias, gardenias, and other large flowers can be used in a similar fashion.

FIGURE 14-5 One or more "glamellias," camellias, or gardenias can be combined into a formal-type corsage.

vogue; sorority functions often call for specific colors and flowers. For these activities, the wearer should be aware of the popular colors and plan her outfit accordingly.

Styles of corsages vary considerably from the "bunchy" grouping of flowers tied together with a bow of ribbon to the finely tailored contemporary versions using a minimum amount of material. However, most corsages do follow certain forms or shapes and are based upon basic lines similar to those described in Chapter 3. The vertical, horizontal, crescent, and Hogarth lines predominate, and the overall shapes are the circle, oval, and triangle. For many corsages, a double triangle or diamond is formed. The circle type usually consists of a single large flower such as a gardenia, "glamellia," or a "nosegay" type arrangement. It can be carried or used as a shoulder, waist, or wrist type corsage. This style or shape will work with most ensembles that a lady will wear. Figure 14-4 shows an informal corsage for either daytime or evening wear.

When making a corsage to be worn on the shoulder, it is important that the neckline of the gown be considered and the line of the corsage conform with it. A "vee" neckline calls for a vertical line, with the line of the corsage placed parallel to that of the gown. For a curved or round neckline, the crescent or Hogarth curve should be used with the crescent line following the neckline; the lower line of the Hogarth curve should follow the curve of the neckline of the gown. If the lines flow in opposite directions, a conflict of interest can result. Both correct and incorrect lines for a corsage are shown in Figure 14-6.

Horizontal lines or Hogarth curves can be used for both waist and wrist corsages. The style and design of the gown will influence the type of corsage to be worn. A corsage suggesting a horizontal line would certainly be out of place on a gown made of material with vertical stripes.

FIGURE 14-6 Flowers worn on the shoulder should follow the neckline of the gown. Top left: A vertical line fits well with a vee neckline but a Hogarth curve conflicts with it. Top right: A crescent line should follow the curved neckline and not flow in the opposite direction. Bottom: With a curved neckline, the lower part of the Hogarth curve should flow with the line of the gown with the top part of the curve over the shoulder.

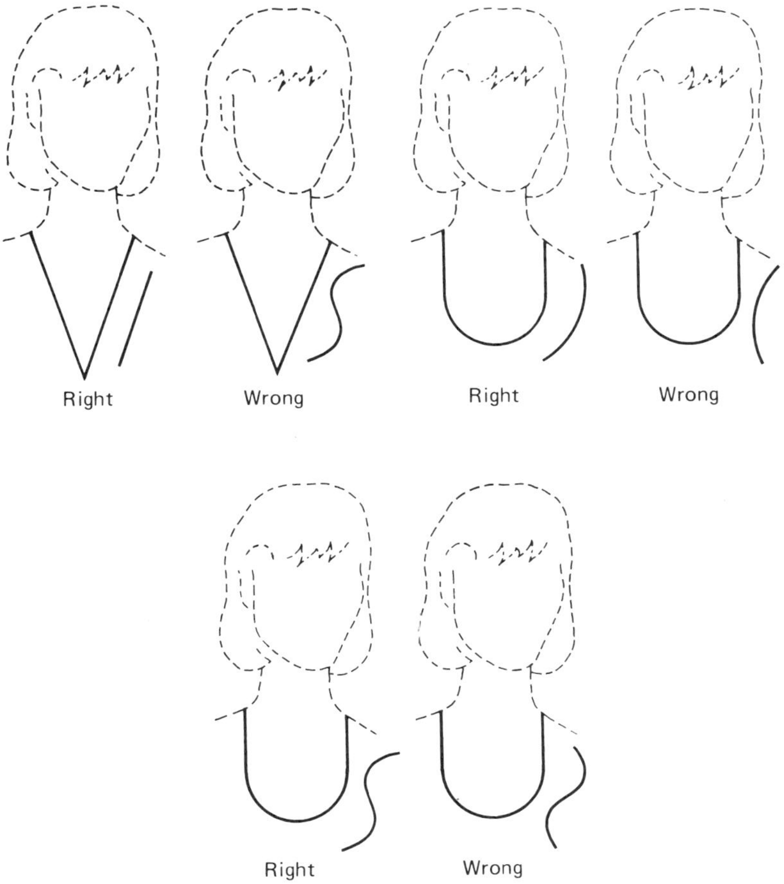

Informal corsages can be made with natural stems or with taped wire suggesting stems exposed as in Figures 14–2 and 14–7. Most will have no stems showing; their overall shape can be that of a circle, oval, or triangle. With most of these, however, the line is more pronounced than the shape. Flowers can be arranged loosely, and a small bow is often used to help conceal the mechanics.

Formal corsages can be either the single- or double-end type. The latter consists of two similar parts joined together at the middle, with a bow of ribbon inserted at the point of junction to help to camouflage the mechanics. The shape of this corsage is an oval or the double triangle. Figure 14–8 shows a double-ended corsage. The single-end type begins with a single flower at the top and gradually increases in size with the greatest concentration of weight at its base. Ribbon may be added if necessary as on the corsages in Figures 14–2 and 14–7.

A nosegay, as shown in Figure 14–9, consists of a grouping of small flowers such as violets clustered tightly together forming a circle; leaves are often used around the outside and help to protect the flowers and at the same time provide a contrasting color to emphasize them. All stems are taped together giving the appearance of a single stem. The arrangement is completed with a bow of ribbon tied to the stem.

Colonial bouquets or nosegays are carried at formal affairs. They are smaller versions of the colonial bouquet carried by some wedding attendants and consist of a series of alternating rings of harmonizing or contrasting colored flowers. They can be completed with a circle of leaves or a paper or lace doily. Sometimes a bow of ribbon is added, either tied to the stem or incorporated into the last row of flowers.

With few exceptions flowers used in corsages are wired into position, allowing the designer to manipulate them into desired lines and shapes. Methods of wiring vary almost as much as the number of people making corsages. Each flower can be wired several different ways, and only experience with each type will determine the method to be used. When wiring flowers, the wire gauge used will depend upon the weight of the flower. Number 20 wire is used on many heavy flowers, whereas for those of medium weight, numbers 24 and 26 are commonly used; numbers 30 and 32 are used for lightweight flowers. Wire that is too heavy may damage the flowers, give them a stiff appearance, and add unnecessary weight to the corsage; wire that is too light will not support or hold the flowers in the

FIGURE 14-7 An informal corsage of chrysanthemums; the end is exposed to add to its informality, and the mechanics are often hidden by using a bow of ribbon.

FIGURE 14-8 A double-end corsage using pompon chrysanthemums. Ribbon in the center completes the arrangement while concealing the mechanics.

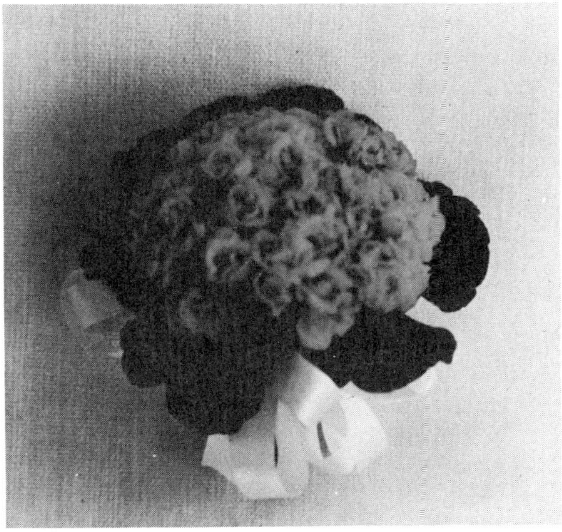

FIGURE 14-9 Geranium flowers surrounded by geranium leaves make an attractive nosegay to be carried. Many variations can be employed; violets with a sweetheart rose centered are often used in a similar style.

desired positions. Florist wire is available in 9-, 12-, and 18-inch lengths. The 12-inch wire is the most versatile and is used more than the others. Therefore, unless one is planning to make many corsages, the investment in other lengths is unnecessary.

Some methods of wiring are discussed in Chapter 8. These can be used in corsage work with some modifications. Most of the flower stem is removed before wiring to avoid bulkiness in the finished arrangement; leaving about an inch of the stem is sufficient to secure the flower firmly on the wire. With some flowers, such as gardenias, the stem is completely removed; with a few (some species of orchids) the stem is left on in its entirety.

The hook method is used with many daisy-type flowers. All the stem except one inch is removed, and a wire of suitable weight is pushed through the remaining stem and flower head. A small hook is made in the end of the wire and is pulled back into the flower head far enough so the wire is not exposed; the lower end of the wire is bent and inserted into the calyx at the point of stem attachment. The wire is cut at the bend, and the piece that has been pushed into the calyx is twisted around the stem two or three times. See Figure 14–10. It is not necessary or desirable that the wires be twisted together for their entire length. Care should be taken to prevent movement of the hook when twisting the wires because this will cause the center of the flower to be ruined.

For flowers with a heavy calyx, for example, roses and carnations, a wire of sufficient weight is pushed through the calyx until equal lengths are exposed on either side as shown in Figure 14–10. It is then pulled down in hairpin fashion; and while one end is held tightly to the stem and calyx, the other end is twisted around them. These flowers are sometimes wired by using florist-type chenille stems. This method involves complete removal of the stem and the insertion of the chenille stem into the base of the calyx. (It should be pushed in far enough to hold the flower securely.)

It is necessary with some flowers for the wire to be pushed through the flower and bent down in a method similar to the one previously described. Two wires inserted at 90 degrees to each other may be necessary for gladioli or similar flowers. When this method is used, care should be taken to expose as little of the wire as possible.

There are many ways to wire orchids. One method is to bend one wire in half and place it along the stem with the curved end against the orchid petals. A second wire is bent in similar fashion, placed along the stem with one section of it

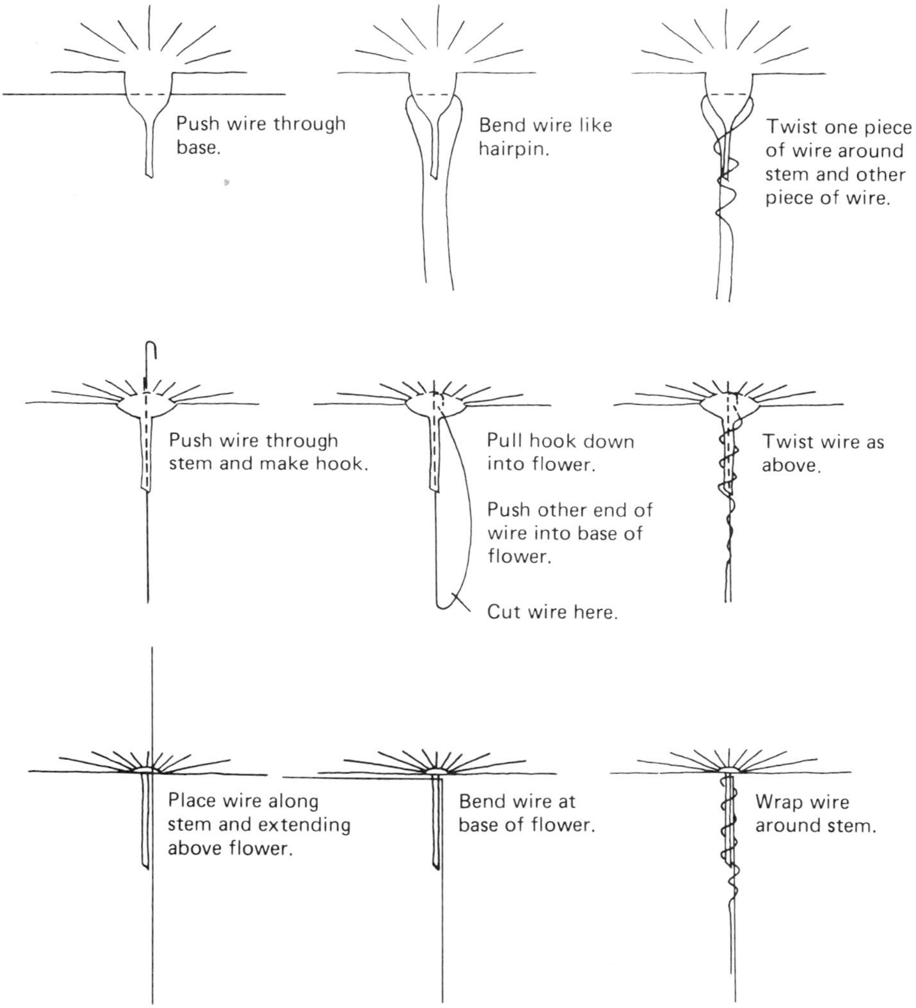

FIGURE 14-10 Methods of wiring flowers. Top: Flower with large calyx (example, carnation). Center: Flower with small but prominent calyx (example, chrysanthemum). Bottom: Flower with no prominent calyx (example, geranium).

twisted around the stem wires. With some flowers where extra support is not needed, only one wire is necessary. Orchids, as well as flowers with a similar structure, are often wired by bending a wire in the form of a hairpin, placing it between the petals at the point of attachment, and twisting one end around the other piece of wire and stem. Wired in this fashion, the wire is held firmly in place and cannot slip down the stem without breaking the flower.

Some flowers are wired by placing the wire parallel along the stem with the flower at the halfway point of the wire. While holding the stem and the lower half of the wire, the top half is wrapped around the stem two or three times to hold it in place. This method is also demonstrated in Figure 14–10.

Individual flower petals used for such things as a Dutchess rose or glamellia are wired as illustrated in Figure 14–11. Many individual leaves are wired by this same method.

Countless variations of these methods are practiced by designers. The main objective, regardless of the method, is to provide a flexible stem so the designer can manipulate it to suit his needs.

After wiring, all stems should be taped with one of the floral tapes made especially for this purpose. This serves to seal the stem and wire, to make a more attractive stem, and to help camouflage the mechanics or construction details. The key to good taping is to *stretch* the tape when applying it. This gives a thin stem which is easy to work with and reduces bulkiness. Taping usually begins as close to the flower head as possible. It is wrapped around the stem two or three times at that point to ensure a good seal; then, holding the tape at about a 45-degree angle to the stem, it is stretched and wrapped down the length of the stem as the stem is rotated. When completed, the tape is broken off or cut off with scissors. Figure 14–12 demonstrates correct use of floral tape.

When enough flowers have been wired and taped, assembly of the corsage can begin. With a combination of flowers of different sizes, smaller flowers are placed at the extremities and the larger ones in the center of a double-end corsage and at the base of a single-end corsage. When flowers are of equal size, greater spaces are left between the more distant ones than among those in the center or base. Two or three large flowers such as gardenias or cymbidium orchids are equally spaced with a bow of ribbon either among them or at the base of the corsage.

Assembly begins by taking two flowers or a piece of wired foliage and a flower, placing them in position, and twisting the wires together for two or three turns. A piece of floral tape can be wrapped around the twisted area to help ensure neatness of the finished product. See Figure 14–13. Another flower is added, twisted, and taped. This is continued until all flowers are in place; care should be taken to use a minimum amount of tape and twisted wire to avoid bulkiness. When all flowers are in place, excess stems are cut off and the end portion taped

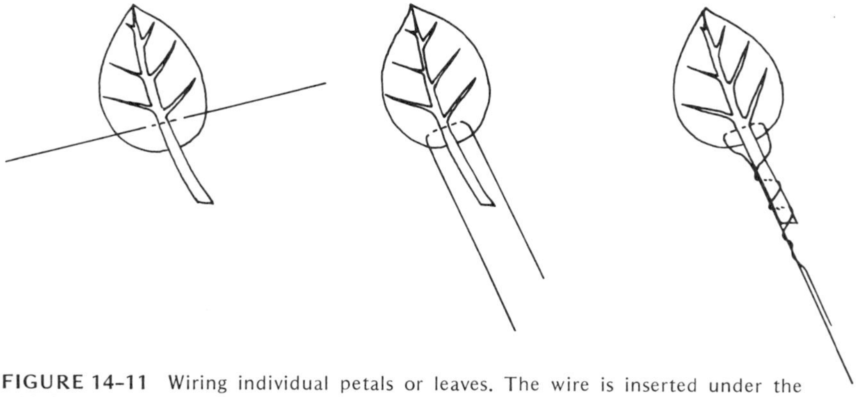

FIGURE 14–11 Wiring individual petals or leaves. The wire is inserted under the midrib and bent downward in the form of a hairpin; then one side is twisted around the other and around the stem.

FIGURE 14–12 Use of floral tape. Left to right: Tape wrapped around the calyx two or three times to hold tightly. The tape is then stretched and twisted down the stem while being held at about a 45-degree angle to the stem. The completed taped stem is shown on the right.

to cover any exposed wire. If the stems are to be left on, they should be trimmed, taped, and placed in desired positions.

Adding a bow of ribbon can be the last step or can be worked into the corsage along with the flowers and foliage. Bows are tied in a number of ways: Four or five loops of Number 2 or 3 ribbon on either side of the center, tied together with a piece of ribbon or wire, is ample for most corsages. If loops are too large, the bow will be out of proportion to the rest of the arrangement, the loops will tend to droop, and the bow may become the dominating factor and the flowers subservient to it.

Except for double-end corsages, flowers should be worn as they grow. This should be kept in mind during construction, keeping the lighter parts pointing upward and concentrating the

FIGURE 14-13 The back of a corsage should be neat and light. Heavy, bulky corsages are uncomfortable to wear.

weight at the base. A high percentage of ladies wear orchids upside down. They are pinned hanging from the shoulder with a bow of ribbon on top and the flower in sort of a drooping position. When hanging this way, the real beauty of the orchid cannot be seen since the most interesting part is in the "throat" of the flower.

There is no hard-and-fast rule regarding where a corsage must be worn. Use it as an accessory and place it where it will be most complimentary to the attire being worn.

Index